Asaṅga's
Mahāyānasaṁgraha
Chapter III

Asaṅga's

Mahāyānasaṁgraha

Chapter III

Translation and Tibetan Text

Chikafumi Watanabe

DK PRINTWORLD
Publishers of Indian Traditions

Cataloging in Publication Data — DK
[Courtesy: D.K. Agencies (P) Ltd. <docinfo@dkagencies.com>]

Asaṅga.
[Mahāyānasaṅgraha. Chapter III. English & Tibetan]
Asaṅga's Mahāyānasaṁgraha, Chapter III : translation and Tibetan text / Chikafumi Watanabe.
p. cm.
In Tibetan (roman); translation and introductory matter in English.
Includes bibliographical references (p.) and index.
ISBN 9788124607190

1. Yogācāra (Buddhism) – Early works to 1800. I. Watanabe, Chikafumi. II. Title.

DDC 294.392 23

First published in India, 2014
ISBN 13: 978-81-246-0719-0

Printed and published by:
D.K. Printworld (P) Ltd.
Regd. Office: "Vedaśrī", F-395, Sudarshan Park
(Metro Station: Ramesh Nagar), New Delhi – 110 015
Phones: (011) 2545 3975, 2546 6019; *Fax:* (011) 2546 5926
e-mail: indology@dkprintworld.com
Website: www.dkprintworld.com

Dedicated to

Fumimaro Watanabe

(1934–1990)

Shinsho Hanayama

(1898–1995)

Shoyu Hanayama

(1931–1995)

Preface

The purpose of this book is to present a translation of the third chapter of Asaṅga's *Mahāyānasaṁgraha*. Although a large number of studies have been made on the *Mahāyānasaṁgraha*, there are very few Western-language translations of the text: *La Somme du Grand Véhicule d'Asaṅga* (*Mahāyānasaṁgraha*) vol. 2 of Étienne Lamotte is a French translation based upon the Tibetan text (vol. 1 is a Tibetan text of the *Mahāyānasaṁgraha*). *The Realm of Awakening* of Noriaki Hakamaya, Paul Griffiths, and others is a translation of the tenth chapter of the text and its commentaries. "*Nirvikalpajñāna*: Awareness Freed From Discrimination" of Leslie Kawamura is a translation of the ninth chapter of the Tibetan text. *The Summary of the Great Vehicle* of John Keenan is a translation of Paramārtha's Chinese translation of the text. "A Translation of *Mahāyānasaṁgraha* III. 1–4," "A Translation of *Mahāyānasaṁgraha* III. 5–7," and "A Translation of *Mahāyānasaṁgraha* III. 5–7" are my English translation of some portions of the third chapter of the Tibetan text (For the details of modern works on the text, see 'Chapter One' of this book, pp. 21–27).

I hope that the translation of the third chapter of the *Mahāyānasaṁgraha* in the present book will be a significant contribution to the study of Yogācāra philosophy in general and of Asaṅga's philosophy in particular.

I would like to thank the late Professor Leslie S. Kawamura of the University of Calgary, who patiently went through the entire translation of the third chapter of the *Mahāyānasaṁgraha* and its commentaries with me, claryfing countless difficult passages. Without his encouragement and help, translation of the text simply could not have been completed.

I am indebted to Professors Tom J. F. Tillemans of the University of Lausanne and Shoryu Katsura of Ryukoku University, who were the Numata Chair of Buddhist Studies visiting professsors at the University of Calgary in 1995 and 1996 respectively. I was influenced much by their lectures on Yogācāra epistemology and Mādhyamika philosophy, etc. Also, Professor Katsura kindly gave me valuable suggestions in reading and translating the third chapter of the *Mahāyānasaṁgraha* and its commentaries.

My special thanks are also due to Professor Lambert Schimithausen of the University of Hamburg for his valuable suggestions in reading and understanding some portions of the *Mahāyānasaṁgraha* and its commentaries, and to Professor Michael Hahn of the Philipps-University of Marburg for his helpful suggestions in reading and understanding a verse quoted in the third chapter of the *Mahāyānasaṁgrahopanibandhana*.

I wish to express my deepest obligations to my *guru*, Professor Ashok N. Aklujkar of the University of British Columbia. When I was an M.A. student at the University of British Columbia, I deepend my understanding of Sanskrit language, Indian linguistics, philosophy, and literature via his lectures and guidance.

I am grateful to Professor Karin Preisendanz, now of University of Vienna, who was my supervisor when I was a first year in the master's programme at the University of British Columbia. I was given much useful information and helpful advice in her classes and in private consultations.

I also would like to acknowledge the generous advice and helpful discussion with Professor Shrikant S. Bahulkar of the University of Pune, who was a visiting professor at the University of British Columbia in 1993, on the *Madhyamakahṛdayakārikā* and *Tarkajvālā*.

It was my good fortune to spend a year (December 1997–December 1998) in Pune, India. Professor Mohan G. Dhadphale of the Department of Sanskrit and Pali at the Fergusson College read Sanskrit texts with me and gave me much valuable advice in reading and understanding Sanskrit texts. Professor Saroja Bhate of the Department of Sanskrit and Prakrit at the University of Pune kindly allowed me to attend her lectures on Sanskrit *vyākaraṇa*.

Study and research in India were made possible through a grant from the Government of India (GOI) through the India Studies Programme of the Shastri Indo-Canadian Institute (SICI). Neither the GOI nor SICI necessarily endorses, however, the views herein expressed.

Thanks are due to Nagoya University Association of Indian and Buddhist Studies, the Zengaku Kenkyukai of Hanazono University, and Nagata Bunshodo for their permission to reproduce my previously published translations of the *Mahāyānasaṁgraha*.

Finally, I would like to express my gratitude to my mother for her constant encouragement. I believe that my late father, Dr. Fumimaro Watanabe, has been protecting me with blessings of the Triple Gem throughout these years.

Chikafumi Watanabe
Kyoto, Japan

Contents

Abbreviations

AKBh	*Abhidharmakośabhāṣya*
AN	*Aṅguttara Nikāya*
AO	Acta Orientalia, Copenhagen.
AS	*Abhidharmasamuccaya*
ASBh	*Abhidharmasamuccayabhāṣya*
BG	Bukkyo-Gaku (Journal of Buddhist Studies), Sankibo-busshorin, Tokyo
BGS	Bukkyo-Gaku Semina (Buddhist Seminar): Otani University
BHS	*Buddhist Hybrid Sanskrit dictionary*
BK	Bukkyogaku Kenkyu (Studies in Buddhism): Ryukoku University
BoBh	*Bodhisattvabhūmi*
BŚ	Buddhaśānta's Chinese translation of the *Mahāyāna-saṁgraha*
BSOAS	Bulletin of the School of Oriental and African Studies: University of London
C	*Co ne* edition of the Tibetan translation of the *Mahāyānasaṁgraha*
CG	Chizan Gakuho (Journal of Koyasan University)
D	*sDe dge* edition of the Tibetan translation of the *Mahāyānasaṁgraha*

DG	Dharmagupta's Chinese translation of the *Mahāyāna-saṁgraha* included in his Chinese translation of the *Mahāyānasaṁgrahabhāṣya*
DG-MSBh	Dharmagupta's Chinese translation of the *Mahāyāna-saṁgrahabhāṣya*
H	Hsüang-tsang's Chinese translation of the *Mahāyāna-saṁgraha*
HBK	Hokke Bunka Kenkyu (Journal of Institute for the Comprehensive Study of Lotus *Sūtra*): Rissho University
H-MSBh	Hsüang-tsang's Chinese translation of the *Mahāyāna-saṁgrahabhāṣya*
H-MSU	Hsüang-tsang's Chinese translation of the *Mahāyāna-saṁgrahopanibandhana*
IBK	Indogaku Bukkyogaku Kenkyu (Journal of Indian and Buddhist Studies), Tokyo
IG	Indo Gakuho (Miscellance Indologica Kiotiensia): Kyoto University
JBORS	Journal of the Bihar and Orissa Research Society, Patna
JIABS	Journal of International Association of Buddhist Studies, Lausanne
JRAS	Journal of Royal Asiatic Society, London
JRS	Journal of Religious Studies: Punjab University
KDB	Koza Daijyo Bukkyo, Hirakawa, A., Kajiyama, Y., and Takasaki, J. eds., Kodansha, Tokyo
KDBKK	Komazawa Daigaku Bukkyogakubu Kenkyu Kiyo (Annual Research for Buddhist Studies): Komazawa University

KDBR	Komazawa Daigaku Bukkyogakubu Ronshu (Journal of Buddhist Studies): Komazawa University
KDBgR	Kinki Daigaku Bungeigakubu Ronshu (Bulletin of the School of Literature, Arts, and Cultural Studies): Kinki University
KJDKK	Komazawa Jyoshi Daigaku Kenkyu Kiyo (Faculty Journal of Komazawa Women's University)
KK	Kenkyu Kiyo (Faculty Journal of Komazawa Women's Junior College)
KRTDK	Kyushu Ryukoku Tanki Daigaku Kiyo (Bulletin of Kyushu Ryukoku Junior College)
L	Lamotte's Tibetan text of the *Mahāyānasaṁgraha*
MAV	*Madhyāntavibhāgabhāṣya*
MB	Mikkyo Bunka (Quartely Report on Esoteric Buddhism): Koyasan University
MCB	Mélanges Chinois et Bouddhiques, Bruxelles.
MDBK	Minobusan Daigaku Bukkyogakubu Kiyo (Bulletin of Faculty of Buddhism): Minobusan University
MS	*Mahāyānasaṁgraha*
MSA	*Mahāyānasūtrālaṁkāra*
MSBh	*Mahāyānasaṁgrahabhāṣya*
MSU	*Mahāyānasaṁgrahopanibandhana*
MVY	*Mahāvyutpatti*
N	*sNar thang* edition of Tibetan translation of the *Mahāyānasaṁgraha*
Na	Nagao's Tibetan text of the *Mahāyānasaṁgraha*
NBK	Nihon Bunka Kenkyu (Studies in Japanese Culture): Komazawa Women's University
NDKR	Nagasaki Daigaku Kyoikugakubu Ronshu (Humanities

	and Science Bulletin): Nagasaki University
NTGK	Nihon Tibetto Gakkai Kaiho (Report of the Japanese Association for Tibetan Studies), Kyoto
ODKN	Otani Daigaku Kenkyu Nenpo (Annual Report of Researchs of Otani University)
OG	Otani Gakuho (Journal of Buddhist Studies and Humanities): Otani University
OsG	Osaki Gakuho (Journal of Nichiren Buddhist Studies): Rissho University
P	Peking edition of Tibetan translation of the *Mahāyānasaṁgraha*
Pa	Pramārtha's Chinese translation of the *Mahāyānasaṁgraha*
Pa-MSBh	Pramārtha's Chinese translation of the *Mahāyānasaṁgrahabhāṣya*
RDBKN	Ryukoku Daigaku Bukkyogakubu Kenkyushitsu Nenpo (Annual Report of Researchs of Department of Buddhist Studies at Ryukoku University)
RDR	Ryukoku Daigaku Ronshu (Journal of Ryukoku University)
SK	Shukyo Kenkyu (Journal of Religious Studies), Tokyo
T	Taipei edition of Tibetan translation of the *Mahāyānasaṁgraha*
Taisho	Taisho Shishu Daizokyo (大正新修大蔵経)
TBKK	Toyo Bunka Kenkyusho Kiyo (The Memoirs of the Institute of Oriental Culture): The University of Tokyo
TDSBK	Taisho Daigaku Sogo Bukkyo Kenkyusho Nenpo (Annual of the Institute for Comprehensive Studies of Buddhism): Taisho University

TG	Toho Gakuho (Journal of Oriental Studies): Kyoto University
WSTB	Wiener Studien zur Tibetologie und Buddhismuskunde, Wien
WZKSO	Wiener Zeitschrift für die Kunde Süd- und Ostasiens, Wien
ZDMG	Zeitschrift der Deutschen Morgenländischen Gesellschaft, Wiesbaden
Y	Yamaguchi's Tibetan text of the *Mahāyānasaṁgraha*
顯揚論	顯揚聖教論, Hsüan-Tsang, tr., Taisho vol. 31, no. 1602, pp. 480b9–583b17.
成唯識論	Shindo: *Ch'eng wei Shih lun* (新導　成唯識論), Saeki, J. ed., Todaiji, Nara, 1940 (fourth ed. 1975)

Prolegomenon

The *Mahāyānasaṁgraha* (hereinafter, MS) has been studied by many scholars, and a great deal of effort has been expended on its philosophical theories, e.g., theory of *ālaya-vijñāna*, theory of three natures (*tri-svabhāva*), theory of the Buddha-body (*buddha-kāya*), etc.[1] What seems to be lacking, however, is a study of praxis and the relation of praxis and the philosophical theory behind it. In order to be released from suffering (*duḥkha*), a fundamental goal of Buddhism, not only philosophical theory but also praxis is important. In such a case, there is to be no differentiation between philosophical theory and praxis. In other words, there is no release from suffering without philosophical theory and there is no release from suffering without praxis. In spite of this, studies to the present have focused upon Asaṅga's philosophical theories and have treated praxis only superficially.[2] Therefore, future research must take into account more fully the theory of praxis. Consequently, translation in the present book aims to advance a scholarly understanding of praxis and the relation of the practical and philosophical theories described in the third chapter (hereinafter, III) of the MS, *Mahāyānasaṁgrahabhāṣya* (herein-

1 Cf. Aramaki 1963, 1964, Katano 1967, Yeh 1975, Takemura 1975, 1976, Hakamaya 1976a, Suguro 1982, Schmithausen 1985, and Yoshimura 1998, 2002, etc.

2 On praxis in the MS, see Watanabe 2001, 2002, and 2013.

after, MSBh) by Vasubandhu (probably around the fifth century)[3], and *Mahāyānasaṁgrahopanibandhana* (hereinafter, MSU) by Asvabhāva (probably the sixth century).[4]

My translations of the MS and some passages of the MSBh and MSU are based upon my own Tibetan texts which will appear in 'Chapter Three' of the present book.

Prior to such textual work, since it will be important to contextualize the text historically, a discussion on Asaṅga and his works, in particular the MS will be given in 'Chapter One.'

---

3 On the person Vasubandhu, see Frauwallner 1951, Jaini 1958, and Schmithausen 1967. Powers lists the works that deal with Vasubandhu's date. See Powers 1992, p. 22, n. 1.

4 The date of Asvabhāva is also uncertain. According to Tāranātha (Chimpa and Chattopadhyaya, 1970, pp. 253–256), Asvabhāva lived after Dharmakīrti (CE. 600–660). Some modern scholars assume his date to be around the fifth to sixth century. Kajiyama dates Asvabhāva to CE. 500–560. However, Katano assumes that Asvabhāva lived between the latter half of the sixth century and the early seventh century. See Kajiyama 1969, p. 314., and Katano, 1975 pp. 38–40.

Chapter One

Asaṅga and His Works

Introduction

In spite of the fact that Asaṅga was an important Buddhist philosopher who composed significant works in which he developed and systematized the Yogācāra philosophy, the exact events of his life are not known. There are, however, four sources for biographical information: (1) the *P'o sou p'an tou fa shih chuan* (婆藪槃豆法師傳) by Paramārtha (CE. 499–569),[1] (2) *Ta t'ang hsi yü chi* (大唐西域記) by Hsüan-tsang (CE. 602–664),[2] (3) *Chos 'byung* by Bu ston (CE. 1290–1364),[3] and (4) *rGya gar chos 'byung* by Tāranātha (the sixteenth century),[4] but these four sources seem to include myth and legend. Only the following particulars which seem to refer to historical facts can be extracted: Asaṅga was born as a son of a brahman woman in Puruṣapura (modern day Peshwar in Pakistan); he was an elder brother of Vasubandhu who was also a very important Yogācāra philosopher and to whom the MSBh is ascribed; he became a Buddhist monk when he was young; he

1 Taisho vol. 50, no. 2049, pp. 188a5–191a17. English translation has been made by Takakusu. See Takakusu 1904.

2 Taisho vol. 51, no. 2087, pp. 867b10–947c1 (especially, 896b20–897a7). English translation has been made by Beal. See Beal 1906.

3 Obermiller 1931a, pp. 136–147.

4 Chimpa and Chattopadhyaya 1970, pp. 154–175.

later converted to the Mahāyāna; he converted his brother Vasubandhu to Mahāyāna; he composed very important works, such as the *Abhidharmasamuccaya*, MS, etc.; and he developed and systematized the Yogācāra philosophy.[5]

The date of Asaṅga has also been a central question among many scholars of Buddhist history both in the East and in the West for a long time. Modern scholars assume that Asaṅga lived between the fourth and the fifth centuries.[6]

Asaṅga's Works

Many works are ascribed to Asaṅga. According to Bu ston, the following works are ascribed to Asaṅga:[7]

---

5 Asaṅga's life has been discussed and summarized by many modern scholars based upon the four sources for biographical information mentioned above. See Lévi 1911, pp. 1–7., Wayman 1961, pp. 19–46., Rahula 1966, pp. 133–136., Warder 1970, pp. 435–437., Rahula 1971, pp. ix–xiii., Willis 1982, pp. 3–12., Nagao 1982, pp. 6–13., Griffiths 1986, p. 174 nn. 7 and 9., and Powers 1992, pp. 22–27.

Herein, where available, English titles of Japanese articles have been taken over from the publications themselves. Where unavailable, English titles of Japanese articles with asterisk have been constructed by the author of this book. Reconstructed Sanskrit titles of the Chinese and Tibetan canonical texts also have been asterisked in Chapters one and two of this book; however, in 'Chapter Two' when Sanskrit terms have been given on the basis of Chinese and Tibetan translations, an asterisk has been added to the technical terms, except the common Sanskrit terms, e.g., Buddha, Bodhisattva, Śrāvaka, etc.

6 Ui and Nakamura date Asaṅga to CE. 310–390. Hikata dates Asaṅga to CE. 395–470. Takasaki dates Asaṅga to CE. 380–460. Lévi dates Asaṅga to CE. 365–440. Warder dates Asaṅga to CE. 290–360. Wayman dates Asaṅga to CE. 375–430. See Ui 1932, Nakamura 1980, Hikata 1954, Takasaki 1982, Lévi 1911, Warder 1970, and Wayman 1961.

7 Obermiller 1931a, pp. 54–56.

(1) *Yogācārabhūmi*[8]

(i) *Sa'i gngos gzhi (*Maulī Bhūmi)*[9]

(ii) *rNam par gtan la dbab pa bsdu ba (Viniścaya-saṁgrahaṇī)*[10]

(iii) *gZhi bsdu ba (Vastusaṁgrahaṇī)*[11]

(iv) *rNam grangs bsdu ba (Paryāyasaṁgrahaṇī)*[12]

---

8 Chinese tradition ascribes this text to Maitreya(-nātha). Tibetan tradition, however, ascribes it to Asaṅga. Many modern scholars think that this work was not composed by a single author. See Frauwallner 1956, p. 265, Schmithausen 1969a, 1969b, 1982, 1987, pp. 220–222., Yokoyama 1971, Suguro 1976, and Hirakawa 1979, pp. 92–119. On the other hand, Wayman and Mukai think that the *Yogācārabhūmi* was composed by a single author, i.e., Asaṅga. See Wayman 1961, pp. 41–45., Mukai 1976, and Mukai 1981.

9 Although in the Tibetan Tripiṭaka, the *Śrāvakabhūmi* and *Bodhisattvabhūmi* are not included, originally they constituted a part of this text. For the details of the *Śrāvakabhūmi* and *Bodhisattvabhūmi*, see nn. 18 and 19 below in this chapter.

Derge no. 4035, Peking no. 5536, translators are unknown. In the *Bodhisattvabhūmi* and *Śrāvakabhūmi*, the translators are ascribed to Jinamitra and Ye shes sde, and Prajñāvarman and Ye shes sde respectively. Chinese translation: *Yü ch'ieh shih ti lun, Pên shih fen* (瑜伽師地論　本事分), Hsüan-tsang, tr., Taisho vol. 30, no. 1579, pp. 279a1–388b2. For the Sanskrit title of this text, see Matsuda 1988, p. 18.

10 Derge no. 4038, Peking no. 5539, Prajñāvarman, Surendrabodhi, and Ye shes sde, tr. Chinese translation: *Yü ch'ieh shih ti lun, Shê chyüeh tsê fen* (瑜伽師地論　攝決擇分), Hsüan-tsang, tr., Taisho vol. 30, no. 1579, pp. 579a1–749c18., *Chyüeh ting tsang lun* (決定藏論), Paramārtha, tr., Taisho vol. 30, no. 1584, pp. 1018b18–1035b25. Tibetan texts: Schmithausen 1969 and Willis 1976, pp. 186–257. Modern translations: Schmithausen 1969 (German translation of some sections in the *Viniścayasaṁgrahaṇī*) and Willis 1976 (English translation of the *Tattvārtha* chapter of the *Bodhisattvabhūmi* in the *Viniścayasaṁgrahaṇī*). Modern works: Ui 1965a, Hakamaya 1978, 1979b, and Matsuda 1988.

11 Derge no. 4039, Peking no. 5540, Prajñāvarman, Surendrabodhi, and Ye shes sde, tr. Chinese translation: *Yü ch'ieh shih ti lun, Shê shih fen* (瑜伽師地論　攝事分), Hsüan-tsang, tr., Taisho vol. 30, no. 1579, pp. 772b10–868b23.

12 Derge no. 4041, Peking no. 5542, Prajñāvarman, Surendrabodhi, and Ye shes sde, tr. Chinese translation: *Yü ch'ieh shih ti lun, Shê i mên fen* (瑜

(v) *rNam par bzhad pa'i sgo bsdu ba* (**Vivaraṇa-saṁgrahaṇī*)[13]

(2) *Abhidharmasamuccaya*[14]

(3) *Mahāyānasaṁgraha*[15]

According to Tāranātha, the following works are ascribed to Asaṅga:[16]

(1) *Yogācārabhūmi*

(i) *Śrāvakabhūmi*[17]

(ii) *Bodhisattvabhūmi*[18]

伽師地論　攝異門分), Hsüan-tsang, tr., Taisho vol. 30, no. 1579, pp. 760a4–772b9.

13 Derge no. 4042, Peking no. 5543, Prajñāvarman, Surendrabodhi, and Ye shes sde, tr. Chinese translation: *Yü ch'ieh shih ti lun, Shê shih fen* (瑜伽師地論　攝釋分), Hsüan-tsang, tr., Taisho vol. 30, no. 1579, pp. 749c19–760a3.

14 Sanskrit editions: Pradhan 1950 and Tatia 1976. Tibetan translation: Derge no. 4049, Peking no. 5550, Jinamitra, Śīlendrabodhi, and Ye shes sde, tr. Chinese translation: *Ta ch'êng a p'i ta mo chi lun* (大乘阿毘達磨集論), Hsüan-tsang, tr., Taisho vol. 31, no. 1605, pp. 663a1–694b10. Modern translations: Rahula 1971, Griffiths 1986, pp. 129–138., and Funahashi 1982, 1986, 1990, 1995. Modern works: Schmithausen 1983, Funahashi 1991a, 1991b, Kritzer 1995, 1999., etc.

15 For the details of this text, see next section, "The *Mahāyānasaṁgraha*," in this chapter.

16 Chimpa and Chattopadhyaya 1970, pp. 393–394.

17 Tibetan translation: Derge no. 4036, Peking no. 5537, Jinamitra and Ye shes sde, tr. Chinese translation: *Yü ch'ieh shih ti lun, Shêng wên ti* (瑜伽師地論　聲聞地), Hsüan-tsang, tr., Taisho vol. 30, no. 1579, pp. 395c1–477c1. Sanskrit editions: Wayman 1961, Shukla 1973, Schmithausen 1982, and Katsube 1981, 1982, 1984, 1985, 1986, 1987, 1988, 1998. Modern translations: Wayman 1961, pp. 58–162 and Katsube 1998.

18 Tibetan translation: Derge no. 4037, Peking no. 5538, Prajñāvarman, and Ye shes sde, tr. Chinese translations: *Yü ch'ieh shih ti lun, P'u sa ti*, (瑜伽師地論　菩薩地), Hsüan-tsang, tr., Taisho vol. 30, no. 1579, pp. 478b2–576b27. *P'u sa ti ch'ih ching* (菩薩地持経), T'an-Wu-Ch'en (曇無讖), tr.,

(iii) *rNam par gtan la dbab pa bsdu ba* (*Nirṇayasaṁgrahaṇī =Viniścayasaṁgrahaṇī*)

(iv) *gZhi bsdu ba* (*Vastusaṁgrahaṇī*)

(v) *'Dul ba bsdu ba* (*Vinayasaṁgrahaṇī*)[19]

(vi) *rNam grangs bsdu ba* (*Paryāyasaṁgrahaṇī*)

(vii) *rNam par bẓhad pa'i sgo bsdu ba* (**Vivaraṇasaṁgrahaṇī*)

(2) *Abhidharmasamuccaya*

(3) *Mahāyānasaṁgraha*[20]

(4) *Chos kyi sku la gnas pa'i yon tan la bstod pa* (*Dharmakāyāśrayāsāmānyaguṇastotra*)[21]

Taisho vol. 30, no. 1581, pp. 888a5–959b14. *P'u sa ti shan chieh ching* (菩薩善戒経), Guṇavarman (求那跋摩), tr., Taisho vol. 30, no. 1582, pp. 960a1–1013c14. *P'u sa ti shan chieh ching* (菩薩善戒経), Guṇavarman, tr., Taisho vol. 30, no. 1583, pp. 1013c15–1018b17. *P'u sa ti chieh chieh mo wên* (菩薩戒羯磨文), Hsüan-tsang, tr.,Taisho vol. 24, no. 1499, pp. 1104c16–1106c1. *P'u sa ti chieh pên* (菩薩戒本), Guṇavarman, tr., Taisho vol. 24, no. 1500, pp. 1107a1–1110a24. *P'u sa ti chieh pên* (菩薩戒本), Hsüan-tsang, tr., Taisho vol. 24, no. 1501, pp. 1110b1–1115c22. *Yu p'o sê wu chieh wei i ching* (優婆塞五戒威儀経), Guṇavarman, tr., Taisho vol. 24, no. 1503, pp. 1116c6–1121b15 (Taisho nos. 1581 and 1582+1583 are complete translations of the *Bodhisattvabhūmi*. Taisho nos. 1499, 1500, 1501, and 1503 are translations of the *śīla* chapter in the *Bodhisattvabhūmi*). Sanskrit editions: Rahder 1926, Wogihara 1930, Dutt 1966, Hatano 1975, and Roth 1977. Modern translations: Frauwallner 1956, pp. 270–279., Demiéville 1957, Ui, 1961a, Willis 1976, pp. 186–257., Willis 1982, and Soma 1986a, 1986b, 1987. Modern works: Bendall & Poussin 1905, 1906, 1911, and Yokoyama and Hirosawa 1997.

19 Derge no. 4040, Peking no. 5541, Prajñāvarman, Jinamitra, and Ye shes sde, tr. Chinese translation: *Yü ch'ieh shih ti lun, Shê shih fen* (瑜伽師地論 攝事分), Hsüan-tsang, tr., Taisho vol. 30, no. 1579, pp. 868c1–882a13.

20 For the details of this text, see next section, "The *Mahāyānasaṁgraha*," in this chapter.

21 Derge no. 1115, Peking no. 2007, Jimamitra, Śīlendrabodhi, and Ye shes sde, tr. Tibetan edition and Modern work: Hakamaya 1983.

(5) *Shes rab kyi pha rol tu phyin ma'i sgrub thabs* (*Prajñāpāramitāsādhana*)[22]

(6) *'phags pa byams pa'i sgrub thabs* (*Āryamaitreya-sādhana*)[23]

(7) *'phags pa dgongs pa nges par 'grel pa'i rnam par bshad pa* (*Āryasaṁdhinirmocanabhāṣya*)[24]

(8) *Sangs rgyas rjes su dran pa'i 'grel pa* (*Buddhānu-smṛtivṛtti*)[25]

(9) *Chos rjes su dran pa'i 'grel pa* (*Dharmānusmṛtivṛtti*)[26]

(10) *Dge 'dun rjes su dran pa'i bshad pa* (*Saṁghānusmṛti-vyākhyā*)[27]

(11) *Theg pa chen po['i] rgyud bla ma'i bstan bcos kyi rnam par bshad pa* (*Mahāyānottaratantraśāstra-vyākhyā*)[28]

---

22 Derge no. 3550, Peking no. 4372, Grags pa rgyal mthsan, tr.

23 Derge no. 3647, Peking no. 4471, Jo bo chen po and Dge bshes ston pa, tr.

24 Derge no. 3981, Peking no. 5481, Jinamitra, Śīlendrabodhi, and Ye shes sde, tr. Modern works: Nishio 1982 and Powers 1992, pp. 29–50.

25 Derge no. 3982, Peking no. 5482, Ajitaśrībhadra and Śākya 'od, tr. Modern work: Goda 1995.

26 Derge no. 3983, Peking no. 5483, translators are unknown. Modern work: Goda 1998.

27 Derge no. 3984, Peking no. 5484, Ajitaśrībhadra and Śākya 'od, tr.

28 Peking no. 5526 (Kārikā with commentary) is ascribed to Asaṅga. Derge no. 4025 (Kārikā with commentary) and both Derge no. 4024 and Peking no. 5525 (Kārikā only) are ascribed to Maitreya(-nātha). This text is, however, ascribed to Chien-Hui (堅慧) by Chih-I (智顗, *Mo ho chih kuan*, chüan 3 (摩訶止観 巻３)). Ui ascribes this text to Chen-Hui. Takasaki ascribes the Kārikā text (Derge no. 4024, Peking no. 5525) to Maitreya(-nātha). Nakamura ascribes the Kārikā text (Derge no. 4024, Peking no. 5525) to Chen-Hui, but he ascribes the Kārikā text with the commentary (Derge no. 4025, Peking no. 5526) to Vasubandhu. See Ui 1959, pp. 80–90., Takasaki 1966, p. 62., and Nakamura 1961, pp. 58–61. Tibetan translation: Derge no. 4025, Peking no. 5526, Sajjana and Blo ldan shes rab, tr. Chinese translation: *Chiu ching i ch'êng pao hsing lun*

(12) *bSam gtan gyi sgron ma zhes bya ba'i man ngag (Dhyānadīpadeśanāmopadeśa)*[29]

In the Chinese Tripiṭaka, the following works are ascribed to Asaṅga:

(1) *Shê ta ch'êng lun* (攝大乘論, Skt. Title: *Mahāyānasaṁgraha*)[30]
(2) *Hsien yang shêng chiao lun* (顯揚聖教論, Skt. Title: **Āryadeśanāvikhyāpana*)[31]
(3) *Hsien yang shêng chiao lun sung* (顯揚聖教論頌)[32]
(4) *Ta ch'êng chuang yen ching lun* (大乘荘嚴經論, Skt. Title: *Mahāyānasūtrālaṁkāra*)[33]

(究竟一乘寶性論), Ratnamati (勒那摩提), tr., Taisho vol. 31, no. 1611, pp. 813a4–848a27. Sanskrit editions: Johnston and Chowdhury 1950, and Nakamura 1961. Modern translations: Obermiller 1931b, Ui 1959, Nakamura 1961, and Takasaki 1966, 1988. Modern works: Ruegg 1969, Takasaki 1974, and Schmithausen 1971.

29 Derge no. 4073, Peking no. 5574, translators are unknown. Modern work: Goda 1994.

30 For the details of this text, see next section, "The *Mahāyānasaṁgraha*," in this chapter.

31 顕揚聖教論, Hsüan-tsang, tr. Taisho vol. 31, no. 1602, pp. 480b9–583b17. Modern works; Yuki 1956, vol. I, pp. 51–60, vol. II, pp. 397–463., Ui 1965b, Mukai 1979, and Hayashima 1988 1997a, 1997b, 1997c, 2004, etc.

32 顯揚聖教論頌, Hsüan-tsang, tr., Taisho vol. 31, no. 1603, pp. 583b18–589b18.

33 In the Chinese tradition, Kārikā text is ascribed to Asaṅga, and commentary is ascribed to Vasubandhu. In the Tibetan tradition, however, this text (Kārikā text only, Derge no. 4020, Peking no. 5521) is ascribed to Maitreya(-nātha). The text (Kārikā with commentary, Derge no. 4026, Peking no. 5527) is ascribed to Vasubandhu. For the discussion on this text and its authorship, see Yokoyama 1971, Hakamaya 1993, pp. 13–23., etc.
大乘荘嚴經論, Prabhākaramitra, tr., Taisho vol. 31, no. 1604, pp.

(5) *Ta ch'êng a p'i ta mo chi lun* (大乘阿毘達磨集論, Skt. Title: *Abhidharmasamuccaya*)

(6) *Lu mên chiao shou hsi ting lun* (六門教授習定論, Skt. Title is not known)[34]

(7) *Chin kang pan jo lun* (金剛般若論, Skt. Title: **Vajracchedikāprajñāpāramitāśāstra*)[35]

(8) *Nêng tuan chin kang pan jo po lo mi to ching lun sung* (能斷金剛般若若波羅密多經論頌, Skt. Title: *Triśatikāyāḥ prajñāpāramitāyāḥ kārikā saptati*)[36]

(9) *Shun chung lun* (順中論, Skt. Title is not known)[37]

589b1–661c21. Sanskrit editions: Lévi 1907, Bagchi 1970, Hayashima 1977, 1978, 1979, 1982, 1983a, 1983b, Odani 1983, pp. 217–232., and Funahashi 1985, pp. 1–55. Modern translations: Léve, 1911, Ui 1961b, Odani 1983 pp. 136–218., etc. Modern works: Funahashi, 1978, 1985, 2000, Hayashima 1973, 1983c, etc.

34 六門教授習定論, I-Ching (義淨), tr., Taisho vol. 31, no. 1607, pp. 774a7–777b3. Modern work: Ui 1963, pp. 567–606.

35 金剛般若論, Dharmagupta, tr., Taisho vol. 25, no. 1510, pp. 757a1–781a24. Modern work: Nagao 1973 (Japanese translation).

36 能斷金剛般若波羅密多經論頌, I-Ching (義淨), tr., Taisho vol. 25, no. 1514, pp. 885a1–886c17. Sanskrit edition: Tucci 1956, pp. 51–92. Tibetan translation: Cordier 1915, p. 495. Modern translations: Tucci 1956, pp. 93–128 (English translation)., Ui 1963, pp. 302–416 (Japanese translation)., and Joshi 1978 (Hindī translation). Modern works: Yamamoto 1961 and Nagao 1978.

There is a commentary ascribed to Vasubandhu, i.e., 能斷金剛般若波羅密多經論釋, I-Ching, tr., Taisho vol. 25, no. 1513, p. 875a1. This commentary contains the Kārikā text (Taisho no. 1514).

37 順中論, Gautama-Prajñāruci, tr., Taisho vol. 30, no. 1565, pp. 39c14–51b15. Modern works: Kataoka 1959, Ozawa 1968, 1970, and Keenan 1989.

The *Mahāyānasaṁgraha*

The MS of Asaṅga is one of the most representative works of the Yogācāra school in Mahāyāna Buddhism. It develops and systematizes the Yogācāra philosophy and praxis discussed in the early *Mahāyāna sūtras*, such as the *Saṁdhinirmocanasūtra*, *Prajñāpāramitāsūtra*, and early Yogācāra texts such as, the *Yogācārabhūmi*, *Mahāyānasūtrālaṁkāra*, *Madhyāntavibhāga*, etc.[38]

The MS (root text) is not extant in Sanskrit, or Sanskrit manuscript might be extant, but we have no detailed information about it. In any case, it is extant in Tibetan translation and four Chinese translations. More recently, a commentary by Mi pham has come to our attention. The text is titled, *Theg chen bsdus pa'i snying po mchan bcas bshugs*.[39]

The MS consists of an introduction (*prastāvana*) and ten chapters: I (*jñeyāśraya*) deals with the theory of *ālaya-vijñāna*; II (*jñeya-lakṣaṇa*) deals with the three natures (*tri-svabhāva*) theory; III (*jñeya-lakṣaṇa-praveśa*) deals with entrance into the realization of the truth that all phenomena are nothing but mental presentations (*vijñapti-mātratā*); IV (*tat-praveśa-hetu-phala*) deals with six kinds of perfection (*pāramitā*); Chapter V (*tat-bhāvanā-prabheda*) deals with ten bodhisattva stages (*bhūmi*); VI (*adhiśīla*) deals with moral conduct (*śīla*); VII (*adhicitta*) deals with concentration (*samādhi*); VIII (*adhiprajñā*) deals with non-discriminative cognition (*nirvikalpa-jñāna*); IX (*phala-prahāṇa*) deals with the transformation of the basis of existence (*āśraya-parāvṛtti*); X (*phala-jñāna*) deals with the three bodies (*tri-kāya*) of the Buddha.

---

38 See Ui 1935, pp. 28–116., Sasaki 1931 (rpt. 1977, pp. 12–25), and Nagao 1982, pp. 41–47.

39 Date and source are unknown, except that it is available in Nepal.

Chinese translations of the MS (root text):

(1) *Shê ta ch'êng lun* (攝大乘論), Buddhaśānta (仏陀扇多) of the Northern Wei dynasty (後魏, CE. 386–534), tr., Taisho vol. 31, no. 1592, pp. 97a1–112b8.

(2) *Shê ta ch'êng lun* (攝大乘論), Paramārtha (眞諦) of the Chou dynasty (陳, CE. 557–589), tr., Taisho vol. 31, no. 1593, pp. 112b9–132c14.

(3) *Shê ta ch'êng lun shih lun* (攝大乘論釋論), Dharmagupta and others (笈多共行矩等) of the Sui dynasty (隋, CE. 589–618), tr., Taisho vol. 31, no. 1596, pp. 271a1–321a8. (This is in fact a translation of Vasubandhu's commentary on the MS, but this text containes the MS.)

(4) *Shê ta ch'êng lun pên* (攝大乘論本), Hsüan-tsang (玄奘) of the Tang dynasty (唐, CE. 618–907), tr., Taisho vol. 31, no. 1594, pp. 132c15–152a18.

Among the four Chinese translations, Buddhaśānta's translation is the oldest and the most difficult. Since it is crude and difficult to comprehend, the original Sanskrit words, phrases, and sentences are not easily reconstituted, and in many cases, even an understanding of his text can not be gained. In MS III. 4, for example, the word "four situations" is rendered in the Tibetan translation by *gnas bzhi*. Whereas other Chinese translations have *ssŭ ch'u* (四處), Buddhaśānta's translation has *chung chung chuang ch'u* (種種荘處).[40] Thus, it is difficult to understand what is to be meant by

40 See 'Chapter Three,' p. 91, n. 27 below. Nagao, too, gives some examples of Buddhaśānta's mistranslations and misunderstandings of the MS.

Buddhaśānta's translation.

Paramārtha's translation is the longest translation among the four. He seemed not to simply translate the Sanskrit original text, but added words, phrases, or sentences in many places. In MS III. 6, for example, Paramārtha's translation has the phrase *yu mieh ch'u ssŭ ch'u chang ku* (由滅除四處障故) which other translations including the Tibetan translation do not have.[41] This additional phrase does not change the meaning of the discussion itself in MS III. 6; rather it makes the context of the discussion of the MS clear. In MS III. 7A, moreover, Paramārtha's translation has the sentence *yüan fa chi i wei ching* (緣法及義爲境), but the Tibetan translation and other Chinese translations have no such sentence.[42] Other than these two, there are many cases where Paramārtha added his own words, phrases, or sentences. Paramārtha's additional words, phrases or sentences may be helpful to some degree in understanding the discussion of the MS, but as Nagao mentions, "Paramārtha is very impressionistic in places and lacks any attempt to standardize the vocabulary."[43]

Dharmagupta's translation, as mentioned above, is in fact a translation of Vasubandhu's MSBh with a translation of the MS. Since the Sanskrit original text is not available, it cannot be known how faithful Dharmagupta's translation is to the Sanskrit. As Nagao states: "The translation of Dharmagupta (originally from Lo-lo 羅羅, in South India) shares with that of Hsüan-tsang a close identity with the Tibetan version, but the former is written in the so-called 'old translation' style. In addition, there are infelicities

See Nagao 1994, p. xiii.

41 See 'Chapter Three,' p. 97, n. 42 below.

42 See 'Chapter Three,' p. 99, n. 51 below.

43 Nagao 1994, p. xii.

in the Chinese style and word usage. In other words, this is a literal translation, from which we can imagine to a considerable extent the Sanskrit which it must represent. From the point of view of reconstituting the Sanskrit originnal of the treatise this can, of course, be a great help."[44]

Hsüan-tsang's translation is probably the most reliable translation among the four. It seems to try to convey the meaning of the MS. For this reason, Hsüan-tsang's translation has been most widely studied by modern scholars. However, it cannot be assumed on that basis that Hsüan-tsang's translation strictly conveys the philosophy of Asaṅga. There are some ambiguities in his translation. The ambiguities, as Nagao states, may be caused by Hsüan-tsang's struggle to express the nuances of the Sanskrit originals in the Chinese medium.[45] In any case, it is true that Hsüan-tsang's translation is a great help in understanding the MS.

Tibetan translation of the MS:

> *Theg pa chen po bsdus pa*, Jinamitra, Śīrendrabodhi, and Ye shes sde, tr., Derge no. 4048, *Co ne* microfiche vol. 55, Peking no. 5549, *sNar thang* no. 3540, Taipei no. 4053.

The Tibetan translation of the MS is dense and terse so that it contains many difficult passages. The surviving Tibetan translation, as Schmithausen reports, contains later additions.[46] As he aptly comments, however, this does not mean that additions have been

44 Ibid., p. xi.
45 Ibid., p. xi.
46 Schmithausen 1985, p. 148.

made by someone other than the author of the MS. They may had been added by the author himself during the process of composition or in the course of a later revision of the work.[47]

There are three commentaries on the MS, i.e., (1) the MSBh, (2) the MSU, and (3) the *Don gsang ba rnam par phye ba bsdus te bshad pa* (**Vivṛtaguhyārthapiṇḍavyākhyā*)

The MSBh is ascribed to Vasubandhu, a younger brother of Asaṅga.[48] This text is not extant in Sanskrit, but it remains in Tibetan translation and three Chinese translations.

---

47 Ibid., p. 148.

48 Researches regarding Vasubandhu's works have been continuing and have produced their results progresssively. Matsuda and Muroji determined the chronological order of the following works ascribed to Vasubandhu through an examination of those works, *Abhidharmakośabhāṣya* (hereinafter, AKBh) — *Vyākhyāyukti* — *Karmasiddhiprakaraṇa* — *Pratītyasamutpādavyākhyā*. For the detailed discussions, see Matsuda 1984a and Muroji 1986.

In examining AKBh, Hakamaya has pointed out eleven places that deal with the idea of *pūrvācārya* (former master), and says that ten among the eleven can be traced to Yogācāra texts. Moreover, he draws our attention to a very interesting sentence in Yaśomitra's *Abhidharmakośavyākhyā* in which it is stated: *pūrvācāryāḥ yogācāra ārya Asaṅgaprabhṛtayaḥ|* (*pūrvācāryās* are the Yogācārins beginning with *ārya*-Asaṅga). See Hakamaya 1986.

Moreover, Matsuda, as a result of his investigation, points out that the theory of two truths in the *Vyākhyāyukti* is the theory of the two truths advocated by Yogācāra school, and it has the same content as the theory of two truths found in the AKBh. In another paper, he points out that the "prescription for the taking refuge in the *triratna*" found in the *Pratītyasamutpādavyākhyā* is applied to the verse of veneration to the Buddha by Vasubandhu found in his MSBh. See Matsuda 1984b and 1985.

Chinese translations of the MSBh:

(1) *Shê ta ch'êng lun shih* (攝大乘論釋), Paramārtha, tr., Taisho vol. 31, no. 1595, pp. 152a19–270b14.

(2) *Shê ta ch'êng lun shih lun* (攝大乘論釋論), Dharmagupta and others (笈多共行矩等), tr., Taisho no. 1596, pp. 271a1–321a8.

(3) *Shê ta ch'êng lun shih lun* (攝大乘論釋論), Hsüan-tsang, tr., Taisho no.1597, pp. 321a9–380a 17.

Paramārtha's translation is more than twice the length of the other two Chinese translations. He has added his own additional comments to the translation of the MSBh. In MSBh III. 1, for example, the Tibetan translation has *mang du thos pas bsgoms pa'i gnas zhes bya ba ni theg pa chen po yongs su bsgoms pa'i bdag nyid kyi ngo bo'o*. While Dharmagupta has *to wên hsün hsi wei i chih chê wei ta ch'êng fa so hsün shên ku* (多聞熏習爲依止者 謂大乘法所熏身故) and Hsüan-tsang has *to wên hsün hsi so i chê wei ta ch'êng fa so hsün tzu t'i* (多聞熏習所依者 謂大乘法所熏自體), Paramārtha has inserted his additional comment, i.e., *tz'u hsün hsi yu shuo chi tz'u i chih* (此熏習有說即此依止), in the translation of the MSBh.[49] Paramārtha's additional comments, according to Keenan, seem to blend the ideas of Asaṅga and Vasubandhu with themes drawn from the *tathāgatagarbha* thought.[50] Nagao, however, states that "Paramārtha has strayed far from Vasubandhu's intentions."[51]

Dharmagupta's translation is close to Hsüan-tsang's transla-

49 Taisho vol. 31, p. 199a11.
50 Hakamaya 1989, p. 41.
51 Nagao 1994, p. xii.

tion. In his translation of the MSBh, moreover, there are many passages, from which the Sanskrit original words and phrases can be reconstituted.[52] Therefore, Dharmagupta's translation is of great help in emending the Tibetan translation of the MSBh. However, it cannot be assumed on that basis that Dharmagupta's translation is an accurate and faithful rendition of the Sanskrit original text. As mentioned above, since the Sanskrit original of the MSBh is not available, to what extent Dharmagupta's translation represents Vasubandhu's original text cannot be known.[53]

Hsüan-tsang's translation is probably the most reliable translation among the three. Although in contrast to the Tibetan and other Chinese translators, there are some places where he has changed the order of the sentences, Hsüan-tsang's translation as well as Dharmagupta's is of a great help in emending the Tibetan translation and in understanding the MSBh. Since Hsüan-tsang is the only scholar who had translated all three texts, i.e., the MS, MSBh, and MSU, his translations are consistent in presenting technical terms and in translation style. It should be noted, however, that in some places, Hsüan-tsang has inserted additional comments, and as Keenan reports, there are places where Hsüan-tsang weaves a Fa-hsiang (i.e., Dharmapāla) interpretation into the text.[54] Therefore, it can be questioned to what extent Hsüan-tsang transmitted accurately and faithfully Vasubandhu's intentions.

---

52 In his excellent monograph, *Ālayavijñāna*, for example, Schmithausen has reconstituted a passage in Dharmagupta's Chinese translation III. 12 into Sanskrit. See Schmithausen 1987, Part II, p. 403, n. 717 below.

53 For the discussion on the characteristics of Dharmagupta's Chinese translation of the MSBh, see Iwata 1983.

54 Hakamaya 1989, p. 43.

Tibetan translation of the MSBh:

Theg pa chen po bsdus pa'i 'grel pa, Dīpaṁkaraśrījñāna and Tshul khrims rgyal ba, tr., Derge no. 4050, Peking no. 5551, Taipei no 4055.

The Tibetan translation of the MSBh, especially the introductory chapter and third chapter, has many displacements and missing portions of the sentences, paragraphs, and sections. It can not be determined when these textual problems occurred, but they might have taken place during the process of the translation or they might have been in the Sanskrit original text of the MSBh with which the Tibetan translators worked. Although there is a general trend to think that the Tibetan translations of Indian works are basically faithful to the Sanskrit originals, since the Sanskrit original of the MSBh is not available, to what extent the Tibetan translation is accurate and faithful to the Sanskrit original cannot be determined. In any case, the surviving Tibetan translation of the MSBh cannot be read and understood without careful emendations.[55]

The MSU of Asvabhāva is also not extant in Sanskrit, but it is extant in Tibetan and Chinese translations.

Chinese translation of the MSU:

Shê ta ch'êng lun shih lun (攝大乘論釋論), Hsüan-tsang, tr.,

55 The introductory chapter of the MSBh has been emended in Nagao 1943. The third chapter of the MSBh has been emended in Shimokawabe 1992.

Taisho no. 1598, pp. 380a18–449b26.

Hsüan-tsang's translation has some passages which are not found in the Tibetan translation. According to Hakamaya, the passages which are not found in the Tibetan translation are additions made by Hsüan-tsang himself.[56] According to Keenan, moreover, Hsüan-tsang's translation of the MSU has places where Fa-hsiang (i.e., Dharmapāla) interpretations are weaved into the original text.[57] This does not, of course, mean that Hsüan-tsang's translation of the MSU is inaccurate. His translation is still a great help in understanding the MSU.

Tibetan translation of the MSU:

> *Theg pa chen po bsdus pa'i bshad sbyar*, Jinamitra, Śīlendrabodhi, and Ye shes sde, tr., Derge no. 4051, Peking no. 5552, Taipei no. 4056.

The Tibetan translation of the MSU is in general a readable text. There are, however, cases where it is not in accord with Hsüan-tsang's Chinese translation, and there are passages which are not accounted for in his translation. With regard to this, Hakamaya reports that the content of the passages which do not accord with Hsüan-tsang's translation is closely aligned to Asvabhāva's own ideas and that the passages which are not found in Hsüan-tsang's translation are regarded to be passages found in the original so that the Tibetan translation of the MSU more faithfully represents the

56 See Hakamaya's articles mentioned above.
57 Hakamaya 1989, p. 43.

original Sanskrit text than Hsüan-tsang's Chinese translation.[58]

The *Don gsang ba rnam par phye ba bsdus te bshad pa* (**Vivṛtaguhyārthapiṇḍavyākhyā*, hereinafter, Vivṛ) is extant only in Tibetan translation and its author is unknown.

Tibetan translation of the Vivṛ:

> *Don gsang ba rnam par phye ba bsdus te bshad pa*, Derge no. 4052, Peking no. 5553, Taipei no. 4057.

According to Bu ston's *Dkar chag* (Nishioka #706), however, the Vivṛ is recorded to have been composed by Dbyig gnyen (*Vasubandhu).[59] This text is a commentary on the first chapter of the MS, but it goes no further than section 49 in Lamotte's numbering.

58 For the detailed discussions on this matter, see Hakamaya 1969, 1970, 1973, 1974b, and 2008, pp. 237–247.

59 Nishioka 1981, p. 57.

Bibliography of Modern Editions and Translations of the MS, MSBh, MSU, and Vivṛ

The MS and its commentaries have been studied by many scholars over a long period of time because the MS is one of the most important texts in the Yogācāra school. Therefore, numerous works have been completed already on the text.

Chiba, Koji. "『秘儀分別摂疏』覚え書 (1)" (A Memo about *Vivṛtaguhyārthapiṇḍavyākhyā* (1)), KJDKK vol. 8, 2001, pp. 209–216 (Japanese translation of some portions of the Vivṛ).

———— "『秘儀分別摂疏』覚え書 (2)" (A Memo about *Vivṛtaguhyārthapiṇḍavyākhyā* (2)), NBK vol. 4, 2002, pp. 117–131 (Japanese translation of some portions of the Vivṛ).

———— "如来の所分別についての一考察—『秘儀分別摂疏』覚え書 (3)" (A Study of *Kalpitatva* for *Tathāgata*: A Memo about *Vivṛtaguhyārthapiṇḍavyākhyā* (3)), KJDKK vol. 9, 2002, pp. 199–210 (Japanese translation of some portions of the Vivṛ).

———— "『秘儀分別摂疏』における真如観について" (On the Concept of *tathatā* in the *Vivṛtaguhyārthapiṇḍavyākhyā*), IBK vol. 52-1, 2003, pp. 376–373 (119–122) (Japanese translation of some portions of the Vivṛ).

———— "所分別と三昧についての一考察—『秘儀分別摂疏』覚え書 (4)" (A Study of *Vikapla* and *Samādhi*: A Memo about *Vivṛtaguhyārthapiṇḍavyākhyā* (4)), KK vol. 37, 2004, pp. 79–85 (Japanese translation of some portions of the Vivṛ).

———— "唯識説におけるBuddha-vacanatvaについて—『秘儀分別摂疏』覚え書 (5)" (On the *Buddha-vacanatva* in Vijñaptimātratāvādin: A Study of *Vivṛtaguhyārthapiṇḍavyākhyā* (5)), KJDKK vol. 11, 2004, pp. 131–140 (Japanese translation of some portions of the Vivṛ).

———— "『秘儀分別摂疏』の考察 (6)" (A Study of *Vivṛta-guhyārthapiṇḍavyākhyā* (6)), KJDKK vol. 12, 2005, pp. 107–117 (Japanese translation of some portions of the Vivṛ).

———— "アーラヤ識縁起説における増益と損減—『秘儀分別摂疏』の考察 (7)—" (*Samaropa* and *Apavāda*, in Thought of *Pratītyasamutpada* based on *Ālayavijñāna*: A study of *Vivṛta-guhyārthapiṇḍavyākhyā* (7)), KJDKK vol. 13, 2006, pp. 167–175 (Japanese translation of some portions of the Vivṛ).

———— "アーラヤ識の存在証明—『秘儀分別摂疏』の考察 (8)—" (Existence Proof of *Ālayavijñāna*: A Study of *Vivṛta-guhyārthapiṇḍavyākhyā* (8)), KJDKK vol. 14, 2007, pp. 131–140 (Japanese translation of some portions of the Vivṛ).

———— "アーラヤ識の存在証明—『秘儀分別摂疏』の考察 (9)—" (Existence Proof of *Ālayavijñāna*: A Study of *Vivṛta-guhyārthapiṇḍavyākhyā* (9)), KJDKK vol. 15, 2008, pp. 103–114 (Japanese translation of some portions of the Vivṛ).

———— "『秘儀分別摂疏』の考察 (10)" (A Study of *Vivṛta-guhyārthapiṇḍavyākhyā* (10)), KJDKK vol. 16, 2009, pp. 117–127 (Japanese translation of some portions of the Vivṛ).

———— "『秘儀分別摂疏』の考察 (11)" (A Study about *Vivṛta-guhyārthapiṇḍavyākhyā* (11)), KJDKK vol. 17, 2010, pp. 149–184 (Japanese translation of some portions of the Vivṛ).

Frauwallner, Erich. *Die Philosophie des Buddhismus*, Berlin, 1956, pp. 335–350 (Includes German translation of some portions of MS I, II, III, VIII, IX, and X).

Goda, Hideyuki. "『摂大乗論』第三章の解明 (1)—チベット訳無性註を中心として—" (An Interpretation of the Third Chapter of the *Mahāyānasaṁgraha* (1)), Toho vol. 9, 1994, pp. 119–129

(Japanese translation of early portions of MSU III).

Hakamaya, Noriaki. "*Mahāyānasaṁgrahopanibandhana*, Its Tibetan and Chinese Text (1)," KDBK vol. 31, 1973, pp. 8–14 (Edition of some portions of the Tibetan and Chinese texts of MSU I).

——— "*Mahāyānasaṁgrahopanibandhana*, Its Tibetan and Chinese Text (2)." KDBK vol. 32, 1974, pp. 1–14 (Edition of some portions of the Tibetan and Chinese texts of MSU I).

——— "*Mahāyānasaṁgrahopanibandhana*, Its Tibetan and Chinese Text (3)." KDBK vol. 33, 1975, pp. 15–33 (Edition of some portions of the Tibetan and Chinese texts of MSU I).

——— "*Mahāyānasaṁgraha* における心意識説" (The Theory of *citta*, *manas*, and *vijñāna* in the *Mahāyānasaṁgraha*), TBKK vol. 76, 1977, pp. 197–307 (Japanese translation of the early portions of MSBh I and MSU I).

Harada, Waso. "「蛇・縄・色等」の比喩と入唯識性 (I)—MS III §§ 8–9 の和訳と評註—" (*An Analogy of 'Snake, Rope, Colour, etc.' and Entrance into *Vijñaptimātratā* (1)), 渡邊隆生教授還暦記念佛教思想文化史論叢 (*A Collection of Papers In Honour of Professor Watanabe Takao On the Occasion of his Sixtieth Birthday, Buddhist Thought and History of Buddhist Culture*), the Committee for the Commemoration of Professor Watanabe Takao's Sixtieth Birthday, ed., Nagata Bunshodo, Kyoto, 1997, pp. 125–152 (Sanskrit reconstitution, edition of the Tibetan text, and Japanese translation of MS III. 8–9).

——— "「蛇・縄・色等」の比喩と入唯識性 (II)—MSU III §§ 8–9 の和訳と評註—" (*An Analogy of 'Snake, Rope, Colour, etc.' and Entrance into *Vijñaptimātratā* (2)), KRTDK, vol. 43, 1997, pp. 135–175 (Sanskrit reconstitution, edition of the Tibetan text, and Japanese translation of MSU III. 8–9).

Iwata, Taijyo. 初期唯識思想研究—世親造『摂大乗論釈』所知相章の漢蔵対照— (A Study of the Early Yogācāra Philosophy: Vasubandhu's *Mahāyānasaṁgrahabhāṣya*: A Comparison of the Chinese and Tibetan Translations: The *Jñeyalakṣaṇa* Chapter), Daizoshuppan, Tokyo, 1981 (Edition of the Tibetan and Chinese texts of MSBh II).

———— "世親造『摂大乗論釈』所知依章の漢蔵対照（一）" (A Comparison of the Chinese and Tibetan Translations of the *Jñeyāśraya* Chapter of Vasubandhu's *Mahāyānasaṁgrahabhāṣya*), HBK vol. 18, 1992, pp. 1–54 (Edition of some portions of the Tibetan and Chinese texts of MSBh I).

———— "世親造『摂大乗論釈』所知依章の漢蔵対照（二）" (A Comparison of the Chinese and Tibetan Translations of the *Jñeyāśraya* Chapter of Vasubandhu's *Mahāyānasaṁgrahabhāṣya*), MDBK vol. 1, 2000, pp. 1–34 (Edition of some portions of the Tibetan and Chinese texts of MSBh I).

———— "世親造『摂大乗論釈』所知依章の漢蔵対照（三）" (A Comparison of the Chinese and Tibetan Translations of the *Jñeyāśraya* Chapter of Vasubandhu's *Mahāyānasaṁgrahabhāṣya*), MDBK vol. 2, 2001, pp. 17–37 (Edition of some portions of the Tibetan and Chinese texts of MSBh I).

———— "世親造『摂大乗論釈』所知依章の漢蔵対照（四）" (A Comparison of the Chinese and Tibetan Translations of the *Jñeyāśraya* Chapter of Vasubandhu's *Mahāyānasaṁgrahabhāṣya*), MDBK vol. 4, 2003, pp. 1–19 (Edition of some portions of the Tibetan and Chinese texts of MSBh I).

Katano, Michio. インド仏教における唯識思想の研究—無性造「摂大乗論註」所知相章の解読— (*A Study of *Vijñaptimātra* Thought—

An Annotated Translation of the *Jñeyalakṣaṇa* Chapter of Asvabhāva's Commentary on the *Mahāyānasaṁgraha*), Buneido, Kyoto, 1975. (Japanese translation of MSU II)

———— "無住涅槃としての転依" (Buddhist Thought of *Apratiṣṭhita-nirvāṇa* in India: An Annotated Translation of Asvabhāva's Commentary on the *Mahāyānasaṁgraha*, the Chap. IX), OG vol. 56-2, 1976, pp. 37–49 (Japanese translation of MSU IX).

———— "無性造「摂大乗論註」序章の解読" (The Annotated Translation of Asvabhāva's Commentary on the Introductory Chapter of the *Mahāyānasaṁgraha*), BGS vol. 27, 1977, pp. 37–54 (Japanese translation of the introductory chapter of the MSU)

Kawamura, Leslie S. "*Nirvikalpa-jñāna*: Awareness Freed From Discrimination," in *From Benares To Beijing: Essays on Buddhism and Chinese Religion in Honour of Prof. Jan Yün-Hua*, Shinohara, K. and Schopen, G., eds. Mosaic Press, 1991 (English translation of MS IX with English translation of Nagao's explanatory comment on the same chapter of the MS).

Hakamaya, Noriaki. (Keenan, J., Griffiths, P., and Swanson, P.), *The Realm of Awakening: Chapter Ten of Asaṅga's Mahāyānasaṁgraha*. Oxford University Press, 1989 (Editions and English translation of the Tibetan texts of MS X, MSBh X, and MSU X. It also includes English translation of the two Chinese translations (Hsüan-tsang and Paramārtha) of MSBh X).

Keenan, John P. *The Summary of the Great Vehicle*, Numata Center, Berkeley, 1992 (English translation of Paramārtha's

Chinese translation of the MS).

Lamotte, Étienne. "L'*ālayavijñāna* (La Réceptacle) dans la *Mahāyānasaṁgraha* (Chaptire II), Asaṅga et ses commentateurs," MCB vol. 3, 1935, pp. 169–255 (French translation of MS II, MSBh II, and MSU II).

——— *La Somme du Grand Véhicule D'Asaṅga* (*Mahāyānasaṁgraha*) Tome I and II. Université du Louvain, Publications de l'Institut Orientaliste du Louvain 8, 1938 (rpt. 1973) (Edition and French translation of the Tibetan text of the MS and French translation of some portions of the Tibetan and Chinese texts of the MSBh and MSU).

Nagao, Gadjin M. "摂大乗論世親釈の漢蔵本対照" (*A Comparison of the Chinese and Tibetan Translations of Vasubandhu's Commentary on the *Mahāyānasaṁgraha*), TG vol. 13-2, 1943, pp. 119–175 (Edition of Tibetan and Chinese texts of the introductory chapter of the MSBh).

——— 摂大乗論—和訳と註解—（上）（下）(*The *Mahāyānasaṁgraha*: A Japanese Translation and Annotation), Kodansha, Tokyo, 1982–1987 (Edition of Tibetan text and annotated Japanese translation of the MS based on both Tibetan and Chinese translations).

Sasaki, Gessho. 漢訳四本対照・攝大乗論 (*Comparison of the Four Chinese Translations of the *Mahāyānasaṁgraha*), Hobunsha, Tokyo, 1931 (rpt. Rinsenshoten 1977), (Edition of the Chinese texts of the MS. It includes Yamaguchi's Tibetan edition of the MS).

Shimokawabe, Kiyoshi. "An Emendation of the Tibetan Translation of Vasubandhu's Commentary on *Jñeyalakṣaṇapraveśa* of the *Mahāyānasaṁgraha*," HBK, vol. 18, 1992, pp. 55–76

(Edition of the Tibetan text of MSBh III).

———— "チベット語訳世親釈『摂大乗論・入所知相分』和訳" (A Japanese Translation of the Tibetan Version of Vasubandhu's Commentary on *Jñeyalakṣaṇapraveśa* of the *Mahāyānasaṁgraha*), HBK vol. 20, 1994, pp. 107–122. (Japanese translation of MSBh III)

Ueda, Yoshifumi. 摂大乗論講読 (*Lectures on the *Mahāyānasaṁgraha*), Kodansha, Tokyo, 1981 (Includes a free translation of MS II).

Ui, Hakuju. 攝大乗論研究 (*A Study of the *Mahāyānasaṁgraha*), Iwanamishoten, Tokyo, 1935 (rpt. 1966) (Includes edition of Paramārtha's Chinese texts of the MS).

Watanabe, Chikafumi. "A Translation of *Mahāyānasaṁgraha* III. 1–4" in 瓜生津隆真博士退職記念論集　仏教から真宗へ (Essays in Honour of Prof. Dr. Ryushin Uryuzu's Retirement from Kyoto Women's University, "From Buddhism to [Pure Land] Shin Buddhism"), Nagata Bunshodo, Kyoto, 2003, pp. 157–176 (Tibetan text and English translation of the MS III. 1–4).

———— "A Translation of *Mahāyānasaṁgraha* III. 5–7," *Nagoya Studies in Indian Culture and Buddhism, SAṀBHĀṢĀ* vol. 24, Nagoya University, Nogoya, 2004, pp. 99–114 (Tibetan text and English translation of the MS III. 5–7).

———— "A Translation of *Mahāyānasaṁgraha* III. 8–11" in 禪學研究　特別號　小林圓照博士古希記念論集　仏教の思想と文化の諸相 (Studies in Zen Buddhism, Special Issue, Aspects of Buddhist Thought and Culture: Essays in Honour of Professor Ensho Kobayashi's 70th Year), Hanazono University, Kyoto, 2005, pp. 73–98 (Tibetan text and English translation of the MS III. 8–11).

The Contents of *Mahāyānasaṁgraha* III

MS III is a discussion on the bodhisattva's entrance into the defining characteristics of what is to be known, i.e., the realization of the truth that all phenomena are nothing but mental presentations (*vijñapti-mātratā*). In order to realize this truth, yogic praxes, such as concentration and meditation, are necessary. According to the Yogācāra school, there is a fivefold path/fivefold yogic stage (*pañca-mārga/pañca-yoga-bhūmi*) in which a yogin practices concentration and meditation. The MS deals with four paths that are summarized in the third chapter into eighteen sections (III. 1–III. 18 below).[60]

III. 1 Introduction

This section is an introduction to the realization of the truth and explains how the bodhisattva is to understand "the entrance into the defining characteristics of what is to be known (*jñeya-lakṣaṇa-praveśa*)."

In explaining "the entrance into the defining characteristics of what is to be known," Asaṅga introduces the concept of mind-talk (*mano-jalpa*). Mind-talk is (1) subsumed under proper attentiveness (*yoniśo-manaskāra*), (2) presents itself as the cognitum which is characterized by the fact that Buddha's teachings and their meanings emerge in it as an appearance, and (3) accompanied by the act of perceiving (*sadṛṣṭi/sadarśana*). This concept of mind-talk plays an important role in praxis. The bodhisattva, listening to the Buddha's teachings, repeats them in his mind and by doing so, the Buddha's teachings are impregnated into the Bodhi-

60 In the following, the divisions of numbering of the MS made by Nagao has been adopted. See Nagao, 1987.

sattva's mind.

III. 2 The subject who realizes the truth

This section deals with the subject of who realizes the truth. It is the bodhisattva who has accumulated the provisions of meritorious acts and knowledge. The reason is that a bodhisattva is someone who has accumulated the roots of wholesomeness by virtue of the mental flow (*citta-saṁtāna*) that has been impregnated by listening to the Mahāyāna teachings many times, who is accomplished in serving the infinite numbers of the Buddhas who have appeared in the world (*aprameya-buddhotpāda*), and who possesses unwavering earnest commitment (*aikāntikādhimuktitva*).

III. 3 The place/object of the realization of the truth

This section deals with the place/object of the realization of the truth. The bodhisattva enters into mind-talk (1) that is accompanied by the act of perceiving, (2) that possesses the appearance (*pratibhāsa*) of Buddha's teachings and their meanings, and (3) that arises from having the Mahāyāna teachings as its cause. It is on the basis of such mind-talk that the bodhisattva enters (I) *adhimukticaryā-bhūmi* (the stage of zealous application), (II) *darśana-mārga* (the path of insight), (III) *bhāvanā-mārga* (the path of cultivation) and (IV) *niṣṭhā-mārga* (the path of fulfilment).

III. 4 The practical means to the realization of truth

This section deals with the means of the realization of the truth. The bodhisattva realizes the truth (1) by stimulating the mind in three ways, (2) by removing the four obstructive situations, and

(3) by being attentive to practicing, constantly and carefully, the meditations of calm and insight that have the teachings and their meanings as their objective reference/support (*ālambana*).

III. 5A Three ways of stimulating the mind

This section explains the "stimulating the mind in three ways" mentioned in section 4. The first incident of stimulating the mind is to think: "Countless sentient beings (*aprameya-sattva*) who are human beings (*manuṣya-bhūta*) in the countless worldly realms (*aprameya-lokadhātu*) shall realize incomparable perfect enlightenment (*anuttarā saṁyak-saṁbodhi*) at every moment." The second incident of stimulating the mind is to think: "I have obtained that intention (*āśaya*) with which I practice fully the perfection of giving (*dāna-pāramitā*), etc., and consequently, with little difficulty (*alpa-kṛcchena*), I will become accomplished fully in the habituation of the perfection." The third incident of stimulating the mind is to think: "If one possesses wholesome qualities (*kuśala-dharma*), even though wholesomeness is obstructed, then immediately at the time of one's death, one will quickly be born with the body completely intact (*saṁpad*) just as one wishes. If that is so, why would someone like I who possess wholesomeness which is not obstructed (*anāvaraṇa-kuśala*) not become immediately born with the body completely intact?"

III. 5B Three Verses from Texts, such as *Mahāyānasūtrālaṁkāra* X. 11

This section quotes three verses which illustrate three ways of stimulating the mind. The first verse is quoted from *Mahāyānasūtrālaṁkāra* X. 11, but text or texts of the second and third verses are not identified.

III. 6 The proper exertion regarding the four obstructive situations

This section explains "removing the four obstructive situations" which was also mentioned in section 4. (1) The bodhisattva removes completely the attentiveness (*yoniśo-manaskāra*) of the Śrāvakas and Pratyekabuddhas by means of removing improper attentiveness, (2) the bodhisattva becomes free of doubt regarding the Mahāyāna teachings by means of getting rid of the harbouring a divided mind (*vimati*) and ambivalence (*kāṅkṣā*), and (3) the bodhisattva removes the attachment to the notion that "I have heard the teachings" and the notion that "the teachings that I have heard and reflected upon are mine," and (4) by means of removing discrimination (*vikalpa*), the bodhisattva, not paying attention to any objectification (*nimitta*) whether it appears before him or whether it is caused to be present in meditation, does not discriminate.

III. 7A The means to the realization of the truth

This section deals with the means by which the truth is realized. That is, a bodhisattva realizes the truth by means of mind-talk (1) that arises owing to the impregnation of listening to the teachings many times, (2) that is subsumed under proper attentiveness, (3) that appears as Buddha's teachings and their meanings, and (4) that is accompanied by the act of perceiving.

It is on the basis of mind-talk that the bodhisattva enters into the truth through the four kinds of investigations (*paryeṣaṇā*), i.e., the investigations into the (i) name, (ii) object, (iii) designation of the intrinsic nature of entities and (iv) designation of specific attributes (*viśeṣa*) of entities, and through the four kinds of wisdom of knowing reality as-it-is (*yathābhūta-parijñāna*): the wisdoms of knowing (i) name as-it-is, (ii) object as-it-is, (iii) designation of the intrinsic nature of entities as-it-is, (iv) designation of specific attributes of entities as-it-is.

III. 7B The realization of the truth

This section deals with the realization of the truth, i.e., the result of the praxis. The bodhisattva who has practiced realizes that all phenomena are nothing but mental presentations. Through the praxis, i.e., the four kinds of investigations and the four kinds of wisdom of knowing reality as-it-is, the bodhisattva understands that a name and an object are nothing but mind-talk.

III. 8A The explanation of the realization of the truth

This section explains the realization of the truth to be "that-only" (*tan-mātra*)—i.e., cognition-only (*vijñapti-mātra*), "the two," i.e., that which is to be cognized and cognizer (*grāhya-grāhaka*), and "various forms (*nānākāra*)."

III. 8B An Analogy regarding the realization of the truth

This section gives an analogy regarding III. 8A.

III. 9 The three natures (*tri-svabhāva*)

This section describes the realization of the truth in terms of three natures (*tri-svabhāva*). The bodhisattva realizes the imagined nature (*parikalpita-svabhāva*) by understanding the defining characteristics of objects that appear from mind-talk. He realizes the other-dependent nature (*paratantra-svabhāva*) by realizing the truth that all phenomena are nothing but mental presentations. He realizes the consummated nature (*pariniṣpanna-svabhāva*) by having reversed even the idea that all phenomena are nothing but mental presentations.

III. 10 A verse regarding the domain of naming

This section summarizes "the name" mentioned in the previous sections by means of a verse.

III. 11 *Darśana-mārga* (the path of insight)

This section describes the contents of *darśana-mārga* (the path of insight). Realizing the truth that all phenomena are nothing but mental presentations, the bodhisattva enters into the first of bodhisattva's ten stages. The bodhisattva who understands *dharmadhātu* is born in the lineage of the *Tathāgata*s and obtains the mind of equanimity regarding all sentient beings, all bodhisattvas, and all Buddhas.

III. 12 The purpose of the realization of the truth

This section explains the purpose of the realization of the truth. The bodhisattva realizes the truth in order to attain the wisdom of an omniscient one. That is, the bodhisattva realizes the truth in order to become a Buddha.

III. 13 The four kinds of *samādhi*s and *nirvedha-bhāgīya*

This section explains the practice in *nirvedha-bhāgīya* (the state leading up to penetration [into truth]). That is, in *uṣma-gata* (the state of heat), the bodhisattva practices the "concentration by which one obtains clarity" (*āloka-labdha-samādhi*). In *mūrdha* (the state of maximum value), the bodhisattva practices the "concentration of increased clarity" (*vṛddhāloka-samādhi*). In *kṣānti* (the state of patience), the bodhisattva practices the concentration which has entered into one part of the object of reality (*tattvārthaika-deśa-praviṣṭa-samādhi*). In *laukikāgra-dharma* (the state of the mundane supreme *dharma*), the bodhisattva practices the uninterrupted concentration (*ānantarya-samādhi*).

III. 14 *Bhāvanā-mārga* (the path of cultivation)

This section describes how the bodhisattva practices *bhāvanā-mārga* (the path of cultivation) by attaining the supramundane knowledge of the meditations of calm and insight (*śamatha-vipaśyanā*) that have the teachings of the Buddha as their objective references/supports and the cognition that is attained subsequent to that supramundane knowledge.

III. 15 The superiority of the realization of the bodhisattva

This section describes the superiority of the realization of the bodhisattva in contrast to the realization of the Śrāvakas. The realization of the bodhisattva is superior in contrast to the realization of the Śrāvakas in view of ten kinds of superiorities, i.e., (1) in view of objective reference (*ālambana*), (2) in view of support (*upastambha*), (3) in view of experience (*prativedha*), (4) in view of *nirvāṇa*, (5) in view of the stages (*bhūmi*), (6) in view of purification (*pariśuddhi*), (7) in view of obtaining an impartial mind (*sama-cittatā-prāpti*), (8) in view of birth [in the family of the Buddha] (*janma*), (9) in view of taking up the rank [of a Buddha] (*utpatti-saṁbhava*), and (10) in view of fruition (*phala*).

III. 16 Three verses from texts, such as *Mahāyānasūtrālaṁkāra* XIX. 47

This section quotes three verses that illustrate the four kinds of investigations, the four kinds of wisdom of knowing reality as-it-is, and the three natures.

III. 17 Two verses from the **Yogavibhāgaśāstra*

This section quotes two verses from the **Yogavibhāgaśāstra* that illustrate the bodhisattva's concentration.

III. 18 Six verses from *Mahāyānasūtrālaṁkāra* VI. 6–10

This section quotes verses VI. 6–10 from the *Mahāyānasūtrālaṁkāra* that summarize the Bodhisattva's practice discussed in MS III, and are understood by the translators and commentators of the MS, MSBh, and MSU as the ones that illustrate the Bodhisattva's fivefold path to the enlightenment.

Chapter Two

Translation of *Mahāyānasaṁgraha* III

Introduction to the Translation

The following translation of MS III is based on the Tibetan text found in 'Chapter Three' of this book. The most important point of translating a text is to express the idea of the author as faithfully as possible. However, in the process of translating, there arise many issues such as the complexities of Tibetan grammar, sentence style, and technical terms that must be understood in order to give an accurate interpretation of the original text. Accordingly attention has been given to such issues in the English translation of MS III that follows, and therefore, care has been taken to choose the most appropriate and fitting English words for the technical terms that appear in the text, to express the nuance of the Tibetan grammar and syntax, and to be mindful of the original Sanskrit terms that Asaṅga may have employed in his original work. Also, in order to keep the sense of the text itself, an attempt was made to keep the translation as literal as possible, without losing the English grammatical construction and the natural flow of English. For example, the following will illustrate the implications of above statements. In MS III 7B, the Tibetan text reads: *yongs su tshol ba bzhi dang yang dag pa ji lta ba bzhin du yongs su shes pa bzhi po dag gis yi ge dang don snang ba'i yid kyi rnam par rtog pa de dag la rnam par rig pa tsam nyid du 'jug go*. This statement might be translated literally thus: By means of the four investigations and the four wisdom of knowing reality as-it-is, one enters into **vijñaptimātratā* with regard to those mental discriminations that appear as sound and meaning. However, a more stylistic English translation might read thus: [In this manner,] by means of the four [kinds of] investigations and the four [kinds of] wisdom of knowing reality as-it-is, [the bodhisattva] understands those mental discriminations that appear as sound and meaning to be **vijñaptimātratā*.

As tools for translation, the Tibetan-English dictionaries[1] by Das and Jäschke are indispensable; however, when the technical terms of Mahāyāna Buddhism and of Yogācāra in particular are of concern, then lexicons such as *Tibetan-Sanskrit Dictionary*,[2] the *Mahāvyutpatti*,[3] edited by Sakaki, the various indexes such as *Index to the Mahāyānasūtrālaṁkāra* (Parts I and II),[4] *An Index to Asaṅga's Mahāyānasaṁgraha* (Parts I and II),[5] *Madhyāntavibhāgabhāṣya* (the index that follows the Sanskrit text),[6] *Index to the Abhidharmakośabhāṣya*,[7] and the academic works of other scholars such as Schmithausen's "The *Darśanamārga* Section of the *Abhidharmasamuccaya* and Its Interpretation by Tibetan Commentators (with special reference to *Bu ston rin chen grub*)"[8] and *Ālayavijñāna, On the Origin and the Early Development of a Cen-*

---

1 Das, 1902 (rpt. 1969) and Jäschke, 1965.
2 Candra, 1959.
3 Sakaki, 1962 (rpt. 1981).
4 Nagao, 1958 (Part I) and 1961 (Part II).
5 Nagao, 1994.
6 Nagao, 1964, pp. 79–220.
7 Hirakawa, 1973.
8 Schmithausen, 1983, pp. 259–274.

tral Concept of Yogācāra Philosophy.[9]

Further, Monier-Williams' *A Sanskrit-English Dictionary*[10] and Edgerton's *Buddhist Hybrid Sanskrit Dictionary and Grammar*[11] are indispensable tools when translating from the Sanskrit.

When reference to Sanskrit words or passages from extant Sanskrit texts are used, these terms are used without the asterisk (*), because these can be verified through the original text. However, when the original Sanskrit technical terms cannot be verified, the terms have been marked with the asterisk (*), except the common Sanskrit terms, e.g., Buddha, Bodhisattva, Śrāvaka, etc.

Square brackets [ ] were used to indicate that additional words or ideas were added to make the passage more comprehensive in English. Selected Tibetan passages from MSBh III and MSU III and Sanskrit passages from other works were also translated in footnotes, and their Tibetan and Sanskrit passages can be found in footnotes of the Tibetan text of the MS in 'Chapter Three' of this book.

Reference to the Chinese translations of the MS and of its commentaries, the MSBh and MSU were noted when the Tibetan texts were not clear or when difficulties in interpretation of passages were encountered.

9 Schmithausen, 1987.
10 Monier-Williams, 1982.
11 Edgerton, 1970.

Translation

MS III. 1

The defining characteristic of what is to be known (**jñeya-lakṣaṇa*) has been explained as above.[12] How is [the bodhisattva] to understand the entrance (**praveśa*) into the defining characteristics of what is to be known?

It is [to be understood as] the basis (**āśraya*) that has been impregnated (**paribhāvita*) by listening [to the Mahāyāna teachings] many times (**bahu-śruta/bāhu-śrutya*).[13] Although it is not what is subsumed under the **ālaya-vijñāna*, like the **ālaya-vijñāna*, it becomes the seed of mind-talk[14] (**mano-jalpa*) that is subsumed

12 See MS II, Lamotte 1973, pp. 87–152, Nagao 1987, pp. 272–440.

13 MSBh: [The statement:] **the basis that has been impregnated by listening [to the Mahāyāna teachings] many times** refers to a body (basis of personal existence, **ātmabhāva*) impregnated fully by the Mahāyāna [teachings].

Pa-MSBh (199a11) has the sentence 此熏習有說即是依止 (tr.: Someone states that this impregnation is the basis).

MSU: [*Ācārya*-Asaṅga] states: **the basis that has been impregnated by listening [to the Mahāyāna teachings] many times**, because it is the situation of [listening to] the Mahāyāna [teachings many times]. **By listening to** the Mahāyāna teachings and [their] meanings **many times**, a person's continuous flow of mind and mental functions (**citta-caitta-saṁtāna*) **has been impregnated**, because there is no realization (**abhisamaya*) in one who has not yet listened [to the Mahāyāna teachings] many times. [In the *Rāhula-sūtra*] *ārya*-Rāhula makes a request to Bhagavat as follows: "I request the Bhagavat to teach me, so that I [will be able to attain] the realization." [Bhagavat] replies: "Rāhula, have you taken up the teachings?" He answers: "Bhagavat, no, I have not yet taken them up." Bhagavat says: "Rāhula, if that is the case, then, take up the teachings only and learn them."

14 In Tibetan text, the word "mind-talk" is used in the plural (*yid kyi brjod pa rnams*), but I have translated it in the singular. See 'Chapter Three,' p. 87, *l*, 2.

under proper attentiveness (*yoniśo-manaskāra-saṁgṛhīta),[15] that presents [itself] as the cognitum (*grāhya-vastu-sthānīya) which is characterized by [the fact that the Buddha's] teachings and [their] meanings emerge [in it] as appearance,[16] and that is accompanied by the act of perceiving (*sadṛṣṭi/sadarśna).[17]

---

15 MSBh: [The statement:] **Although it is not what is subsumed under the *ālaya-vijñāna** and [the statement:] **like the *ālaya-vijñāna, it becomes the seed** [**of mind-talk**] **that is subsumed under proper attentiveness** mean that in the manner that ***ālaya-vijñāna** is the cause of impure *dharmas (*saṁkliṣṭa-dharma), in the same manner, it becomes the cause of the pure *dharmas. [This means that the statements] beginning with **of mind-talk that is subsumed under the proper attentiveness** up to **mind-talk ... that is accompanied by the act of perceiving** refer to the cause because representation (*ākāra) of **the** [**Buddha's**] **teachings and** [**their**] **meanings** emerges from **proper attentiveness.**

MSU: [The statement:] **it is not what is subsumed under the *ālaya-vijñāna** means that [it] is not the nature of that [*ālaya-vijñāna*], because [it] flows out of *dharma-dhātu completely freed of impurities and because [it] is the antidote (*pratipakṣa) of that [*ālaya-vijñāna*], and [the basis] **is not subsumed under** that [*ālaya-vijñāna*] because [it] is opposite [of the *ālaya-vijñāna*]. [The statement:] **like the *ālaya-vijñāna, it becomes the seed** means that in the manner that the ***ālaya-vijñāna** is the cause of impure *dharmas, in the same manner also this **basis** is the cause of pure *dharmas; [basis] is conformity with (*anurūpa) the analogy (*dṛṣṭānta) [i.e., *ālaya-vijñāna*,] only in so far as a cause, but not otherwise.

16 MSBh: [The statement: **mind-talk that**] **presents** [**itself**] **as the cognitum** means that [mind-talk] becomes a form (*rūpa).

MSU: [The statement:] **teaching** (*dharma) refers to *sūtra*, etc. [The statement:] **meaning** (*artha) refers to non-self (*nairātmya, *anātman*), etc., that are to be taught precisely therein. Because [mind-talk] has its own characteristics of emerging in the form of those [teachings and their meanings], **it is characterized by** that [**fact that the Buddha's teachings and their meanings**] **emerge** [**in it**] **as appearance.** [The statement: **mind-talk that**] **presents** [**itself**] **as the cognitum** is [stated] because [it] appears in the likeness of that [object].

17 MSBh: [The statement:] **accompanied by the act of perceiving** means [that mind-talk is] **the act of perceiving.** That very [mind-talk] is es-

MS III. 2

In this case (**atra*), who is it that enters into the defining characteristics of what is to be known?[18]

It is a bodhisattva who has accumulated properly the provisions of meritorious acts and knowledge (**puṇya-jñāna-saṁbhāra*) because he has properly accumulated the roots of wholesomeness (**kuśala-mūla*) [by virtue of the fact that his] mental flow (**citta-saṁtāna*) has been impregnated by listening to the Mahāyāna teachings many times,[19] [he is one who] is accomplished in serving the infinite numbers of the Buddhas who have appeared [in the world] (**aprameya-buddhotpāda*),[20] and [he is

---

tablished as the knowledge (**vijñāna*) possessing the objective aspect (**nimitta*) and **the act of perceiving**.

MSU: [The statement:] **accompanied by the act of perceiving** means **accompanied by** the auditory-cognition. **Various mind-talks** refer to **various** **manovijñāna*. Or, [mind-talk] **accompanied by** the aspect of **the act of perceiving** is established as the cognitum (**grāhya*) and the cognizer (**grāhaka*), just as explained before (See MS II. 12, Lamotte, 1973 pp. 101–103, Nagao 1987, pp. 307–312).

18 MSU: [The statement:] **who is it that enters into [the defining characteristics of what is to be known]** is a question in the form of investigating [**who it is that**] **enters** and realizes [the defining characteristics of what is to be known].

H-MSU (413c12–13): 用及用具皆待作者　故問入者誰能悟入 (tr.: All the activity and means possess the doer. Accordingly, [the statement:] **Who is it that** can **enters [into the defining characteristics of what is to be known]** asks one who enters).

19 MSBh: Therein, the word "**Mahāyāna**" is stated with the intention of rejecting [other] vehicle, the Śrāvaka, etc.

20 MSBh: [The statement: **he is one who] is accomplished in serving the infinite numbers of the Buddhas who have appeared [in the world]** means that **[the bodhisattva is] one who is accomplished in serving** innumerable **Buddhas who have appeared [in the world]**. It means that [the bodhisattva] has encountered **the Buddhas** directly.

MSU: In [the statement: **his] mental flow has been impregnated by**

one who] has unwavering earnest commitment (*aikāntikādhi-*muktitva*).[21]

---

listening to the Mahāyāna teachings many times, etc., [the statement:] **serving the infinite numbers of the Buddhas who have appeared [in the world]** refers to encountering [many Buddhas], and accordingly, by being **accomplished in** that [serving, the bodhisattva] is said [to be one who] **is accomplished in** encountering **the infinite numbers of the Buddhas who have appeared [in the world]**.

21 Another possible translation of the MS: "It is a bodhisattva who has accumulated the provisions of meritorious acts and knowledge because he has accumulated the roots of wholesomeness, whose mental flow has been impregnated by listening to the Mahāyāna teachings many times, who is accomplished in serving the infinite numbers of the Buddhas who have appeared [in the world], and who has unwavering earnest commitment." Translation in the body of this section, however, is supported by the MSBh and MSU.

The first half of the MSBh (MSBh1) seems not to make sense, and DG-MSBh and H-MSBh make better sense. Following is a tentative translation of MSBh, according to the MSBh, DG-MSBh, and H-MSBh. See 'Chapter Three,' p. 88, n. 19 below.

MSBh1: [The statement: **he is one who**] **has unwavering earnest commitment** means that [a bodhisattva is one] whose **earnest commitment** cannot be distracted from the Mahāyāna, [and] bad friends (*mi dge ba'i grogs po*, **akalyāna-mitra*) cannot move [him] away [from the Mahāyāna]. Since, by the above-mentioned three kinds of causes for **[properly] accumulating the roots of wholesomeness**, [a bodhisattva] has accumulated the provisions of meritorious acts and knowledge, [he] is called **the bodhisattva who has properly accumulated the provisions of meritorious acts and knowledge**.

MSBh2: Moreover, by means of what order does he fully accomplish **the provisions of meritorious acts and knowledge**? [They are accomplished] by (1) the force of the cause (**hetu-bala*), (2) the force of good friends (**kalyāna-mitra-bala*), (3) the force of proper attentiveness (**manasikāra-bala*), and (4) the force of support (**upastambha-bala*). Among these, [the first] two phrases [in *ācārya*-Asaṅga's text] are to be known as [the first] two forces in the manner [that they were] numbered. Among these, by the force of proper attentiveness, [the bodhisattva] is caused to become **unwaveringly earnestly committed**. It in its turn is caused by the impregnation of [listening to] the Mahāyāna [teachings many times]. With regard to that, if there is unwavering earnest commitment, [the bodhisattva] properly engaged in the praxis (**pratipatti*). If [the bodhisattva] properly stays in the praxis, there will be the accumu-

MS III. 3

Wherein (**kutra*) does [a bodhisattva] enter?[22]

[A bodhisattva enters] that very mind-talk that is accompanied by the act of perceiving, that possesses the appearance (**pratibhāsa*) of [the Buddha's] teachings and [their] meanings, and that arises from having the Mahāyāna teachings as its cause.[23]

---

lation of the roots of wholesomeness. Thus, since, by the force of proper attentiveness, there will be **the accumulation of the provisions of meritorious acts and knowledge**, [we speak of] the order (**anukramanaya*) in that manner.

MSU: [The statement: **he is one who**] **has unwavering earnest commitment** refers to [the bodhisattva who] believes entirely in the Mahāyāna teachings and cannot be distracted by any bad friends. By these three [reasons], i.e., **listening to the Mahāyāna [teachings] many times**, etc., **because he has properly accumulated the roots of wholesomeness,** [*ācārya*-Asaṅga answers the question by stating] **it is a bodhisattva who has accumulated properly the provisions of meritorious acts and knowledge**.

22 According to Pa-MSBh and H-MSU, this question has two meanings. That is, one is the domain that the bodhisattva enters and the other is the stages that the bodhisattva enters. See Pa-MSBh (199c5–7): 論曰 諸菩薩於何處 入唯識觀 釋曰 此問有二意 一問何處是唯識境界 二問何處是唯識位, H-MSU (413c24–25): 釋曰 何處能入者 問所入境及能入位. DG-MSBh and H-MSBh seem also to have the same understanding. However, I am not certain of the meanings of the words, 相, 行相, and 類, in their translations. DG-MSBh (295a11–12): 釋曰 入如是相此入行相 今當顯示, H-MSBh (349c20): 釋曰 入如是類及入行相 今當顯示. MSBh and MSU do not state that the question in the MS has two meanings.

MSBh: In order to explain the basis for entering by such kinds, [the content of MS III] is stated [by *ācārya*-Asaṅga]. Nagao reads: かくの如きの姿をもって悟入することの階位 (tr.: the stages of entering by means of having such forms/figures ...). See Nagao 1987, p. 14, n. 1.

MSU: [The statement:] **Wherein does [the bodhisattva] enter** is asked by one who intends to ascertain the domain [that the bodhisattva enters].

23 MSBh: **Mind-talk** refers to the mental discrimination (**mano-vikalpa*). That [mind-talk] becomes the cause for the arising of any Mahāyāna teachings. [The statement: **mind-talk ... that**] **arises from having the**

[The bodhisattva] enters (I) **adhimukticaryā-bhūmi* (the stage of zealous application), (II) **darśana-mārga* (the path of insight), (III) **bhāvanā-mārga* (the path of cultivation), and (IV) **niṣṭhā-mārga* (the path of fulfillment), because [on (I) *adhimukticaryā-bhūmi*] he applies himself to the proclamation (**anuśrāvaṇa*) that [all phenomena are] nothing but [mental] presentations (**vijñapti-mātra*), because [on (II) *darśana-mārga*] he experiences [that all phenomena are nothing but mental presentations] just as-they-are, because [on (III) *bhāvanā-mārga*] he cultivates himself only in the antidote (**pratipakṣa*) against all obstructions (**sarvāvaraṇa*), and because [on (IV) *niṣṭhā-mārga*] he is [completely] freed of [any] obstructions (**nirāvaraṇa*).[24]

Mahāyāna teachings as its cause means that [**mind-talk**] has the demonstrated **teachings** as its objective-reference/support (**ālambana*).

MSU: In [the statement:] **accompanied by the act of perceiving**, etc., since **mind-talk** of one who enters and that **arises** as the appearance (**ākāra*) [of Buddha's teachings and their meanings] **from having the Mahāyāna teachings as its cause** is the domain to be entered, it is intended to be taught as the foundation (*gzhi*, **ādhāra*) [of one who wishes to realize on the different stages].

24 MSBh: Moreover, [the bodhisattva who] enters that very [mind-talk] by means of the very excellent mind-talk enters ***adhimukticaryā-bhūmi***. That is, when **he applies himself to the proclamation that all phenomena are nothing but [mental] presentations, zealous conduct** takes place [in the bodhisattva], and consequently, it is said that that [bodhisattva] enters therein. Since the manner in which [the bodhisattva] enters ***darśana-mārga*** must be explained, [*ācārya*-Asaṅga states that] **he experiences [that all phenomena are nothing but mental presentations] just as-they-are** and [this means that] mind-talk **experiences [all phenomena as nothing but mental presentations] just as-they-are**. How does that [mind-talk] **experience [that all phenomena are nothing but mental presentations] just as-they-are**? It is any experience of mind-talk in the manner: "teachings do not exist, meanings do not exist, cognitum does not exist, and cognizer does not exist." Since the entrance into ***bhāvanā-mārga*** must be explained, [*ācārya*-

MS III. 4

By means of what (**kena*) [does the bodhisattva] enter?[25]

[The bodhisattva enters] by generating (**ādhāna*) the strength of the root of wholesomeness (**kuśala-mūla-bala*). [That is, the bodhisattva] enters by (1) stimulating the mind (**cittottāpana*) in three ways, by (2) removing the four [obstructive] situations[26]

Asaṅga states that] **he cultivates himself only in the antidote against all obstructions**. To **cultivate himself** means to be actively engaged in the praxis of that very experience. Accordingly, whatever is experienced by non-discrimination (**nirvikalpa*), etc., that very experience removes the obstructions. In order to explain the entrance into that ***niṣṭhā-mārga**, [*ācārya*-Asaṅga states that] **because [... he is completely] freed of [any] obstructions**. The situation (**avasthā*) of a very pure wisdom wherein there does not exist even the most minuscule obstruction (**sukṣmāvaraṇa*) is the entrance into ***niṣṭhā-mārga**.

MSU: One who enters that mind-talk enters ***adhimukticaryā-bhūmi**, because by merely listening [to the Mahāyāna teachings many times], he applies himself to [the idea that] all phenomena are nothing but [mental] presentations. One enters ***darśana-mārga**, because he experiences mind-talk **just as-it-is**. Here, [the statement:] **experiences just as-it-is** means that [the bodhisattva] **experiences** thus: "sentient beings do not exist, teachings do not exist, cognitum does not exist, and cognizer does not exist." One enters ***bhāvanā-mārga**, because by means of **cultivating himself only in the** very **antidote against all obstructions** of afflictions (**kleśa*) and of what is to be known, he is purified. One enters ***niṣṭhā-mārga**, **because he is [completely] freed of [any] obstructions**. Thus, the experience (**prativedha*) [of the path] is of four kinds.

25 MSU: [The statement:] **by means of what [does the bodhisattva] enter** is an inquiry about the cause (**hetu*) and is synonymous with [asking] by what skillful means (**upāya*) [does the bodhisattva enter].

26 As Nagao states, it is not clear how *gnas* (probably Skt. *sthāna* in this case) should be understood. The four Chinese translations have 處 which originally means "place," "spot," etc. BŚ (104b24–25): 種種莊處滅故, Pa (122c 11): 由滅除四處障故, DG (295a29): 滅除四處故, and H (142b19): 断四處故. Nagao understands *gnas* as "場合" (case), but he says that "主題点" (subjective points), "あり方" (state), and "道理" (propriety) are also possible translations. See Nagao 1987, p. 17, n. 3. Lamotte understands *gnas* as arrêt. See Lamotte 1973, p. 156.

(**sthāna*), and by (3) being attentive (**apramāda*) to practicing (**prayoga*) constantly and carefully the cultivating of calm and insight (**śamatha-vipaśyanā-bhāvanā*) that have the teachings and their meanings as their objective references/support (**dharmārthālambana*).[27]

---

27 MSBh: **By means of what [does the bodhisattva] enter?** [The bodhisattva enters] **by generating the strength of the root of wholesomeness. [That is, the bodhisattva] enters by (1) stimulating the mind in three ways,** up to **by (3) being attentive to practicing constantly and carefully the cultivating.** [The statement:] **generating the strength of the root of wholesomeness** is, moreover, to be contextually connected with the eight subjects explained above [in *ācārya*-Asaṅga's text]. [The statements: **by**] **generating the strength of the root of wholesomeness** and **stimulating the mind in three ways** are answers to [the question:] **By means of what does [the bodhisattva] enter?** The bodhisattva who possesses **the strength of the root of wholesomeness** is firm by means of its strength, therefore [his] mind does not become depressed. Moreover, because the mind is stimulated in three ways, the mind is encouraged. … [The bodhisattva, moreover, enters] by **being attentive [...] that have the teachings and their meanings as their objective references/supports**, etc. Therein, [the word:] **constantly** means "to do continually" (**nitya-kāratva*); [the word:] **practicing [...] carefully** means "to honor" (**guru-kāratva*); [the word:] **being attentive** means to be attentive to whatever aspect/representation (**ākāra*) [of the teaching] that is taught whatever it may be. On the basis of **stimulating the mind in three ways** that arises from **the strength of the root of wholesomeness**, [the bodhisattva] practices attentively because [the bodhisattva's praxis] is possessed of uninterrupted reverence.

MSU: That [means by which the bodhisattva enters] is explained by [the statement:] **generating the strength of the root of wholesomeness**, etc. With regard to [a bodhisattva who] thinks "although [I] possess the strength of the root of wholesomeness, I am still desponded," [*ācārya*-Asaṅga] states [that one should overcome the dread by] **stimulating the mind in three ways.**

MS III. 5A

The first [incident of] stimulating the mind is to think: "Countless sentient beings (**sattva*) who are born as human beings (**manuṣya-bhūta*) in the countless worldly realms (**aprameya-loka-dhātu*) shall realize incomparable perfect enlightenment (**an-uttarā saṁyak-saṁbodhi*) at every moment."[28]

The second [incident of] stimulating [the mind] is to think: "I have obtained that intention (**āśaya*) with which [I] practice fully (?**samudācāra*, proper/right practice) the perfection of giving, etc. (**dānādi-pāramitā*), and consequently, with little difficulty (**alpa-kṛcchrena*), I will become accomplished fully in the cultivation of the perfection."[29]

---

28 MSBh: When the bodhisattva hears that it is difficult to realize the supreme (**parama*), deep (**gaṁbhīra*), and profound (**udāra*) incomparable perfect enlightenment, [he] becomes fearful. **The first [incident of] stimulating the mind** is the antidote of that [fearful mind].

MSU: In [the statement:] **the countless worldly realms**, etc., **the first [incident of] stimulating the mind** is clear [because it] has been already clarified by the explanation.

Although Asvabhāva states that the first incident of stimulating the mind is clear, both Asaṅga's explanation and Vasubandhu's explanation of the first incident of stimulating the mind are not clear. H-MSU differs from MSU. See H-MSU (414a20–21): 無量諸世界等者　此言顯示初練磨心　引多例已　令心增盛　無有退屈. (Tr.: The statement **countless worldly realms** shows the first [incident of] stimulating the mind. The other example has been already given. [If a bodhisattva] makes the mind active, there is no shame/back sliding.

29 MSBh: Moreover, the bodhisattva fears the practice of perfection (**pāramitā*) which is the supreme, deep, and difficult to understand (**durbodha*). As the antidote of that [fearful mind], **the second [incident of] stimulating** the mind is stated. In [the statement:] **intention with which [I] practice fully the perfection of giving**, [the word] **intention** refers to belief (**śraddhā*) and desire (**chanda*). The belief of the bodhisattva is to trust in the existence (**astitva*), in one who possesses good qualities (**guṇavat*), in one's capability (**sāmarthya*) and in

The third [incident of] stimulating [the mind] is to think: "If one possesses wholesome qualities (**kuśala-dharma*), even though wholesomeness is obstructed, then immediately at the time of one's death, one immediately will be born with the body completely intact (**saṁpad*) just as one wishes. If that is so, why would not someone like I who possess wholesomeness which is not obstructed (**anāvaraṇa-kuśala*) become immediately one [who is born] with the body completely intact?"[30]

---

perfection. The desire [of the bodhisattva] is the wish to apply himself [to the practice] that arises from the belief. The bodhisattva who has obtained **intention** having such belief and desire as its nature becomes accomplished in practicing the six [kinds of] perfection **with little difficulty**.

MSU: [The statement:] **I have obtained that intention** means that there is no bondage (**pratibandha/vibandha*), because there is no avarice (**mātsarya*), there is no discrimination with regard to desire (**rāga-vikalpa*), there is no malice (**vyāpāda*), there is no laziness (**kausīdya*), there is no torpor and drowsiness (**styāna-middha*) and there is no ignorance (**avidyā*). Therefore, **the second [incident of] exciting [the mind]** means to think: "**With little difficulty, [I] will become accomplished fully in the cultivation of the** six [kinds of] **perfection**," when if one obtains the most excellent intention, [the perfections of] giving, etc., arise naturally.

30 MSBh: Furthermore, when the bodhisattva dwells in the expertise (**kauśalya*) regarding the examination (**pravicaya*) of the Buddha's deep and profound teachings, he thinks like this: 'That [one] should attain incomparable perfect enlightenment that belongs to each moment is difficult." Accordingly, because the one becomes fearful [in this manner], there is **the third [incident of] stimulating** the mind as the antidote of that [fearful mind]. [The statement:] "**I who possess wholesomeness which is not obstructed**, etc.," [is stated] because it is connected with [the phrase:] "I am like one who has accumulated properly the provisions of knowledge by traversing all ten stages completely." [The statement:] **wholesomeness which is not obstructed** means that the diamond-like concentration (**vajropama-samādhi*) restrains barriers/badness (**dauṣṭhulya*) possessing attachment (**rāga*) and destroys the obstructions which are difficult to remove. Being freed of all obstruc-

MS III. 5B

With regard to this, there are verses:

> One should not become despondent (*laya*), for countless sentient beings who are born as human beings attain perfect enlightenment at every moment.[31] //1//[32]

---

tions immediately after [attaining] that concentration, [the bodhisattva's] basis (*rten*) will obtain the transformation of the basis (**āśraya-parāvṛtti*) by that [diamond-like concentration]. **Death** only is claimed to have the same quality as freedom (**visaṁyojana*). [The word:] **perfection** means omniscience regarding all features (**sarvākārajñātā*).

For the diamond-like concentration, see MS X. 4, Lamotte 1973, pp. 273–276, Nagao 1987, p. 333., and Hakamaya 1989, pp. 93–97.

MSU: **The third [incident of] stimulating** the mind means to think: "If I am one who possess wholesomeness because of wholesomeness freed of obstructions owing to the fact that I have removed the antidote, **why would someone like I not become** a Buddha [who is born] **with body [completely] intact?**" This means that the mind being activated is made sharp (**tīkṣa*).

31 MSBh: [The statement:] **One should not become despondent** means that the mind should not dwell in despondency. Such is the meaning derived from thinking: "I cannot realize incomparable enlightenment."

MSU: The very meaning [of three incidents of stimulating the mind] is summarized by verses: **for countless sentient beings who are born as human beings attain perfect enlightenment at every moment**, etc. [The word:] **despondent** refers to a confused (**ākula*) mind, and [this] is synonymous with saying that [one] should not be like that [i.e., one with confused mind]. [That is, one] should not think that one does not have ability by thinking "I cannot [attain] incomparable supreme enlightenment." As stated:

> Whosoever obtained the citadel of a Well-gone (**sugata*) may have had fallen into a very lowly state. Even you who have fallen into anxiety should not blame yourself, [because] a person who [thinks I am a] self-blamer destroys happiness.

32 Cf. MSA X. 11, p. 52, *ll.* 17–20:

> [One] should not become despondent, for countless sentient beings who are born as human beings attain perfect enlightenment at every moment.

For three reasons, "despondence" (*laya*) is not proper. For those "who

Although one with a proper mind [is engaged in] the act of giving, etc., by some intention, only [the act of] giving, etc., of those steadfast ones, [i.e., bodhisattvas], who have obtained that intention is said to be [the perfection of giving, etc.][33] //2//

---

are born as human beings attain" enlightenment; [They] "attain" [it] always, and countless [sentient beings] "attain" [it].

33 MSBh: [The statement:] **with a proper mind** means neither an unwholesome nor a neutral mind. To be exact, the neutral is a distracted mind by which some do [the act of] giving, etc. Likewise, heretics (**tīrthika*), etc., do [the act of] giving, etc., with an unwholesome mind, but [the bodhisattvas] are not [like that], because [they] desire incomparable perfect enlightenment. Moreover, those who have obtained the highest root of wholesomeness by [those] intentions are steadfast ones. With regard to [the statement:] **the act of giving, etc.**, here, it means that because [bodhisattvas] habituate themselves in doing the perfection **of giving, etc.**, after having obtained whatever [intention] which is in accord with that intention [of giving], [they] obtain the mind which is free from avarice, etc., i.e., the adherent of that [giving]. [The statement:] **only [the act of] giving, etc., of those steadfast ones, [i.e., bodhisattvas,] who have obtained that intention is said to be [the perfection of] giving, etc.** explains only [the act of] **giving, etc**. By the word **etc.**, [everything] from [the perfection of] moral conduct (**śīla*), etc., up to the perfection of wisdom (**prajñā-pāramitā*) is included.

MSU: [The word:] **intention** [in the statement:] **by some intention** has been explained before. **[Intention]** is the cause to be engaged in [the perfection of] giving without attachment. [The statement:] **with a proper mind** [means] by those with a wholesome mind, but not by those with an unwholesome or neutral (**avyākṛta*) mind. In the manner that because even those who have wholesomeness, unwholesomeness, or neutral mind wish transmigratory existence (**bhava*) and enjoyment (**bhoga*), [they] are engaged in [the act of] giving, etc., so too the bodhisattvas are not like that, because [they] are engaged in incomparable supreme enlightenment. [The statement:] **have obtained that intention** means that with some **intention** that has arisen naturally and which has been explained above, [the bodhisattvas] **have obtained** the cultivation of the perfections. [The statement:] **of those steadfast ones** means of bodhisattvas. How so? **Only [the act of] giving, etc., ... is said to be [the perfection of giving, etc.,]** because it is determined that it is not

At the time of one's death, one who possesses wholesomeness will obtain, just as one wishes, the body intact. Why would one possessed of wholesomeness who has removed [obstructions] not obtain the [body] intact even now?[34] //3//

MS III. 6

[The bodhisattva enters into the defining characteristics of what is to be known by removing the four obstructive situations,] because, (1) by means of removing [improper] attentiveness, [the bodhisattva] removes completely the attentiveness of the Śrāvaka and Pratyekabuddha,[35] (2) by means of removing the harboring a

---

antidote, it is explained that [bodhisattvas] are engaged in [the perfection of giving, etc.,] without making effort, because the antidotes have been overcome. [One should understand] the word '**etc.**' means the perfection of moral conduct, and the rest.

34 MSBh: [The statement:] **will obtain, just as one wishes, the body intact** means that [bodhisattva] **will obtain**, i.e., will be born in, the sphere of neither consciousness nor non-consciousness (**naivasaṁjñānā-saṁjñā-yatana*). [The statement:] **has removed** means that [bodhisattva] **has removed** obstructions. [The statement:] **the [body] intact** means that [bodhisattvas obtain] Buddhahood (**Buddhatva*).

MSU: [The statement:] **At the time of one's death, one who possesses wholesomeness** means that one who possesses **wholesomeness** by means of worldly wholesomeness dies. [The statement:] **will obtain, just as one wishes, the body intact** means that worldly people will be born even into the highest state of existence (**bhavāgra*). [The statement:] **one possessed of wholesomeness who has removed [obstructions]** means those who possess **wholesomeness** by virtue of wholesomeness that **has removed** obstructions. [The statement:] **the [body] intact** means that [the bodhisattvas attain] the Buddhahood as they desire.

35 MSU: [The statement:] **by means of removing [improper] attentiveness** is stated because [the bodhisattva] rejects **attentiveness** of the Śrāvaka[-yāna] and of the Pratyeka-buddhayāna.

divided mind (*vimati*) and ambivalence (*kāṅkṣā*), [the bodhisattva] becomes doubtless regarding all doubts (*vicikitsā*) towards the Mahāyāna teachings,[36] (3) by means of removing attachment (*abhiniveśa*) to teachings, [the bodhisattva] removes completely the attachment to the notion of I [have heard teachings] and the notion of mine (*ahaṁkāra-mamakāra*) with regard to the teachings that [he] has heard and reflected upon,[37] and (4) by means of removing conceptual discrimination (*vikalpa*), [the bodhisattva] neither pays attention to (*amanaskāra*) nor conceptually discriminates (*avikalpa*) any objective aspects (*nimitta*) which appear before [him] (*purataḥ-sthita*) or which are caused to be present

---

36 MSBh: [The statement:] **by means of removing the harboring a divided mind and ambivalence** means that [the bodhisattva] **removes the harboring a divided mind and ambivalence** towards the Mahāyāna teachings that is deep and profound.

MSU: [The statement:] **by means of removing the harboring a divided mind and ambivalence** means that [the bodhisattva] must not **harbor a divided mind** mistakenly and [must not] doubt the vastness and deepness of the Mahāyāna [teachings].

37 MSBh: [By the statement: **the bodhisattva] removes completely the attachment to the notion of I [have heard teachings] and the notion of mine with regard to the teachings that [he] has heard and reflected upon**, [*ācārya*-Asaṅga] asserts removing of only **attachment to teachings.** [*Ācārya*-Asaṅga states:] **by means of removing attachment to teachings** [because] as far as [the bodhisattva] has [the attachment to the notion of] I [have heard teachings] and [the notion of] mine with regard to the teachings that [he] has heard and reflected upon, [he] does not become aware of [the truth].

MSU: **by means of removing attachment to teachings, the attachment to the notion of I and the notion of mine with regard to the teachings that [he] has heard and reflected upon** should be removed. Because [the attachment] is an obstacle to realization, [the bodhisattva] should not attach [himself] to [the notions]: "[I] myself reflect upon [the teachings,"] "I realize the teachings," "[the teachings that] I have heard are mine," "the meaning [of the teachings] is mine."

(*sthāpita) [in meditation].[38]

With regard to this, there is a verse:[39]

---

38 MSBh: [*Ācārya*-Asaṅga states:] **by means of removing conceptual discrimination, [the bodhisattva] neither pays attention to nor conceptually discriminates any objective aspects which appear before [him] or which are caused to be present [in meditation]**, [because by doing so, bodhisattva's] fixed mind (**samāhita-citta*)] dwells entirely in the state/situation (*gnas skabs*, **avasthā*) of proper attentiveness that is present in non-discriminative wisdom that has arisen from the practice (**prayoga*). [*Ācārya*-Asaṅga states:] **by means of removing conceptual discrimination**, [because the bodhisattva] enters [into truth] by means of skillful means of non-discrimination to colour/form (**rūpa*), etc., that appear before [him] or to that which is to be discriminated by means of not paying attention to all objective aspects that become the objective reference/support, such as the skeleton, etc., through meditation. Otherwise, if [he] discriminates, [he] does not enter [into truth].

39 Cf. MSA XIX. 50, p. 169, *ll*. 9–17:

> The wise, who does not discriminate whatsoever objective aspect as caused to be present [in meditation] or as present naturally [in the external world], attains the supreme awakening.

With regard to that, [the statement:] "whatsoever objective aspect as caused to be present [in meditation]" refers to that which is conceptually constructed (*parikalpita*) which is objectified by the practice [based upon] listening to, reflecting upon, and cultivating [Buddha's teachings]. [The statement:] "present naturally" refers to that which is conceptually constructed which has [arisen] without making effort, which becomes an objective reference/support naturally (*prakṛtyālambanībhūta*). Non-causing to be present for that [objective aspect] is cessation (*vigama*) and non-being objective reference/support (*anālambanī-bhāva*). Non-conceptual construction is the means for that and an antidote of the objective aspect (*nimitta-pratipakṣa*). Moreover, both are [not discriminated] in order, for at first that which is caused to be present in meditation [is not discriminated], and then that which is present naturally [is not discriminated]. With regard to that, a yogin who does not discriminate the mark/form of a person who follows the four kinds of perversions (*catur-viparyāsa*) attains awakening of the Śrāvaka or awakening of the Pratyeka[-buddha]. One who does not discriminate the mark/form of all teachings [attains] the great awakening. By this, it is thoroughly illustrated that, [in a bodhisattva who,] has understood properly the truth, i.e., who is released, wisdom as-it-is arises.

The wise, who does not discriminate whatsoever objective aspect as caused to be present [in meditation] or as present naturally [in the external world], attains the supreme awakening.

MS III. 7A

By what and how [does the bodhisattva] enter?[40]

[The bodhisattva] enters by mind-talk that arises owing to the impregnation of listening to [the Mahāyāna teachings many times] that is subsumed under the proper attentiveness, that appears as [the Buddha's] teachings and [their] meanings, and that is accompanied by the act of perceiving.[41]

[Moreover, the bodhisattva enters by means of] the four [kinds of] investigations (**paryeṣaṇā*), i.e., the investigations into (i) name (**nāma*), (ii) object (**artha*), (iii) designation (**pra-*

---

40 MSU: [The statement:] **By what and how [does the bodhisattva] enter** is an inquiry about the means [of entering] (**karaṇa*) and what is to be done (**iti-kartavyatā*). When one who enters enters the object of entering, the means [of entering] and what is to be done—an action (**kriyā*) characterized by realization is to be done in such and such a manner—become undoubtedly necessary. For this reason, the two are described.

41 MSBh: **By what and how [the bodhisattva] enters** must be stated. With regard to that, [the statement: **mind-talk that**] **arises owing to the impregnation of listening to [the Mahāyāna teachings many times]** means that [mind-talk] is conformable to (*rjes su mthun pa*, **anurūpa*) **the impregnation of listening to [the Mahāyāna teachings many times]**. The place where [the bodhisattva] enters has been explained before (III. 3), and because that also **arises** from **the impregnation of [listening to]** the Mahāyāna [**teachings many times**], it is to be seen as that subsumed under the consummated nature.

MSU: By [the statement: **mind-talk that**] **arises owing to the impregnation of listening to [the Mahāyāna teachings many times]**, etc., the means [of entering] is stated.

jñapti) of the intrinsic nature (**svabhāva*) [of entities] and (iv) [designation of] specific attributes (**viśeṣa*) [of entities],[42] [and by means of] the four [kinds of] wisdom of knowing reality as-it-is (**yathā-bhūta-parijñāna*):[43] by means of knowing (i) name as-it-is, (ii) thing as-it-is, (iii) designation of the intrinsic nature [of entities] as-it-is, (iv) [designation of] specific attributes [of entities] as-it-is, because they are not perceivable.[44]

---

42 On the four *paryeṣaṇā* in other Yogācāra texts, see BoBh, pp. 53, *ll.* 6–13, MSA, p. 168, *l.* 18–p. 170, *l.* 1., and 顯揚論, Taisho vol. 31, no. 1602, p. 507c14–22.

43 On the four *yathābhūta-parijñāna* in other Yogācāra texts, see BoBh, p. 53, *l.* 14–p. 55, *l.* 3, MSA, p. 168, *l.* 24–p. 169, *l.* 2., and 顯揚論, Taisho vol. 31, no. 1602, pp. 507c23–508a23.

44 The MS has the phrase: "the intrinsic nature as-it-is, and specific attributes as-it-is" after the phrase: "(iv) [designation of] specific attributes [of entities] as-it-is," but they seem to be superfluous according to all four Chinese translations of MS. See 'Chapter Three,' p. 100, n. 56 below.

MSBh: [The word:] **investigation** refers to examination. [The word:] **wisdom of knowing reality as-it-is** refers to non-perception.

MSU: By **the four [kinds of] investigations** and (3) **the four [kinds of] wisdom of knowing reality as-it-is**, what is to be done is shown. [The bodhisattva] investigates in the state of the practice (**prayogāvasthā*). [That is, the bodhisattva] sees an aspect (**ākāra*) of analysis (**nirūpaṇa*), which means that [the bodhisattva] fully understands the entrance into an aspect of [the fact that] objective references/supports do not exist. A determined cognition (**niścita-jñāna*) [by which the bodhisattva understands that] objective references/supports do not exist is a result (**phala*) [of the four kinds of investigations], and [it is] a **wisdom of knowing reality as-it-is**. With regard to that, the **name** refers to form (**rūpa*), etc. **The investigation into name** is to understand that [name is] nothing but mind-talk, because [name] exists as a designation, owing to [the fact that name] does not exist [as something] other than mind-talk. The investigation of thing (**vastu-paryeṣaṇā*) is to understand that in the manner that [five] aggregates (**skandha*) and [eighteen] elements (**dhātu*) are expressed by the words (**nāma-kāya*), [things] do not exist substantively, because when the link between cause (**gotra*) and that which possesses cause (i.e., effect) is not related, speech (**jalpa*) which possesses that [link] would not be possible. ... [The statement:]

MS III. 7B

Thus, the bodhisattva who endeavours in that manner to enter [into the truth that all phenomena are] nothing but [mental] presentations (**vijñapti-mātra*) understands properly that the name which is based upon sound (**akṣara*) in that mind-talk, that appears as sound (**akṣara*) and [its] meaning (**artha*), is also nothing but mental construction (**mano-kalpa-mātra*). [The bodhisattva] understands properly that even the meaning which takes its stand on sound is also nothing but the very mind-talk (**mano-jalpa-mātra*). [The bodhisattva] understands properly that even that name is nothing more than the designation (**prajñapti-mātra*) of the intrinsic nature and specific attributes [of entities].[45]

Next,[46] when [all phenomena are] perceived as nothing but mind-talk (**mano-jalpa*), neither a name nor what is designated is perceived. Nor is the designation of intrinsic nature or [the des-

---

because they are not perceivable means **because** it is certain that name, etc., **are not perceivable**.

45 MSU: [The bodhisattva] understands that whatever is a thing "named" which is an object to be spoken about and which is to be spoken about on the basis of name, even that is nothing more than mind-talk. [The bodhisattva,] turning about his attachment to the external images, analyzes the internal. The words "form," etc., on the one hand, are of the nature of the designation having intrinsic nature and are [those things] called body (**kāya*), feeling (**vedanā*), etc., because [the bodhisattva,] although [it] does not exist, designates an intrinsic nature, just as **pudgala* [is a designation]. [The things "matter," etc.,] on the other hand, have the defining characteristics of designated specific attributes and [those things are] called "impermanence" (**anitya*), "suffering" (**duḥkha*), etc., because [the bodhisattva] designates the specific attributes on what is not existing.

46 Here Tibetan has *de'i phyir*, but Pa has the sense of after that or next (次). See 'Chapter Three,' p. 102, n. 65 below.

ignation of] the specific attributes perceived. Nor is the defining characteristics of an object (*artha-lakṣaṇa*) [that is perceived as] possessing intrinsic nature or specific attributes perceived. [In this manner,] by means of the four [kinds of] investigations (*paryeṣaṇā*) and the four [kinds of] wisdom of knowing reality as-it-is (*yathā-bhūta-parijñāna*), [the bodhisattva] understands those mental discriminations (*mano-vikalpa*) that appear as sound and meaning to be *vijñapti-mātratā*.

MS III. 8A

[The bodhisattva] enters into that *vijñapti-mātratā*. In which state does [he] enter? [And] what is [the entrance] like?[47]

[The bodhisattva] enters into (1) a state of that-only (*tan-mātratā*), (2) a state of the two, i.e., having object and subject (*sa-nimitta-dṛṣṭi-dvayatā*), and (3) a state of various forms (*nānākāra-tā*), (1) because (i) name (*nāman*), (ii) object (*artha*), (iii) the designation (*prajñapti*) of the intrinsic nature (*svabhāva*), (iv) [the designation of] specific attributes (*viśeṣa*), (v) the intrinsic nature and (vi) specific attributes—these six kinds of topics (*artha*) do not exist as [external] objects, (2) because they are present as cognitum and cognizer (*grāhya-grāhaka-bhāva*) and (3) because [they] arise simultaneously with the appearance of

47 MSU: If, since objects do not exist, [the bodhisattva] enters [into the truth that all phenomena are] nothing but mental presentations, [then] by [the statement: "**The bodhisattva] enters into that *vijñapti-mātratā*. In which state does [he] enter?**," [your position] is negated, [because in such a case] that very [*vijñapti-mātratā*] is thought to be an object [of the entrance].

various forms (*nānākārārthābhāsa).[48]

MS III. 8B

[The manner in which a bodhisattva] enters is in the manner that a rope (*rajju) appears to be a snake (*sarpa) in the dark.[49] For

---

48 MSBh: With regard to that, [the statement:] **a state of that-only** refers to *vijñapti-mātratā. [The statement:] **a state of the two, i.e., having object and subject** explains a knowledge **having object and subject**. ... [The statement:] **because [they] arise simultaneously with the appearance of various forms** means that **because [they] arise with the appearance of various [forms]**, such as a name, word, and letters, and [it means that] **because** the objects which are based upon them **arise with the appearance of various forms.**

MSU: In order to negate that [objection], [*ācārya*-Asaṅga] states: **that-only**. An object is non-existent not only as an external [object], but also as an object of the cognition (*vijñapti). If the object is truly non-existent, how [do you] follow the teachings regarding the twelve spheres (*dvādaśāyatana), etc., and conventional usage (*vyavahāra) regarding the worldly things. Then, [*ācārya*-Asaṅga] states: **the two, i.e., having object and subject**. When the cognition which appears as an external object, although object does not exist, is established owing to the impregnation of words for the object (*arthābhilāpa-vāsanā), the appearance of the cognition also is designated as the subject, accordingly, there is no contradiction (*virodha/viruddha). Is it the case that [the bodhisattva] enters into [the fact that] these cognitions which appear as the subject and object become other? Or not? Then, [*ācārya*-Asaṅga states: **the bodhisattva] enters into various forms**. By the division of form into the cognitum and cognizer, only one mind appears in different forms variously at one time, accordingly, [the bodhisattva] enters [into various forms]. [The word:] **various** means that a single cognition perceives itself (*svasaṁvedana) many forms. By explaining these three kinds of concepts, the three—i.e., **the six kinds of topics,** such as **name**, etc., **do not exist as [external] objects**, etc.,—has been explained.

49 MSBh: With regard to that, entering into the three natures is described by an analogy with the rope.

MSU: An analogy of what is spoken about in the statement: **What is [the entrance] like** is explained by the statement: **[The manner in which a bodhisattva] enters is in the manner that a rope appears to be a snake in the dark**, etc. By the analogy, understanding of the three

instance, because a snake [superimposed upon] a rope is non-existent, it is a misperception (an error, **bhrānti*),[50] [therefore,] those who are aware of the reality of that object, turning away from the notion of the non-existent snake, dwell in the notion of a rope.[51] Moreover, when [this notion of a rope is] analyzed more minutely, [even the notion of a rope] is misperception (an error), because its defining characteristics are colour (**varṇa*), odour (**gandha*), taste (**rasa*) and what is to be touched (**spraṣṭavya*). With regard to that, just as even the notion of a rope is to be removed on the basis of the notion of colour, etc., so too, the notion of cognition-only (**vijñapti-mātra*) is to be destroyed on the basis of the notion of consummated nature (**pariniṣpanna-svabhāva*), when the six kinds [of topics]—mind-talk that appears as the six kinds [of objects], such as letter, meaning—become negated as real objects just as the notion of a snake [is negated].[52]

---

natures is described.

50 MSU: [*Ācārya*-Asaṅga states:] **For instance, because a snake [superimposed upon] a rope is non-existent, it is a misperception (an error)**, and in the same manner, name, etc., [superimposed upon] the other-dependent [nature]—mind-talk that appears as words and [their] meanings that comprise the six kinds of objects, such as name, etc.,—are also an error.

51 MSU: With regard to that, in the manner that [the bodhisattva,] on the basis of the notion of a rope, **turns away from the notion of the non-existent snake**, because it is an error, in the same manner, [he,] on the basis of the other-dependent [nature,] turns away from the notion of the imagined six kinds of topics, such as name, etc.

52 MSU: In the manner that when [the bodhisattva,] on the basis of colour, odour, etc., divides a rope into parts, [he] removes **even the notion of a rope**. [For instance,] it is stated [in **Hastavāla-prakaraṇa* k. 1]:

> [The bodhisattva] perceives a rope as a snake. Seeing/ Knowing [that the snake is actually] a rope, [he understands that such] object (i.e., snake) does not exist. Even when [the

MS III. 9

Thus, this bodhisattva by entering into the defining characteristics of objects that appear from mind-talk enters into the imagined nature (**parikalpita-svabhāva*).[53] By entering into [the idea that all phenomena are] nothing but [mental] presentations (**vijñapti-mātra*), he enters into the other-dependent nature (**paratantra-svabhāva*).[54]

[Then,] how does the bodhisattva enter into the consummated nature (**pariniṣpanna-svabhāva*)?

[The bodhisattva] enters [into the consummated nature] from

---

bodhisattva] sees a portion of that [rope], [he understands that] cognition is an error, just as a snake [is an error].

In the same manner, in [the statement:] **when the six kinds [of topics] ... become negated as real objects just as** that **[notion of a snake is negated]**, [the words:] **become negated** means to be divided and non-existence. On the basis of the consummated [nature] characterized by the non-existence of the six kinds of topics which are not real objects, the erroneous other-dependent [nature] is also to be removed and is to be negated.

For the details of the **Hastavāla-prakaraṇa*, see Thomas and Ui 1918, Frauwallner 1959, Akashi 1932, Nagasawa 1955, Ui 1958, pp. 336–345., Tola and Dragonetti 1980, and Harada 1993.

53 MSBh: [The statement:] **by entering into the defining characteristics of objects that appear from mind-talk** means that since the object is nothing but that which is imagined, [the bodhisattva] **enters into the imagined [nature]** in that manner.

MSU: [The statement:] **by entering into the defining characteristics of objects that appear from mind-talk** means that although this **mind-talk** appears as objects, objects which are to be imagined do not exist, accordingly [the bodhisattva] **enters into the imagined [nature]**.

54 MSU: [The statement:] **By entering into [the idea that all phenomena are] nothing but [mental] presentations** means that this cognition-only is mistaken owing to the power of ignorance (**avidyā*), and there appears a form of an object which is the error with regard to non-existing object, accordingly [the bodhisattva] **enters into the other-dependent [nature]**.

having turned away from even the idea (*saṁjñā) that [all phenomena are] nothing but [mental] presentations (*vijñapti-mātra), at which time, in that bodhisattva who has abandoned the idea of object, that mind-talk that has arisen owing to the impregnation of having listened to the teachings [many times] lacks the opportunity of arising as all appearances of objects.[55] Accordingly, [mind-talk] does not arise even as an appearance of cognition-only (*vijñapti-mātra).[56]

[The bodhisattva,] dwelling in the name which is non-discriminating regarding all objects, dwells in *dharma-dhātu* owing to the operation of direct intuition. At that time, there occurs in that bodhisattva non-discriminatory wisdom wherein what is to be perceived and that which perceives (*ālambya-ālambaka) are exactly alike (*sama-sama).[57] In this manner, this bodhisattva has

---

55 MSBh: [The statement: **mind-talk ...**] **lacks the opportunity of arising as all appearances of objects** [is stated]. When even [mind-talk] does not arise as the appearance of cognition-only, how is it that [mind-talk] as the appearance of that object arises. Accordingly, if *vijñapti-mātratā* is discriminated, [it] again becomes an object. Therefore, after that [understanding], *tathatā* is directly intuited. That step is inexpressible, since it is to be understood individually.

MSU: With regard to the entrance into the consummated [nature], [*ācārya*-Asaṅga] states that [**the bodhisattva who**] **has abandoned the idea of object**. [It] means that [the bodhisattva] negates **the idea of object**. [The statement: **mind-talk ...**] **lacks the opportunity of arising as all the appearances of objects** means that arising [of mind-talk] even by whatever is **the appearances of objects** is impossible.

56 MSU: [The statement:] **Accordingly, [mind-talk] does not arise even as an appearance of cognition-only** means that when the cognitum does not exist, the cognizer does not exist, accordingly, from having made the *vijñapti-mātra* its an object, **[mind-talk] does not arise**.

57 MSU: By [the statement:] **dwelling in the name which is non-discriminating regarding all objects**, etc., [it is meant that] **dwelling in**

entered into the consummated nature.[58]

MS III. 10

With regard to this, there is a verse:[59]

> Matter (**dharma*), person (**pudgala*), teaching (**dharma*), [its] meaning (**artha*), the concise

---

[the fact that] this everything is **name**-only (**nāma-mātra*) when it is not affected/infected (**aparāmṛṣṭa*) by the teachings of a **sūtra* which are the domain of **the name**. Just as it is stated [in *Madhyānta-vibhāga-kārikā* V. 18ab]:

> That everything is just name-only prevents all discriminations from arising. The cognition which appears as name designates (**upacāra*) the name.

[The statement: **The bodhisattva ...**] **dwells in **dharma-dhātu* owing to the operation of direct intuition** means that [the bodhisattva] **dwells** [in *dharma-dhātu*] through **the direct intuition** by oneself (**pratyātma*), but not by zealous conduct (**adhimukti*). [The statement:] **wisdom wherein what is to be perceived and that which perceives are exactly alike** means that in the manner that **what is to be perceived** does not exist, in the same manner, **that which perceives** also does not exist, accordingly, the two, i.e., **what is to be perceived and that which perceives, are exactly a like.**

58 MSU: [The statement:] **In this manner, this bodhisattva has entered into the consummated nature** explains the fulfillment (**niṣṭhāna*) of activities of one who enters. Since entrance into the imagined [nature] and the other-dependent [nature] has remaining [to be done], activities for entering are not fulfillment. Accordingly, [the word] "enter" is shown [in the present tense] because it is intended to express that [the bodhisattva is still] the doer/performer.

59 MSBh: On the basis of the meaning [of the questions:] "what is the name? And how many kinds does [the name have]?" [*Ācārya*-Asaṅga states: **the bodhisattva,**] **dwelling in the name which is non-discriminating regarding all objects.** [In order to answer the questions,] distinction of the name is stated by a verse.

MSU: The distinctions of the name, which possess the domain that is stated as [**dwelling**] **in the name which is non-discriminating regarding all objects**, is stated by a verse.

(*samasta*), the extended (**vyasta*), cause (**gotra*), the impure (**aśuddha*), the pure (**śuddha*) and extreme (**paryanta*): [These constitute] the domain of naming by virtue of their distinctions.[60]

60 MSBh: The name of **matter** refers to form (**rūpa*), feeling (**vedanā*), eye (**cakṣus*), etc. The name of **person** refers to the Buddha, good friend (**kalyāṇa-mitra*), one who practices in accordance with belief (**śruddhānusārin*), etc. The name of **teaching** refers to **sūtra*, etc. The name of [**its**] **meaning** refers to the meaning based on teaching. The name of **the concise** refers to one who is called sentient being (**sattva*). The name of **the extended** refers to individual name of that very [sentient being]. The name of **cause** refers to alphabet of the letters. The name of **the impure** refers to [the name] of ignorant people (**pṛthag-jana*). The name of **the pure** refers to [the name] of the disciple (**śaikṣa*). The name of **extreme** refers to a perception of the combined teachings.

Briefly, cognition of bodhisattva's name is ten kinds. That is, the name of **matter** refers to eye, etc. The name of **person** refers to self, sentient being, etc. [The name of] **teaching** refers to twelve kinds of **sūtras*. [The name of **its**] **meaning** refers to meaning of the twelve kinds of **sūtras*. **The concise** name refers to that all existences are the conditioned (**saṁskṛta*) and the non-conditioned (**asaṁskṛta*), etc. **The extended** name refers to form, feeling, etc., and sphere (**ākāśa*), etc. The name of **cause** refers to the [alphabets] beginning with the first letter *a* to the last letter *ha*. The name of **the impure** refers to the ignorant person who possesses the object. The name of **the pure** refers to those who saw the truth. The name of **the extreme** refers to a perception of the combined teaching by means of the two wisdom, i.e., supra-mundane [wisdom] and [wisdom that is] attained subsequent to [supramundane wisdom]. It is like the ten stages depending upon all the various teachings. In that case, all objects are the objective references/supports of wisdom that perceives the combined teaching. Such kinds are domain of a bodhisattva's name.

MSU: [The word:] **matter** refers to form, etc. [The word:] **person** refers to *devadatta* and one who practices in accordance with belief (**śruddhānusārin*), etc. [The word:] **teaching** refers to *sūtra*s which are the secret writings of the Buddha and songs (**geya*), etc. [The word: **its**] **meaning** refers to that which is to be stated (**abhidheya*) of those [*sūtra*s], and [the meaning of the statement that] having killed father, mother, the two, i.e., king and **brāhmaṇa*, country and the victo-

MS III. 11

Thus, by entering [into the truth that all phenomena are] nothing but [mental] presentations (**vijñapti-mātratā*), this bodhisattva has entered the defining characteristics of what is to be known (**jñeya-lakṣaṇa*). By having entered there, [he] has entered the stage of joy (**pramuditā*); that is, [this bodhisattva] has fully realized **dharma-dhātu*, [he has] been born in the lineage (**gotra/kula*) of the Tathāgatas, has obtained an impartial mind (**sama-citta*) regarding all sentient beings, all bodhisattvas and all Buddhas.[61]

---

rious one who follows retinue, a man becomes pure, etc. [The word:] **the concise** refers to [the statement that] all of the existences are non-self (**anātman*, **nairātmya*), etc. [The word:] **the extended** refers to the [statement that] form is non-self, etc. [The word:] **cause** refers to letter *a*, etc., because it is a cause of words (**pada*) and speech (**vacana*), etc. [The word:] **the impure** refers to ignorant people, because they become those who possess impurity due to the afflictions (**kleśa*), etc. [The word:] **pure** refers to the respectable people (**ārya*), because they remove the impure, etc. [The word:] **extreme** refers to the combined perception (**saṁbhinnālambana*), because they perceive the combined objects (**saṁbhinnārtha*), such as the perfection of wisdom (**parijñā-pāramitā*), the ten stages (**daśa-bhūmi*), etc.

61 MSBh: [*Ācārya*-Asaṅga states: **has obtained**] **an impartial mind regarding all sentient beings**, because [the bodhisattva] thinks that as he is released, all sentient beings are released. ... [*Ācārya*-Asaṅga states: **has obtained**] **an impartial mind regarding all Buddhas**, because by means of that [impartial] mind, [the bodhisattva] **has obtained** the state/stage (*gnas skabs*) of the *dharma*-body of the Buddhas, and by means of obtaining that [impartial mind], [he] **has obtained an impartial mind regarding all Buddhas**. [The statement:] **an impartial mind regarding all sentient beings** refers to that [the bodhisattva] wishes to remove their sufferings as well as his [suffering] by the understanding that self and others are exactly alike. [The statement:] **an impartial mind regarding all bodhisattvas** refers to that intention of the practice is impartial with all bodhisattvas. [The statement:] **has obtained an impartial mind regarding all Buddhas** refers to that [the bodhisattva] sees that there is no difference between **dharma-dhātu* [attained by] them and [*dharma-dhātu* attained by] him in its nature.

This is his **darśana-mārga*.

MS III. 12

Moreover, for what purpose does [the bodhisattva] enter into that [truth that all phenomena are] nothing but [mental] presentations (**vijñapti-mātra*)?[62]

[The bodhisattva] enters [into the truth] in order to attain the wisdom of the omniscient one (**sarvajña-jñāna*). [This wisdom is attained by means of the following processes:] By that supramundane cognition of [the meditations of] calm and insight (**śamatha-vipaśyanā*) which has the combined teaching (**sambhinna-dharma*) as its objective reference/support and by a cogni-

---

MSU: [*Ācārya*-Asaṅga states: **this bodhisattva**] **has fully realized *dharma-dhātu*** because [the bodhisattva] has intuitively perceived that [*dharma-dhātu*]. [In the statement: **he has**] **been born in the lineage of the Tathāgatas, the lineage of the Tathāgatas** refers to **dharma-dhātu*. [That is, the bodhisattva] **has been born** there because [he] has realized that [*dharma-dhātu*], because [he] has been born [as one who] possesses a superior wisdom that perceives that [*dharma-dhātu*], and because [his] previous basis (**pūrvāśraya*) has been transformed and the other basis has arisen [in him]. ... [*Ācārya*-Asaṅga states: **the bodhisattva ...**] **has obtained an impartial mind regarding all sentient beings** because [the bodhisattva] sees impartially that all [sentient beings] are non-self. For instance, just as stated that all sentient beings are **tathāgata-garbha*. [*Ācārya*-Asaṅga states: **the bodhisattva has obtained**] **an impartial mind regarding all bodhisattvas** because [the bodhisattva] thinks that the [other bodhisattvas'] basis (*gnas*) and his own [basis] are [equal]. [*Ācārya*-Asaṅga states: **the bodhisattva**] **has obtained an impartial mind regarding all Buddhas** because [the bodhisattva] thinks that the *dharma*-bodies are obtained by himself too.

62 MSU: [The statement:] **Moreover, for what purpose does [the bodhisattva] enter into that [truth that all phenomena are] nothing but [mental] presentations** is an enquiry about the purpose [of entering into the truth].

tion that is the presentation of various forms (*nānākāra-vijñapti-jñāna*) and that is attained subsequent to that [supramundane knowledge] (*tat-pṛṣṭha-labdha*), [the bodhisattva first] removes all of the seeds of the *ālaya-vijñāna* together with the cause, and then increases the seeds of coming into the contact with the *dharma-kāya*. [Thus, the bodhisattva] transforms the basis, and properly accomplishes all qualities of the Buddha[, and thereupon, attains the wisdom of the omniscient one].[63]

The wisdom that is attained subsequent to [the supramundane knowledge] (*tat-pṛṣṭha-labdha-jñāna*) comes forth as that which is naturally freed of perversion (*aviparīta*) because [it] sees that everything arises from the *ālaya-vijñāna* and that all the characteristics of [mental] presentations are like illusion. Accordingly, the bodhisattva is at all times free of perversion regarding even the teaching consisting of [the doctrine of] cause (*hetu*) and effect

---

63 MSBh: ***Ālaya-vijñāna*** possesses the **seed** of impure **dharmas* (**saṁkleśa-dharma*). Moreover, the word: **cause** (**nimitta*) is used in order to explain that that **seed** is the cause of the perception. Thinking in that manner, [the statement: **removes all of the seeds of the *ālaya-vijñāna together with the cause**] explains removal of the **seeds** possessing the cause and effect.

MSU: [The statement:] **all of the seeds of the *ālaya-vijñāna together with the cause** refers to that **together with** the impregnators that appear as colour/form, etc., and [it] explains the removal of the **seeds** which has cause and effect. ... [*Ācārya*-Asaṅga states:] **transforms the basis** [because] the pure mind and mental function arise through the realization of **tathatā*, or because **tathatā* is completely pure (**viśuddhi*). [The statement: **properly**] **accomplishes all qualities of the Buddha** means that [the bodhisattva properly accomplishes all qualities of the Buddha,] such as [five kinds of] forces (**bala*), [four kinds of] self confidences (**vaiśāradya*). [The statement:] **in order to attain the wisdom of the omniscient one** means in order to obtain pure and unimpeded **wisdom**.

(*phala), just as a magician [who is free of perversion] regarding things (*dharma) made by magic (*māyā-kṛta).[64]

MS III. 13

When [a bodhisattva] enters into [the truth that all phenomena are] nothing but [mental] presentations, how should [he] see the four [states] leading up to penetration [into truth] (*nirvedha-bhāgīya)[65] that are supported by the four [kinds of] concentrations?

(1) When by means of the four kinds of investigations [a bodhisattva] understands, although weakly, that [external] objects do not exist, [he practices] the *āloka-labdha-samādhi (concentration by which one obtains clarity), and [it] is a support (*āśraya) for *uṣma-gata (the state of heat) within the context of [the four states] leading up to penetration [into truth].[66]

---

64 MSU: In [the statement:] **The wisdom that is attained subsequent to [the supramundane knowledge]**, etc., [the statement:] **everything arises from the *ālaya-vijñāna** means that [the *ālaya-vijñāna*] is that which becomes the cause. [The statement:] **all the characteristics of [mental] presentations** refers to those which become effect, and since [the wisdom that is attained subsequent to the supramundane knowledge] sees the other-dependent nature as-it-is, [it] understands those which appear as cognitum and cognizer without perversion (**viparyāsa*) and error.

65 On *nirvedha-bhāgīya*, see MSA XIV. 23-27, p. 93, *ll.* 6–25.

66 MSBh: By the words ***āloka-labdha**, the understanding [of the idea] that [**external**] **objects do not exist** is stated. The ***āloka-labdha-samādhi** is an observation by ***samādhi** that depends properly upon [the understanding] that [external] objects do not exist.

MSU: [The statement:] **When ... [a bodhisattva] understands, although weakly, that [external] objects do not exist** means that [**a bodhisattva**] **understands weakly** [**that external**] **objects do not exist**. The [word:] ***āloka** refers to clearness (*gsal ba*, **prakāśa*), and [by

(2) When [that] understanding/intellectual receptivity increases [by means of the four kinds of investigations, the bodhisattva practices], the **vṛddhāloka-samādhi* (concentration of increased clarity), and [it] is a support for **mūrdha* (the state of maximum value) [within the context of the four states leading up to penetration into truth].[67]

(3) When by the four kinds of wisdom of knowing reality as-it-is [the bodhisattva] enters into [the truth that all phenomena are] nothing but [mental] presentations and determines that [external] objects do not exist, [the bodhisattva practices] the **tattvārthaika-deśa-praviṣṭa-samādhi* (concentration of having entered into one part of a real object), and [it] is a support for **kṣānti* (the state of patience) which conforms with the truth (**satyānulomikī*) [within the context of the four states leading up to penetration into truth].[68]

---

means of it] it should be known that [**external**] **objects do not exist.** [*Ācārya*-Asaṅga states:] ***labdha** because [the bodhisattva] wishes [the understanding that external objects do not exist]. Accordingly, **the *āloka-labdha-samādhi** means [the concentration by which one] **obtains clarity.**

67 MSBh: In [the statement:] **When [that] understanding** [of the idea that external] objects do not exist **increases,** [the word] **understanding/ intellectual receptivity** here refers to wish (**icchā*) and desire (**abhilāṣa*).

68 MSBh: In [the statement: **it is**] **a support for *kṣānti which conforms with the truth, the truth** is **dharma-nairātmya*. ***Kṣānti* which conforms with** that is **the state of patience which conforms with the truth.**

MSU: The ***tattvārthaika-deśa-praviṣṭa-samādhi*** [is the *samādhi* in which the bodhisattva] determines that the [external] objects do not exist. Since objective thing (**vastu*) of cognitum only is negated, it is called ***eka-deśa.*** Thus, [the bodhisattva is] aware of [the fact] that the [external] objects do not exist, but [he does] not [become aware of] even

(4) After that, the destruction of idea of cognition-only (**vi-jñapti-mātra-saṁjñā*) is the **ānantarya-samādhi* (uninterrupted concentration), and [it] is a support for **laukikāgra-dharma* (the state of mundane supreme *dharma*) [within the context of the four states leading up to penetration into truth].

These concentrations are to be understood as that which is akin (**antika*) to realizetion.[69]

MS III. 14

In that manner, the bodhisattva has entered the [first] stage, has obtained **darśana-mārga* and has entered [into the truth that all phenomena are] nothing but [mental] presentations (**vijñapti-mātratā*): How does one cultivate [oneself in the praxis] on **bhāvanā-mārga*?

Having transformed [his] basis (**āśraya*), that [bodhisattva], for the purpose of cultivating [himself] for one hundred thousands **niyuta koṭi* of **kalpa*s, practices [on *bhāvanā-mārga*] in order to obtain the three bodies of Buddha by means of [the two kinds of cognition]—[non-discriminating] supramundane [cognition] that has the combined [teachings] as its objective reference/support and the cognition of calm and insight (**śamatha-vipaśyanā-jñāna*)

[the idea] that [all phenomena are] nothing but mental presentations. For that very reason, that [*samādhi*] is **a support for *kṣānti which conforms with the truth**. [*Ācārya-* Asaṅga states:] ****anugata*** because it is akin, and depending upon [the idea] that cognitum does not exist, [the bodhisattva] understands that cognizer does not exist.

69 MSU: [The statement:] **These concentrations are to be understood as that which is akin to realization** means that at the time of **realization**, [the bodhisattva's basis] is transformed.

that is attained subsequent to that [supramundane knowledge] in the bodhisattva's ten stages (*daśa-bhūmi) that have been established as described [by the Buddha] and that is present as the summary of all of [Buddha's] teachings.[70]

MS III. 15

What difference is there between the two, i.e., realization of the Śrāvakas and realization of the Bodhisattvas?[71]

It should be known that the realization of the bodhisattvas is peculiarly superior to the realization of the Śrāvakas in view of ten [kinds of] superiorities:

(1) [The realization of the Bodhisattvas is superior] in view of superiority of objective reference/support (*ālambana-viśeṣa*), because [it] takes the Mahāyāna teachings as its object.[72]

---

70 MSBh: [The statement:] **the combined [teachings] as its objective reference/support** refers to that the wise perceives the basis of **objective reference/support. Supramundane [cognition]** is non-discriminating [cognition]. **[The cognition ... that] is attained subsequent to that [supramundane cognition]** is [a cognition] that is established [in the conventional world]. That is said to be [that which belongs to] the [conventional] world, because it, indeed, conforms with the [conventional] world. ... [The statement:] **having transformed [his] basis, that [bodhisattva]** refers to that [the bodhisattva] has transformed the excellent basis of wisdom that combines [teachings] as its objective reference/support. [The statement:] **obtain the three bodies of Buddha** [refers to that the bodhisattva, thinking that I will] **obtain the three bodies of Buddha**, should cultivate [himself in the practice].

71 Realization of the bodhisattva is discussed in the AS, see AS, p. 94, *ll.* 7–13 and ASBh § 150, p. 123, *l.* 3–p. 124, *l.* 6.

72 MSU: **Superiority of objective reference/support** means that the bodhisattva perceives the Mahāyāna teachings by means of three [kinds of] wisdom, such as [wisdom] arising from listening, etc. [The bodhisattva does] not [perceive] the teachings of the Śrāvakas.

(2) [The realization of the Bodhisattvas is superior] in view of superiority of support (*upastambha/upasevana-viśeṣa), because [it] takes as its stand the great provisions of meritorious acts and knowledge (*mahā-puṇya-jñāna-saṁbhāra).[73]

(3) [The realization of the Bodhisattvas is superior] in view of superiority of penetration (*prativedha-viśeṣa), because [it] penetrates into the selflessness of person and things (*pudgala-dharma-nairātmya).[74]

(4) [The realization of the Bodhisattvas is superior] in view of superiority of *nirvāṇa, because [it] cognizes (dwells in) the non-dwelling *nirvāṇa* (*apratiṣṭhita-nirvāṇa).[75]

(5) [The realization of the Bodhisattvas is superior] in view of superiority of stages, because [it] takes one out of [saṁsāric existences] by means of [traversing] the ten stages.[76]

(6) [The realization of the Bodhisattvas is superior] in view of superiority of the complete purity (*pariśuddhi-viśeṣa), because

73 MSU: **Provisions of meritorious acts** refer to the practice of giving (*dāna), moral conduct (*śīla) and patience (*kṣānti). **Provisions of knowledge** is [a wisdom based upon] listening.

74 MSU: **Superiority of penetration** means that the Śrāvaka realizes only *pudgala-nairātmya. [However,] the bodhisattva realizes *pudgala-dharma-nairātmya.

75 MSBh: **Superiority of *nirvāṇa** means that the bodhisattvas cognize **the non-dwelling *nirvāṇa**, but the Śrāvaka does not [cognize it].

MSU: **Superiority of *nirvāṇa** means that the bodhisattvas' [*nirvāṇa*] is **the non-dwelling *nirvāṇa**. Since [the bodhisattva] grasps [it] completely by the skillful means of wisdom and compassion (*karuṇā), [he does] not dwell in *samsāra and *nirvāṇa. The Śrāvaka dwells in *asaṁskṛta-nirvāṇa.

76 MSU: **Superiority of stages** means that the bodhisattva departs through the ten stages. In the Śrāvaka, [such ten] stages are not established.

[it] removes the impregnation of afflictions and purifies the Buddha-lands (*buddha-kṣetra*).[77]

(7) [The realization of the Bodhisattvas is superior] in view of superiority of obtaining an impartial mind regarding all sentient beings and one's self (**sarva-sattvātma-sama-cittatā-prāpti-viśeṣa*), because the praxis that makes sentient beings mature is not interrupted.[78]

(8) [The realization of the Bodhisattvas is superior] in view of superiority of birth [in the family of the Buddha] (**janma-viśeṣa*), because [it] comes forth in the lineage of the *Tathāgatas*.[79]

(9) [The realization of the Bodhisattvas is superior] in view of superiority of taking up the rank [of a Buddha] (?**utpatti-saṁbhava*), because [it] is present at all times in the assemblies of the Buddhas.

(10) [The realization of the Bodhisattvas is superior] in view

---

77 MSBh: With regard to **superiority of the purity**, indeed the bodhisattvas **remove afflictions** together with **the impregnation** [of afflictions] **and purifies the Buddha-lands**, but the Śrāvakas do not [remove afflictions together with the impregnation and does not purifies the Buddha-land].

78 MSU: **Superiority of obtaining an impartial mind regarding all sentient beings and one's self** means that by means of **obtaining an impartial mind regarding** one's self and others, **the praxis that makes sentient beings mature is not interrupted** by the bodhisattva. The Śrāvaka, since the discrimination of one's self and others arises [in him], practices for the sake of one's self, but [he] does not practice for the sake of others.

79 MSU: **Superiority of birth** means that the bodhisattva is born in **dharma-dhātu* that is the lineage of the *Tathāgatas* and becomes the son of the Buddha, just like the one who possesses the characteristics of a prince who is born in the lineage of the ruler of a **Cakra* (**cakra-vartin*). The Śrāvaka is not like that, [but] is like a servant [who is born in] the lineage of the low [caste].

of superiority of result (*phala-viśeṣa*), because [it] accomplishes countless qualities (*aparimita-guṇa*) as its result: that is, ten [kinds of] forces,[80] [four kinds of] confidences[81] and [eighteen kinds of] exclusive qualities of a Buddha.[82]

---

80 Ten kinds of forces of a Buddha are: (1) *sthānāsthāna-jñāna-bala*, (2) *karma-vipāka-jñāna-bala*, (3) *nānādhimukti-jñāna-bala*, (4) *nānā-dhātu-jñāna-bala*, (5) [*sattva-*]*indriya-parāpara-jñāna-bala*, (6) *sarvatra-gāminī-pratipaj/-pratipatti-jñāna-bala*, (7) [*sarva-*]*dhyāna-vimokṣa-samādhi-samāpatti-saṁkleśa-vyavadāna-vyutthāna-jñāna-bala*, (8) *pūrva-nivāsānusmṛti-jñāna-bala*, (9) *cyuty-upapatti-jñāna-bala*, (10) *āsrava-kṣaya-jñāna-bala*. See AN vol. V. pp. 33-36, *ll.* 7–19, MVY nos. 119– 129, p. 9, *l.* 1–p. 10, *l.* 3, BoBh, p. 384, *ll.* 18–25, etc. MSU X. 9 lists these items. See Hakamaya p. 125, *ll.* 18–26.

81 Four kinds of confidences of a Buddha are: (1) *sarva-dharmābhisaṁbodhi-vaiśāradyam* (confidence of being perfectly enlightened as to all *dharmas*), (2) *sarvāsrava-kṣaya-jñāna-vaiśāradyam* (confidence of cognition that all impurities are destroyed for him), (3) *antarāyika-dharmānanyathātva-niścita-vyākaraṇa-vaiśāradyam* (confidence of having described precisely and correctly the obstructive conditions [to religious life]), (4) *sarva-saṁpad-adhigamāya nairyāṇika-pratipat-tathātva-vaiśāradyam* (confidence of the correctness of his way of salvation for realization of all [religious] success). See MVY, nos. 131–134, p. 10, *ll.* 4–23, BHS pp. 512–513. MSU X. 9 lists these items. See Hakamaya p. 125, *ll.* 27–39.

82 MSU: **Superiority of result** refers to that the result of the bodhisattva is the ornament (*alaṁkāra*) through the provision of qualities, such as [ten kinds of] forces, a potentiality of the action performed with a special purpose for the sentient beings (*sattvārthākriyā-śakti*) without effort, and realization of the *dharma*-body. The result of others is non-arising of the impurity (*sāsravānutpatti*).

Eighteen kinds of exclusive qualities of a Buddha are: (1) *nāsti tathāgatasya skhalitam*, (2) *nāsti ravitam*, (3) *nāsti muṣita-smṛtitā*, (4) *nāsty asamāhita-cittam*, (5) *nāsti nānātva-saṁjñā*, (6) *nāsty apratisaṁkhyāyopekṣā*, (7) *nāsti chandasya hāniḥ*, (8) *nāsti vīryasya hāniḥ*, (9) *nāsti smṛti-hāniḥ*, (10) *nāsti samādhi-hāniḥ*, (11) *nāsti prajñāyā hāniḥ*, (12) *nāsti vimukti-hāniḥ*, (13) *nāsti vimukti-jñāna-darśana-hāniḥ* (14) *sarva-kāya-karma jñānāpūrvaṁgamaṁ jñānānu-parivarti*, (15) *sarva-vāk-karma-jñāna-pūrvaṁgamaṁ jñānānuparivṛttiḥ*, (16) *sarva-manas-karma-jñāna-pūrvaṁgamaṁ jñānānuparivṛttiḥ*, (17) *atīte 'dhvany asaṅgama-pratihata-jñānam*, (18) *pratyutpanne 'dhvany asaṅgama-*

MS III. 16

With regard to this, there are verses:

> [The bodhisattva] investigates [the fact that] both name and substance are incidental. [Here, the bodhisattva] investigates [the fact that] the two kinds of designnations are that-only (**tan-mātra*).[83] //1//

---

pratihata-jñāna-darśanaṁ. See MVY nos. 135–153, p. 10, *l*. 24–p. 12, *l*. 16. MSU X. 9 lists these items. See Hakamaya p. 126, *l*. 10–p. 127, *l*. 5.

83 Cf. MSA XIX. 47, p. 168, *ll*. 18–24:

> [The bodhisattva] investigates [the fact that] both name and substance are incidental. Here, moreover, [the bodhisattva] investigates [the fact that] the two kinds of designations are that-only.

There are four kinds of investigations of *dharma*s; (1) investigation of name, (2) investigation of thing, (3) investigation of the designation of intrinsic nature [of entities], and (4) investigation of the designation of specific attributes [of entities]. Among these [four kinds of investigations], it should be known that the investigation of name (*nāma-paryeṣaṇā*) is an investigation [of the fact] that name is incidental to substance. It should be known that the investigation of substance (*vastu-paryeṣaṇā*) is an investigation [of the fact] that substance is incidental to name. It should be known that the investigation of the designation of intrinsic nature and specific attributes is an investigation [of the fact that in the combination of these two], designation of intrinsic nature and [designation of] specific attributes are nothing but incidental.

MSBh: In [the statement: **The bodhisattva**] **investigates** [**the fact that**] **both name and substance are incidental**, **name** is incidental to the substance and **substance** is incidental to name. ... **Investigation** is that which is to be seen by meditation.

MSU: [*Ācārya*-Asaṅga states: **Here, the bodhisattva**] **investigates** [**the fact that** ...] **that-only**. What is the object [of investigation]? [*Ācārya*-Asaṅga] states: **the two kinds of designations**; [that is,] designation of intrinsic nature and designation of specific attributes. How [does the bodhisattva investigate]? "This is nothing but designation; There is only designation of conventional usage, but in this case, the designation of intrinsic nature and [the designation of] specific attributes do

[Even when it is understood] by means of [the four kinds of] wisdom of knowing reality as-it-is (**yathā-bhūta-parijñāna*) that [external] objects do not exist, there [still remain] three [kinds of] discriminations (**kalpa-traya*). [The bodhisattva] understands that because those [external objects] do not exist, those [three kinds of discriminations] do not exist. [Thus, there is] entrance into three [natures].[84] //2//

---

not exist."

84 MSBh: [The statement: **Thus, there is**] **entrance into three** means that **there is entrance into three** natures. With regard to that, if [a bodhisattva] sees that both name and substance are incidental, [he] has entered into the imagined nature. If [a bodhisattva] sees that intrinsic nature and specific attributes of name are nothing but designation, [he] has entered into the other-dependent nature. If [a bodhisattva] does not see that very designation, [he] has entered into consummated nature. Thus, [the bodhisattva] enters into three.

MSU: [The statement: **external**] **objects do not exist** refers to being freed of [**external**] **objects**. [The statement:] **there** [**still remain**] **three kinds of discriminations** means that **there** [**still remain**] **discrimination** of name, **discrimination** of the designation of intrinsic nature, and **discrimination** of the designation of specific attributes. [The statement:] **because those** [**external objects**] **do not exist** means **because** [**external**] **objects do not exist**. [The statement: **external**] **objects do not exist** means that [the bodhisattva] sees that three kinds of discriminations **do not exist**. [The statement: **Thus, there is**] **entrance into three** means that **there is entrance into three** natures. By the first half of the first verse, [it is stated that the bodhisattva], having seen that both name and substance are incidental each other, has entered into imagined nature. By the latter half of the first verse, [it is stated that the bodhisattva], having seen that the designations of intrinsic nature and specific attributes are nothing but discriminations, realizes the other-dependent nature. By the second verse, [it is stated that] there exists only discrimination, but [it] is not a substantial existence, accordingly, by seeing that discrimination also does not exist, [the bodhisattva] enters into the consummated nature. Otherwise, since the pure and impure do not exist [in truth], [existences of] the bondage and enlightenment are not

MS III. 17

Now, moreover, verses of doctrine (**avavāda*) from the **Yoga-vibhāga*[*-śāstra*]:[85]

> A bodhisattva who is fixed in meditation sees the images (**pratibimba*) [as his own] mind (**manas*). The one who has abandoned the idea of objects (**artha-saṁjñā*) takes hold of [his] own idea (**sva-saṁjñā*). //1//[86]

---

accomplished.

85 According to Chinese tradition, the **Yogavibhāgaśāstra* is ascribed to Maitreya(-nātha). A Sanskrit manuscript is not extant. Tibetan and Chinese translations of this work are also not extant. The first verse and first half of the second verse are quoted in the AS, p. 82, *ll.* 20–21, the ASBh, p. 100, *l.* 21, and 成唯識論, vol. 9, p. 402, *l.* 1.

86 MSBh: With regard to [the statement: **A bodhisattva ...**] **sees the images** [**as his own**] **mind**, [a bodhisattva] **sees** that **the images** which appear as teachings and [their] meanings are [his own] **mind**. [The statement:] **The one who has abandoned the idea of objects takes hold of** [**his**] **own idea** means that at that time [of meditation the bodhisattva,] having removed **the idea of objects**, understands that his own mind is a representation (**ākāra*) of teachings and [their] meaning.

MSU: Who is the one who, investigating in that manner, obtains the result? And for whom, bringing into that subject which is taught in such a way, are verses stated? [To these questions, *ācārya*-Asaṅga states:] **A bodhisattva who is fixed in meditation sees the images** [**as his own**] **mind**, etc. [That is, a bodhisattva who is fixed in meditation] **sees the images** of the meditation, which appear as teachings and [their] meanings, [as his own] **mind**. [In a *sūtra*,] for instance, it is stated:

> I declare that mind (**vijñāna*) that possesses the object appears through the cognition.

Who sees [the images as his mind]? [It is] **a bodhisattva who is fixed in meditation**, and [the one possessed of] the one-pointed [mind] (**cittaikāgra*). [The statement:] **The one who has abandoned the idea of objects** refers to that [the bodhisattva] has removed **the idea of objects** from the images. [The statement: **The one ...**] **takes hold of** [**his**] **own idea** means that [the bodhisattva] thinks that that very mind of

> In that manner, [the one whose] mind dwells within (**adhyātma-citta-stha*), realizes that cognitum does not exist. Then, [he] realizes that cognizer does not exist. Then, [he] comes into contact with the non-perception (**anupalambha*). //2//[87]

MS III. 18

Now, moreover, verses regarding the realization are stated in *Mahāyānasūtrālaṁkāra* [VI. 6– 10]:

> Having accumulated the limitless provisions of meritorious acts and knowledge, the bodhisattva, because [his] reflection on the teachings became determined well, understands the objects [reflected in teachings] in accordance with speech. //1//[88]

---

mine which **is fixed in the meditation** appears like teachings and [their] meanings.

87 MSBh: [The statement:] **realizes that cognitum does not exist** means that [the bodhisattva] understands that **cognitum does not exist**. … **Then, [he] realizes that cognizer does not exist**; for, because the objects to be cognized do not exist, the mind, i.e., cognizer, too, is not reasonable.

MSU: [The statement:] **In that manner, [the one whose] mind dwells within** means that at that time, **mind dwells** in his very mind. [The statement:] **realizes that cognitum does not exist** [means that the bodhisattva] should understand that **cognitum does not exist**. [*Ācārya-*Asaṅga states:] **Then, [he] realizes that cognizer does not exist**, because it is not admitted that when cognitum does not exist, **cognizer** exists. [The statement:] **Then, [he] comes into contact with the non-perception** [means that the bodhisattva] becomes aware of, i.e., realizes **tathatā* that is freed of perception of the two natures.

88 Cf. MSA VI. 6, p. 24, *ll.* 7-9: The first [verse] shows the entrance into that [state] because [the bodhisattva,] relying upon the *samādhi*, culti-

From knowing that the objects are nothing but speech (*japla-mātra*), he dwells in [the state that all phenomena are] nothing but mind (*citta-mātra*) which appears as them. Therefore, *dharma-dhātu* freed of the two characteristics [i.e., cognitum and cognizer] is directly intuited. //2//[89]

---

vates himself in the accumulation of provisions and in the well-determination of the reflection upon the teachings, and because [the bodhisattva] perceives and understands the meanings of the teachings through mind-talk. [The word:] shore (*pāra*) refers to time of immeasurable distinction, and [the word:] limitless (*ananta-pāra*) refers to accomplishment of this [shore].

MSU: **Provisions of meritorious acts** refer to three kinds of perfections, such as giving, etc. **Provisions of knowledge** refer to the perfection of wisdom. The [perfection of] valour (**vīrya*) belongs to both. When meditation (**dhyāna*) perceives [four kinds of] immeasurable [mind, i.e., love, compassion, joy, and equanimity], [it belongs to] **provisions of meritorious acts**. Others are member/part of [**provisions of**] **knowledge**. ... [*Ācārya*-Asaṅga states:] **because [his] reflection on the teachings became determined well** because after **samādhi*, [the bodhisattva's reflection on] the **sūtra*s, etc., is ascertained well, and because [the bodhisattva] has no doubt [towards the teachings]. [The statement: **the bodhisattva** ...] **understands objects [reflected in teachings] in accordance with speech** [means that the bodhisattva] knows that the cause of objects is mind-talk. For instance, it is like saying that **dharma*s arise from the impregnation of speech, etc. ... This verse shows **saṁbhāra-mārga*.

89 Cf. MSA VI. 7, p. 24, *ll.* 9–12: By the second [verse, it is shown that] having known that objects are nothing but mind-talk, [the bodhisattva] stays in [the state that all phenomena are] nothing but mind which appears as them. This [state] is bodhisattva's state leading up to penetration [into truth]. Then, by other [*pāda*s, it is shown that] when *dharma-dhātu* is directly intuited, [the bodhisattva] is freed of two characteristics, i.e., characteristics of cognitum and cognizer. This is the state—the path of insight.

MSBh: [*Ācārya*-Asaṅga states:] **he dwells in [the state that all phenomena are] nothing but mind which appears as them** because [he] understands that those which appear as objects in that manner are **nothing but mind**.

From knowing by intelligence/intellect (*buddhi*) that there does not exist something other than the mind, [he] understands that [even] the mind (*citta*) does not exist. The wise, having understood that the two [i.e., cognitum and cognizer] do not exist, the one dwells in *dharma-dhātu* which lacks them [i.e., cognitum and cognizer]. //3//[90]

MSU: [The statement:] **Therefore, *dharma-dhātu freed of the two characteristics is directly intuited** means that dwelling in [the state of] mind-only that is accompanied by the understanding that objects do not exist, ***dharma-dhātu* freed of** the two **characteristics** of cognitum and cognizer,—i.e., having no two,—**is directly intuited**, and it is because it certainly arises. This verse explains **prayoga-mārga*.

90 Cf. MSA VI. 8, p. 24, *ll.* 12–16: By the third [verse], it is shown how *dharma-dhātu* is directly intuited. Then, how is *dharma-dhātu* directly intuited? Having understood **by intelligence/intellect that there does not exist** objective reference/support, i.e., cognitum, **other than the mind**, [the bodhisattva] **understands** that that very **mind** also **does not exist** because when cognitum does not exist, cognizer does not exist. Moreover, having known that those two do not exist, [the bodhisattva] stays in *dharma-dhātu* that lacks them. Likewise, *dharma-dhātu* that is freed of the characteristics of the cognitum and cognizer is directly intuited.

MSBh: With regard to [the statement:] **From knowing by intelligence/intellect that there does not exist something other than the mind, [he] understands that [even] the mind does not exist**, when **there does not exist** an object which is to be perceived **other than the mind**, because that does not exist, mind, i.e., perceiver, too, does not exist. Having understood that the two do not exist, the bodhisattva **dwells in *dharma-dhātu that lacks them.** It means that the bodhisattva is freed of those objects and the mind.

MSU: [The statement:] **From knowing by intelligence/intellect that there does not exist something other than the mind, [he] understands that [even] the mind does not exist** connects with [the statement:] the object which is to be perceived **does not exist other than the mind** and since that [object] does not exist, perceiver, too, is not admitted. ... [The statement:] **the one dwells in *dharma-dhātu which lacks them** means that [the bodhisattva dwells] in [*dharma-dhātu* that is]

The wise expels his basis (*āśraya*) which is a thicket-like accumulation of the faults, by the force of the non-conceptual wisdom (*akalpanā-jñāna-balena*) which is always and everywhere followed by equality (*samānu-yātena*), just as [the doctor] expels poison by a good medicine. //4//[91]

The steadfast one who has been established well in the good teachings, which are taught by the Muni, placing [one's] thought in the fundamental *dharma-dhātu* and from knowing that activity of the memory is nothing but concept (*kalpa-mātra*), goes immediately to the other shore of the ocean of merits. //5//[92]

---

freed of cognitum and cognizer. ... By this verse, *_darśana-mārga_ is shown.

91 Cf. MSA VI. 9, p. 24, *ll.* 16–20: By the fourth [verse, Asaṅga] shows the entrance into ultimate cognition (*pāramārthika-jñāna*) because the basis is transformed in the state of the path of cultivation. By the non-discriminative cognition that is always and everywhere followed by equality, [the bodhisattva] follows that [equality], because in the other-dependent nature [he expels] his basis which has entered into a distant place, which is accumulation of the faults, which has the characteristics of barrier/badness, just as [the doctor] expels poison by a good medicine.

MSBh: [The statement:] **his basis which is a thicket-like accumulation of the faults** refers to the **basis** of his impure *_dharma_s (*_saṁkliṣṭa-dharma_) and is the cause. [The statement:] **thicket** refers to difficulty of understanding. [The statement:] **accumulation of the faults** means that which has the nature of impregnation of the impure *_dharma_s.

MSU: [The statement:] **by the non-conceptual wisdom** means by virtue of the non-discriminative **wisdom**. ... [The statement:] **a thicket** refers to difficulty of knowing and difficulty of understanding. [The statement: **accumulation of the faults**] refers to a store-house (*_kośa_),—i.e., *_ālaya_,—of the impregnation of the impure *_dharma_s. ... By this verse, *_bhāvanā-mārga_ is shown.

92 Cf. MSA VI. 10, p. 24, *ll.* 21–26: [The following is] a verse on greatness of the ultimate cognition. ... That bodhisattva who has entered into the

ultimate cognition regarding that which is well-established in the good teachings which are taught by the Buddha, placing [his] thought in *dharma-dhātu* of the fundamental mind that possesses the accumulated teachings as its objective reference/support, understands that all activities of the memory which is obtained are nothing but concepts. Thus, [the bodhisattva] goes immediately to the other shore of the ocean of merits, i.e., Buddhahood. This is greatness of the ultimate cognition.

MSBh: With regard to [the statement:] **The steadfast one who has been established well in the good teachings which are taught by the Muni, placing [one's] thought in the fundamental *dharma-dhātu***, [the bodhisattva] places [his] **thought** in any objective reference/support by means of the mind having **the foundation**. [That is, the bodhisattva places his thought] in that **tathatā*. ... The summary of the meaning of these verses is: by the first [verse], **saṁbhāra-mārga* [is shown]; by the first half of the second [verse] **prayoga-mārga* is shown. By the latter half [of the second verse] and third [verse] **darśana-mārga*. By the fourth [verse], **bhāvanā-mārga*; by the fifth **niṣṭhā-mārga*.

MSU: [The statement:] **the fundamental** refers to the **Daśabhūmika*[-*sūtra*]. It is because it is a mother (**mātṛkā*) of all the *sūtra*s. Its teachings are the entrance of [other] teachings. [The statement:] ***dharma-dhātu** refers to emptiness (**śūnyatā*), and by means of the wisdom that is attained subsequent to that [supramundane knowledge, the bodhisattva] thinks of [*dharma-dhātu*] and dwells [therein]. [The statement:] **from knowing that activity of the memory is nothing but concept** refers to that **activity of the memory** enters into **the fundamental *dharma-dhātu**.

Chapter Three

Tibetan Text

Introduction to the Tibetan text

For the edition appended here, the *sDe dge*, Tokyo edition, has been utilized as the basic text upon which the *Co ne*, Peking, *sNar thang*, and the Taipei editions have been compared. Variant readings, from both the Chinese and Tibetan translations of the MS and selected passages from the MSBh and the MSU have been noted in the footnotes. The passages from the MSBh and the MSU were selected for the explicit purpose of not only clarifying the contents of the MS but to show the differences in interpretation of particular passages by Vasubandhu in his MSBh and by Asvabhāva in his MSU. In editing the Tibetan text, the most likely Sanskrit original form was kept in mind and in such cases as ambiguity in the MS reading, the comparison between MSBh and MSU often aided in thinking through the possible Sanskrit passage that would yield such a difference in interpretation and from which the Tibetan translation could also be edited.

The various texts used for the appended Tibetan text are as follows:

Tibetan translation of the MS:

Theg pa chen po bsdus pa (*Mahāyānasaṁgraha*), Jinamitra, Sīlendrabodhi, and Ye shes sde , tr., Derge no. 4048, folio

Ri 23a7–26b3, *Co ne* microfiche vol. 55, folio Ri 23a7–26b3, Peking no.5549, folio Li 26b6–30b4, *sNar thang* no. 3540, folio Li 25a7–28b7, Taipei no. 4053, folio Ri 23a7–26b3.

Tibetan translation of the MSBh:

Theg pa chen po bsdus pa'i 'grel pa (*Mahāyānasaṁgraha-bhāṣya*), Dīpaṁkaraśrījñāna and Tshul khrims rgyal ba, tr., Derge no. 4050, folio Ri 157b2–168a5, Peking no. 5551, folio Li 189a5–198b8.

Tibetan translation of the MSU:

Theg pa che po bsdus pa'i bshad sbyar (*Mahāyānasaṁ-grahopanibandhana*), Jinamitra, Sīlendrabodhi, and Ye shes sde, tr., Derge no. 4051 folio Ri 242a5–251a1, Peking no. 5552, folio Li 295a7–305b3.

Chinese translations of the MS:

(1) *Shê ta ch'êng lun* (攝大乘論), Buddhaśānta (仏陀扇多), tr., Taisho vol. 31, no. 1592, pp. 104b15–105c11.

(2) *Shê ta ch'êng lun* (攝大乘論), Paramārtha (眞諦), tr., Taisho vol. 31, no. 1593, pp. 122b25–124a24.

(3) *Shê ta ch'êng lun shih lun* (攝大乘論釋論), Dharmagupta and others (笈多共行矩等), tr., Taisho vol. 31, no. 1596, pp. 294c3–299a11.

(4) *Shê ta ch'êng lun pên* (攝大乘論本), Hsüan-tsang (玄奘), tr., Taisho vol. 31, no. 1594, pp. 142b5–143c20.

Chinese translations of the MSBh:

(1) *Shê ta ch'êng lun shih* (攝大乘論釋), Paramārtha (眞諦), tr., Taisho vol. 31, no. 1595, pp. 198c16–212c18.

(2) *Shê ta ch'êng lun shih lun* (攝大乘論釋論), Dharmagupta and others (笈多共行矩等), tr., Taisho vol. 31, no. 1596, pp. 294c3–299a11.

(3) *Shê ta ch'êng lun shih lun* (攝大乘論釋論), Hsüan-tsang (玄奘), tr., Taisho vol. 31, no. 1597, pp. 349b4–354b6.

Chinese translation of the MSU

Shê ta ch'êng lun shih lun (攝大乘論釋論), Hsüan-tsang (玄奘), tr., Taisho vol. 31, no. 1598, pp. 413b6–419a17.

Lamotte's Edition of the Tibetan Text of the MS

La Somme du Grand Véhicule D'Asaṅga (*Mahāyānasaṁgraha*) Tome I. Université du Louvain, Publications de l'Institut Orientaliste du Louvain 8, 1973 (first ed. 1938).

Nagao's Edition of the Tibetan Text of the MS

摂大乗論 和訳と注解 下 (**Mahāyānasaṁgraha*: A Japanese Translation and Annotation), Kodansha, Tokyo, vol. 2, pp. 56–125(left).

Yamaguchi's Edition of the Tibetan Text of the MS

西蔵譯「攝大乘論」(*Tibetan Translation of the *Mahāyānasaṁgraha*) in Sasaki Gessho's 漢訳四本対照・攝大乗論 (*Comparison of the Four Chinese Translations of the *Mahāyānasaṁgraha*), Hobunsha, Tokyo, 1931 (rpt. Rinsenshoten, Kyoto, 1977).

Signs employed in the following Tibetan text.

om.	omit
em. to	emended to
[ ]	folio no.
< >	addition

Tibetan Text

MS III. 1

DCT23a7, P26b6, N25a7

shes bya'i mtshan nyid de ltar bshad pa la shes bya'i mtshan nyid la 'jug pa P26b7 ji ltar blta[1] zhe na/[2]

mang du thos pas bsgos C23b1 pa'i gnas/[3] N25b1 kun gzhi rnam par shes pas bsdus pa[4] ma yin la/ kun gzhi rnam par shes pa DT23b1 ltar[5] tshul bzhin yid la byed pas bsdus pa/[6] chos dang don snang ba 'byung

---

1 D, C, T, P, Y, L, Na *blta*; N *lta*

2 BŚ (104b15): 入智相云何, Pa (122b26): 如此已説應知勝相　云何應知入勝相, DG (294c7): 如此已説應知相　入應知相云何可見, H (142b6): 如是已説所知相　入所知相云何應見.

3 MSBh [D159b2–3, P192a1]: ***mang du thos pas bsgos pa'i gnas*** *zhes bya ba ste/ theg pa chen po yongs su bsgoms pa'i bdag nyid kyi ngo bo'o//*

MSU [D242a5–242b1, P295a8–b3]: ***mang du thos pas bsgos pa'i gnas*** *zhes bya ba ni theg pa chen po'i skabs yin pa'i phyir ro// theg pa chen po'i chos dang don* ***mang du thos pas*** *sems dang sems las byung ba'i rgyud* ***bsgos pa*** *yin te/ mang du ma thos pa la ni mngon par rtogs pa med pa'i phyir ro// 'di ltar bcom ldan 'das la 'phags pa sgra gcan zin gyis gsol ba/ bcom ldan 'das kyis bdag la mngon par rtogs par bgyi ba'i slad du/ gdams su gsol/ bka' stsal pa/ sgra gcan zin khyod kyis phung po pa bzung ngam/ des gsol ba/ bcom ldan 'das ma bzung lags so// bcom ldan 'das kyis bka' stsal pa/ sgra gcan zin de lta bas na phung po pa nyid rje zung shig/ kun chub par gyis shig ces bya ba la sogs pa'o//*

4 D, C, T, Y, L, Na *pa*; P, N *pas*

5 After *ltar*, L places *sa bon yin pa/* which is originally placed after *yid kyi brjod pa rnams kyi* in the last sentence of this section.

6 MSBh [D159b3–5, P192a1–4]: ***kun gzhi rnam par shes pas bsdus pa ma yin la*** *zhes bya ba dang/* ***kun gzhi rnam par shes pa ltar tshul bzhin yid la byed pas bsdus pa'i sa bon yin no*** *zhes bya ba ni ji ltar* ***kun gzhi rnam par shes pa*** *kun nas nyon mongs pa'i chos rnams kyi rgyu yin pa de bzhin du de rnam par byang ba'i chos rnams kyi yang rgyur 'gyur ro zhes bya ba'i tha tshig go//* ***tshul bzhin yid la byed pas bsdus pa*** *zhes bya ba nas brtsams te/* ***lta ba dang bcas pa'i yid kyi brjod pa rnams kyi*** *yang ste/* ***tshul bzhin yid la byed pa*** *las* ***chos dang don*** *gyi rnam pa 'byung bar 'gyur bas rgyu yin no//*

MSU [D242b1–2, P295b3–5]: ***kun gzhi rnam par shes pas bsdus pa ma yin*** *zhes bya ba ni chos kyi dbyings shin tu rnam par dag pa'i rgyu*

P26b8
ba'i tshul can gzung ba'i dngos po'i gnas lta bu/[7] lta ba dang bcas pa'i yid kyi brjod[8] pa rnams[9] kyi sa bon yin N25b2 pa'o[10]//[11]

---

mthun pa dang/ de'i gnyen po yin pa'i phyir/ de'i rang bzhin ma yin te/ 'gal ba'i phyir des ***bsdus pa ma yin*** *no//* ***kun gzhi rnam par shes pa ltar sa bon yin pa*** *zhes bya ba ni ji ltar* ***kun gzhi rnam par shes pa*** *kun nas nyon mongs pa'i chos rnams kyi rgyu yin pa de bzhin du* ***gnas*** *'di yang rnam par byang ba'i chos rnams kyi rgyu yin te/ rgyu'i dngos po tsam du dpe dang bstun pa yin gyi/ gshan du ni ma yin no//*

7 MSBh [D159b5, P192a4–5]: ***tshul can gzung ba'i dngos po<'i gnas> lta bu*** *zhes bya ba ni gzugs su gyur pa zhes bya'i don to//*

MSU [D242b2–3, P295b5–7]: ***chos*** *ni mdo la sogs pa'o//* ***don*** *ni de dag nyid kyi brjod par bya ba bdag med pa la sogs pa'o// 'di dag ni de'i rnam par 'byung ba'i rang tshul can yin pas der* ***snang ba 'byung ba'i tshul can*** *no//* ***gzung ba'i dngos po'i gnas lta bu*** *zhes bya ba ni de dang 'dra bar snang ba'i phyir ro//*

8 P, N, Y, L, Na *brjod*; D, C, T *rjod*

9 MSBh [D159b5, P192a5–6]: ***lta ba dang bcas pa'i*** *zhes bya ba ni* ***lta bar*** *gyur pa rnams so// de dag nyid ni rgyu mtshan dang* ***lta ba dang bcas pa'i*** *rnam par shes par rnam par 'jog par 'gyur ro//*

MSU [D242b3–4, P295b7–8]: ***lta ba dang bcas pa*** *zhes bya ba ni rna ba'i rnam par shes pa* ***dang bcas pa****'o//* ***yid kyi brjod pa rnams*** *zhes bya ba ni yid kyi rnam par shes pa* ***rnams*** *so// yang na* ***lta ba****'i cha* ***dang bcas pa****'i gzung ba dang 'dzin pa'i dngos por rnam par gzhag pa rnams te/ ji skad sngar bshad pa bzhin no//*

10 D, C, T, P, N, Y, Na *kyi sa bon yin pa'o*; L *yid kyi brjod pa rnams so*

11 BŚ (104b15–17): 多聞薰身故　非阿犁耶識所攝　如阿犁耶識種子成　寂靜思惟所攝　諸法義現相所生　可取事處有見者意言處, Pa (122b27–29): 多聞所熏習依止　非阿黎耶識所攝　如阿黎耶識成種子　正思惟所攝　似法及義顯相所生　似所取種類有見意言分別, DG (294c8–10): 多聞所熏習依止　非阿梨耶識所攝　如阿梨耶成種子　正思惟所攝　似法似義所生　似所取物有見意言, H (142b6–9): 多聞熏習所依　非阿賴耶識所攝　如阿賴耶識成種子　如理作意所攝　似法似義而生　似所取事有見意言.

Skt. reconstituted by Schmithausen: *bāhuśrutyabhāvita āśraya ālayavijñānāsaṁgṛhīta ālayavijñānavad bījabhūto yoniśomanasikārasaṁgṛhītānāṁ … manojalpānām/* See Schmithausen 1987, p. 374.

MS III. 2

'di la shes [C23b2] bya'i mtshan nyid la 'jug pa su zhe na/[12]

sems[13] kyi rgyud theg pa chen po'i chos [P27a1] mang du thos [DT23b2] pas bsgos pa/[14] sangs rgyas 'byung ba tshad med pa mnyes par bya ba thob pa/[15] gcig tu mos pa can </> dge ba'i rtsa ba legs par bsags[16] pa'i phyir [N25b3] bsod nams dang ye shes [P27a2] kyi[17] tshogs legs [C23b3] par bsags[18] pa'i byang chub sems dpa'o//[19]

---

12 BŚ (104b17–18): 是中誰入智相, Pa (122b29–c1): 何人能入應知相, DG (294c19): 於中何人能入應知相, H (142b10): 此中誰能悟入所應知相.

MSU [D242b4–5, P295b8]: ***'jug pa su zhe na*** *zhes bya ba ni* ***'jug par*** *byed pa mngon par rtogs par byed pa po dpyod pas 'dri ba gleng slong ngo//*

H-MSU (413c12–13): 用及用具皆待作者 故問入者誰能悟入.

13 BŚ, Pa, DG, H om. *sems*. See n. 19 below.

14 MSBh [D159b6, P192a6]: *de la* ***theg pa chen po*** *smos pas ni nyan thos la sogs pa'i theg pa spang ba'i don to//*

15 MSBh [D159b6–7, P192a6–8]: ***sangs rgyas 'byung ba tshad med pa mnyes par bya ba thob pa*** *zhes bya ba ni grangs las shin tu 'das pa'i* ***sangs rgyas 'byung ba mnyes par bya ba*** *gang gis* ***thob par*** *gyur pa ste/* ***sangs rgyas*** *mngon sum du byas zhes bya ba'i tha tshig go//*

MSU [D242b5–6, P295b8–a2]: ***sems kyi rgyud theg pa chen po'i chos mang du thos pas bsgos pa*** *zhe bya ba la sogs pa la/* ***sangs rgyas 'byung ba tshad med pa mnyes par bya ba*** *ni mngon du byed pa ste/ 'dis de* ***thob pas sangs rgyas 'byung ba tshad med pa*** *mngon du byed pa* ***thob*** *ces bya ba'i tha tshig go//*

16 D, C, T, Y, L, Na *bsags*; P, N *brtsams*

17 D, C, T, Y, L, Na *kyi*; P, N *kyis*

18 D, C, T, Y, L, Na *bsags*; P, N *brtsams*

19 BŚ (104b18–20): 大乘所薫多聞相續身　無量諸親近得故　信欲一向故 善集善根故　善助功徳智行菩薩, Pa (122c1–4): 大乘多聞熏習相續 已得承事無量出世諸佛　已入決定信樂正位　由善成熟修習增長善根　是故善得福徳智慧二種資糧諸菩薩, DG (294c19–21): 大乘多聞熏習相續已故　得親近無量出世諸佛故　一向信解善集善根故 善滿足福智資糧諸菩薩, H (142b10–14): 大乘多聞熏習相續　已得逢事無量諸佛出現於世　已得一向決定勝解　已善積集諸善根故　善備福智資糧菩薩.

MSBh1 [D159b 7–160a1, P192a8–b1]: ***gcig tu mos pa can*** *zhes bya ba ni gang gi* ***mos pa*** *theg pa chen po las bskyod par mi nus pa ste/ ma*

MS III. 3

gang du 'jug ce na/[20]

DT23b3

lta ba dang bcas pa'i chos dang don snang ba'i yid kyi brjod pa theg pa chen po'i chos kyi rgyu las byung ba de nyid la/[21]

---

thag par bshad pa'i ***dge ba'i rtsa ba bsags pa****'i rgyu rnam pa gsum po dang/* ***bsod nams dang ye shes kyi tshogs legs par bsags pa*** *ni mi dge ba'i grogs po zhes bya ba'i tha tshig go//* [D157b3, P189a6] ***bsod nams dang ye shes kyi tshogs legs par bsags pa'i byang chub sems dpa'o*** *zhes bya ba'o//*

The MSBh1 seems not to make sense, and DG-MSBh and H-MSBh make better sense. DG-MSBh (294c25–295a2): 一向信解者　於大乘中決定信解　不爲惡知識之所動壞故　即此次前所説三因縁中　善集善根故　名爲善集福智資糧菩薩, H-MSBh (349c4–7): 已得一向決定勝解者　謂於大乘所得勝解　非諸惡友能動壞　即由無間所説三因　已善積集諸善根故　及得名爲善備福智資糧菩薩.

MSBh2 [D 157b3–5, P189a7–b2]: *yang de ni rim pa ji lta bus* ***bsod nams dang ye shes kyi tshogs*** *yongs su rdsogs par byed ce na/ rgyu'i stobs dang/ dge ba'i bshes gnyen gyi stobs dang/ yid la byed pa'i stobs dang/ nye bar ston pa'i stobs kyis so// de la tshig gnyis kyis ni stobs gnyis la grangs bzhin du rig par bya'o// de la yid la byed pa'i stobs kyis ni* ***gcig tu mos par*** *byed pa'o// de yang theg pa chen po'i bag chags kyi rgyu can no// de la gcig tu lhag par mos pa yod na sgrub pa la yang dag par 'jug go// sgrub pa la yang dag par gnas na dge ba'i rtsa ba nye bar sogs par 'gyur te/ de ltar na yid la byed pa'i stobs kyis* ***bsod nams dang ye shes kyi tshogs legs par bsags par*** *'gyur pas go rim gyi tshul ni de ltar ro//*

MSU [D242b6–7, P296a2–3]: ***gcig tu mos pa can*** *zhes bya ba ni gang theg pa chen po'i chos la mngon par yid ches te/ bshes gnyen ngan pa gang gis kyang dbyer mi phyed pa'o//* ***theg pa chen po mang du thos pa*** *la sogs pa rnam pa 'di gsum gyis/* ***dge ba'i rtsa ba legs par bsags pa'i phyir bsod nams dang ye shes kyi tshogs legs par bsags pa'i byang chub sems dpa'o//***

20 BŚ (104b20): 何處入還, Pa (122c4): 於何處入唯識觀, DG (295a10): 於何處入, H (142b14): 何處能入.

MSBh [D160a1, P192b1]: *de lta bu'i rnam pas 'jug pa'i gnas bstan par bya ba'i phyir smras pa/*

MSU [D242b7, P296a3–4]: ***gang du 'jug ce na*** *zhes bya ba ni yul dmigs kyis dbye ba lhur len pas 'dri ba'o//*

21 BŚ (104b20–21): 彼現見法義現相意語處　因大乘法生故, P (122c4–5): 有見似法義顯相意言分別　大乘法相所生, DG (295a10–11): 即於彼有見似法及

(I) mos pas [P27a3] spyod pa'i sa dang (II) [N25b4] mthong ba'i lam dang (III) bsgom pa'i lam dang (IV) mthar phyin pa'i lam la 'jug ste/ [C23b4] chos thams cad rnam par rig pa tsam du rjes su sgrogs pa la mos pa dang ji lta ba bzhin du[22] de rab tu [P27a4] rtogs [DT23b4] pa dang sgrib pa thams cad kyi gnyen po sgom pa dang [N25b5] sgrib pa med pa'i phyir ro//[23]

義意言　大乘法相所生中故, H (142b14–15): 謂卽於彼有見似法似義意言　大乘法相等所生起.

MSBh [D160a1, P192b1–2]: ***yid kyi brjod pa*** *ste* </> *yid kyi rnam par rtog pa'o// de ni theg pa chen po'i chos gang 'byung ba'i rgyur gyur pa'o//* [D157b6, P189b3–4] ***theg pa chen po'i chos kyi rgyu las byung ba*** *zhes bya ba ste/ bstan pa'i* ***chos*** *la dmigs pa zhes bya ba'i don to//*

MSU [D242b7–243a1, P296a4–a5]: ***lta ba dang bcas pa'i*** *zhes bya ba la sogs pa la/* ***theg pa chen po'i chos kyi rgyu las*** *de'i rnam par* ***'byung ba*** *'jug pa po'i* ***yid kyi brjod pa*** *ni 'jug par bya ba'i yul yin pas gzhi nyid du brjod par 'dod pa'o//*

22 L adds *yang dag pa* before *ji lta ba bzhin du.*

23 BŚ (104b21–23): 信解地中見道行修道行　及盡至一切法唯記爾　随順聞信因故　如是彼分別證因故　一切障對治及離障故, P (122c5–10): 於願樂行地入謂随聞信樂故　見道謂如理通達故　修道謂能對治一切障故　究竟道中謂出離障垢最清淨故　一切法實唯有識　如説随聞信樂故　如理通達故　能對治一切障故　出離障垢最淸淨故, DG (295a15–17): 信解行地中見道中　修道中 究竟道中　一切法唯識随聞信解故　如理通達故　對治一切障故　無障礙故, H (142b15–17): 勝解行地　見道修道究竟道中　於一切法唯有識性　随聞勝解故　如理通達故　治一切障故 無一切障故.

MSBh [D160a1–5, P192b2–8]: *yang de nyid du yid kyi brjod pa'i bye brag gis gang dag 'jug pa de ni* ***mos pas spyod pa'i sa*** *la 'jug par 'gyur te/ 'di ltar de* ***chos thams cad rnam par rig pa tsam du rjes su sgrogs pa la mos pa*** *skyed par byed de/ des na de ni der zhugs pa zhes brjod do// de ji ltar* ***mthong ba'i lam*** *la 'jug pa de bstan par bya ba'i phyir/* ***ji lta ba bzhin du de rab tu rtogs pa dang*** *zhes bya ba ste/ yid kyi brjod pa de* ***ji lta ba bzhin du rab tu rtogs pa****'o// ji ltar na de* ***ji lta ba bzhin du <de> rab tu rtogs*** *zhe na/ ji ltar chos med pa/ don med pa/ gzung ba med pa/ 'dzin pa med pa'o zhes yid kyi brjod pa rtogs pa gang yin pa'o//* ***bsgom pa'i lam*** *la 'jug pa bstan par bya ba'i phyir*</> ***sgrib pa thams cad kyi gnyen po sgom pa*** *zhes bya ba ste/ rab tu rtogs pa de nyid goms par byed pa ni* ***sgom par*** *gyur pa'o// de lta bas na rnam par mi rtog pa la sogs pa de dag gis gang rtogs pa de nyid kyis sgrib pa rnam par sbyong bar byed pa'o//* ***mthar phyin pa'i lam*** *la 'jug pa de bstan pa'i phyir*</> ***sgrib pa med pa'i phyir*** *zhes bya ba ste/ shin tu rnam par dag pa'i ye*

MS III. 4

gang gis[24] 'jug ce na/[25]

dge ba'i rtsa ba'i stobs bskyed pa dang/ rnam pa gsum gyis[26] [C23b5] sems sbyong ba dang/ gnas bzhi [P27a5] spong ba dang/ chos dang don la dmigs pa'i zhi gnas dang lhag mthong bsgom pa [DT23b5] rtag tu dang gus par [N25b6] byas te sbyor ba la bag yod pas 'jug go//[27]

---

shes kyi dus skabs na shin tu phra ba'i sgrib pa yang med pa ni ***mthar phyin pa'i lam*** *la 'jug pa'o//*

MSU [D243a1–4, P296a5–8]: *yid kyi brjod pa de la 'jug pa kha cig ni* ***mos pas spyod pa'i sa*** *la 'jug ste/ thos pa tsam gyis chos thams cad rnam par rig pa tsam nyid du mos pa'i phyir ro// kha cig ni* ***mthong ba'i lam*** *la 'jug ste/* ***ji lta ba bzhin du*** *yid kyi brjod pa rab tu rtogs pa'i phyir ro// de la* ***ji lta ba bzhin du rab tu rtogs pa*** *ni 'di yin te/ 'di ltar sems can med pa dang/ chos med pa dang/ gzung ba med pa dang/ 'dzin pa med par* ***rab tu rtogs pa****'o// kha cig ni* ***bsgom pa'i lam*** *la 'jug ste/ nyon mongs pa dang/ shes bya'i* ***sgrib pa thams cad kyi gnyen po*** *nyid du* ***sgom pas*** *de rnam par dag pa'i phyir ro// kha cig ni* ***mthar phyin pa'i lam*** *la 'jug ste/* ***sgrib pa med pa'i phyir ro*** *// de ltar na rab tu rtogs pa rnam pa bzhi'o//*

24 MSBh, MSU, Y, L, Na *gang gis*; D, C, T *ji ltar gang gis*, P, N *gang gi*

25 BŚ (104b24): 從何處入, Pa (122c10): 云何得入, DG (295a28): 何縁得入, H (142b18): 由何能入.

MSU [D243a4, P296a8]: ***gang gis 'jug ce na*** *zhes bya ba ni rgyu yongs su 'dri ba ste/ thabs gang gis 'jug ce na zhes bya ba'i tha tshig go//*

26 D, C, T, Y, L, Na *gyis*; P, N *gyi*

27 BŚ (104b24–26): 善根力持故　三種相心轉明　種種莊處滅故　念法義定慧一切時正行　及不放逸故, Pa (122c10–13): 由善根力持故　由有三相練磨心故　由滅除四處障故　縁法義爲境　無間修　恭敬修　奢摩他毘鉢舍那　無放逸故, DG (295a28–b1): 善根力持故　三種練治心故　滅除四處故　法義爲所縁故　奢摩他鉢舍那常修正修無放逸等故, H (142b18–20): 由善根力所住持故　謂三種相練磨心故　断四處故　縁法義境止觀恒常殷重加行無放逸故.

MSBh [D157b6–7, P189b4–5]: ***gang gis 'jug ce na/ dge ba'i rtsa ba'i stobs bskyed pa dang/ rnam pa gsum gyis sems sbyong ba*** *zhes bya ba nas/* ***rtag tu dang gus par byas te sbyor ba la bag yod pas 'jug go*** *zhes bya ba'i bar gyis so//* ***dge ba'i rtsa ba'i stobs bskyed pa*** *ni yang ji skad bstan pa'i tshig brgyad la sbyar bar bya'o//* [D160a5–b1, P192b8–193a4] ***gang gis 'jug*** *pa ston par byed pa ni* ***dge ba'i rtsa ba'i stobs bskyed pa dang/ rnam pa gsum gyis sems sbyong ba*** *zhes bya ba ste/* ***dge ba'i rtsa ba'i stobs*** *skyed pa'i byang chub sems dpa' ni de'i stobs*

MS III. 5A

’jig rten gyi khams dpag tu med pa rnams kyi mir gyur pa’i [P27a6] sems can dpag tu med pa dag skad cig skad cig[28] [C23b6] la bla na med pa yang dag par rdzogs pa’i byang chub mngon par rdzogs par ’tshang [N25b7] rgya’o snyam pa ni sems sbyong ba dang [DT23b6] po’o//[29]

bsam[30] pa gang gis sbyin pa la [P27a7] sogs pa’i[31] pha rol tu phyin pa rnams la kun tu spyod pa’i bsam pa de bdag gis thob ste/ des bdag tshegs chung ngus pha rol tu phyin pa bsgom pa yongs su [C23b7] rdzogs

---

kyis brtan pa’i phyir sems ’gong bar mi ’gyur te/ rnam pa gsum gyis sems sbyong bas kyang sems gzengs bstod pa nyid do// … ***chos dang don la dmigs pa*** *la sogs pa nas/* ***bag yod pa*** *zhes bya bar gyis so// de la* ***rtag tu*** *zhes pa ni rtag tu byed pa nyid do//* ***gus par byas te sbyor ba*** *ni bla mar byed pa nyid do// gang gang du bstan pa’i rnam pa nyid de de ni* ***bag yod pa****’o//* [D158b5, P190b7] ***dge ba’i rtsa ba’i stob****s las byung ba’i* ***sems sbyong ba rnam pa gsum*** *la rten nas ’di ltar rtag tu gus pa dang bcas pas bag yod par sbyor ba’o//*

MSU [D243a4–5, P296a8–b1]: ***dge ba’i rtsa ba’i stobs bskyed pa*** *zhes bya ba la sogs pas ni de ston to// dge ba’i rtsa ba’i stobs can du gyur du zin kyang sems zhum pa yang yod do snyam pa la/* ***rnam pa gsum gyis sems sbyong ba*** *zhes bya ba smos so//*

28 Y, L, Na *skad cig skad cig*; D, C, T, P, N *skad cig gcig*

29 BŚ (104b26–c1): 諸世界無量衆生類 無量念念中成阿耨多羅山藐三菩提 初轉心者, Pa (122c13–15): 十方世界無數量故 不可數量在人道衆生 刹那刹那證得無上菩提 是名第一練磨心, DG (295b1–3): 無量世界中無量人道衆生刹那刹那正覺無量阿耨多羅三藐三菩提 是爲第一練治心, H (142b21–22): 無量諸世界無量人有情 刹那刹那證覺無上正等菩提 是爲第一練磨其心.

MSBh [D158a1–2, P189b6–7]: *de yang ’di ltar byang chub sems dpa’ mchog tu zab cing rgya che ba’i bla na med pa yang dag par rdzogs pa’i byang chub mngon par rdzogs par ’tshang rgya bar rtogs par dka’ ba thos pa na zhum par ’gyur te/ de’i gnyen por ni* ***sems sbyong ba dang po’****o//*

MSU [D243a5–6, P296b1–2]: ***’jig rten gyi khams dpag tu med pa rnams kyi*** *zhes bya ba la sogs pa la* ***sems sbyong ba dang po’o*** *zhes bya ba ni gsal bar byed pa ste/ bshad pa nyid kyis gsal bar byas zin to//*

H-MSU (414a20–21): 無量諸世界等者 此言顯示初練磨心 引他例已令心增盛 無有退屈.

30 D, C, T, Y, L, Na *bsam*; P, N *bsams*

31 Y, L, Na *pa’i*; D, C, T, P, N *pa*

N26a1 par ’gyur ro snyam pa ni sbyong ba gnyis pa’o//[32]

P27a8 dge ba sgrib pa dang bcas pa yang DT23b7 dge ba’i chos rnams dang ldan na ’phral du[33] shi la/ ’phral du ’dod pa bzhin du lus thams cad phun sum tshogs par skye na/ bdag dge ba sgrib pa med pa’i dge ba N26a2 dang shin tu P27b1 ldan pa lta ’phral du thams cad C24a1 phun sum tshogs par cï’i phyir mi ’gyur snyam pa ni sbyong ba gsum po’o//[34]

---

32 BŚ (104c1–3): 随所心布施等波羅蜜助集行　彼心我已得　是故我不加用諸波羅蜜　修道能滿成　第二轉明者, Pa (122c15–17): 由此正意施等波羅蜜必得生長　是我信樂已得堅住　由此正意我修習施等波羅蜜　進得圓滿則爲不難 是名第二練磨心, DG (295b11–13): 由專心故能行施等諸波羅蜜　我已得此專心由此故我修諸波羅蜜當得圓滿　不足爲難　是爲第二練治心, H (142b22–25): 由此意樂能行施等波羅蜜多　我已獲得如是意樂　我由此故　少用功力修習施等波羅蜜多當得圓滿　是爲第二練磨其心.

MSBh [D158a2–4, P189b7–190a3]: *yang byang chub sems dpa’ mchog tu zab cing rgya che ba rtogs par dka’ ba’i pha rol tu phyin pa sgrub pa la zhum par ’gyur te/ de’i gnyen por sems* ***sbyong ba gnyis pa*** *bstan te/* ***bsam pa gang gis sbyin pa la sogs pa’i pha rol tu phyin pa rnams la kun tu spyod pa’i bsam pa*** *zhes bya ba de la/* ***bsam pa*** *ni dad pa dang ’dun pa’o// yod pa dang/ yon tan dang ldan pa dang/ nus pa nyid dang/ pha rol tu phyin pa la yid ches pa nyid de ni byang chub sems dpa’i dad pa’o// dad pas bskyed pa’i nan tan byed par ’dod pa nyid ni ’dun pa’o// de lta bu’i dad pa dang ’dun pa’i ngo bo nyid kyi* ***bsam pa*** *thob par gyur pa’i byang chub sems dpa’ ni* ***tshegs chung ngu*** *nyid kyis pha rol tu phyin pa drug sgom pa yongs su rdzogs par ’gyur ro//*

MSU [D243a6–b1, P296b2–4]: ***bsam pa de bdag gis thob pa ste*** *zhes bya ba ni bgegs med ces bya ba’i tha tshig go// gang gi phyir ser sna med pa dang/ ’dod pa la rnam par rtog pa med pa dang/ gnod sems med pa dang/ le lo med pa dang/ gnyid dang rmugs pa med pa dang/ ma rig pa med pa de’i phyir/* ***tshegs chung ngus pha rol tu phyin pa*** *drug po dag* ***bsgom pa yongs su rdsogs par ’gyur ro snyam pa*** *ni sems* ***sbyong ba gnyis pa*** *ste/ bsam pa khyad par du ’phags pa thob na sbyin ba la sogs pa rang gi rang gis ’byung ba’i phyir ro//*

33 L om. *’phral du*

34 BŚ (104c3–6): 諸禪法成就已　死後尋得随所須一切身事　得有障善根者　況我善修善根得無障善根　尋卽一切諸勢不成　第三轉明者, Pa (122c18–21): 若人與衆善法相應　後捨命時於一切受生中　可愛富樂自然而成　是人得有礙善此義尚應成　云何我得圓滿善及無礙善　一切如意可愛富樂當不成　是名第三練磨心, DG (295b19–22): 雖彼有礙善者善法具足已　卽於死時　隨所念欲

MS III. 5B

DT24a1
'dir tshigs su bcad pa/

gang phyir sems can dpag med pa//

mir gyur skad cig re re la//

P27b2
rdzogs pa'i byang chub thob gyur pa//

N26a3
de phyir zhum par mi bya'o//[35]<1//>[36]

一切具足身　彼時得生　況我此最勝善無礙善　於彼時一切具足何爲不得 是名第三練治心, H (142b25–28): 若有成就諸有障善　於命終時卽便可愛一切自體圓滿而生　我有妙善無障礙善 云何爾時不當獲得一切圓滿　是名第三練磨其心.

MSBh [D158a4–7, P190a3–8]: *yang byang chub sems dpa' sangs rgyas rnams kyi zab cing rgya che ba'i chos rab tu 'byed pa la mkhas par gnas pa na 'di ltar sems par byed de/ 'di ltar bla na med pa yang dag par rdzogs pa'i byang chub skad cig ma gcig tu gtogs pa thob par bya'o zhes bya ba ni rtogs par dka'o zhes zhum par 'gyur bas de'i gnyen por sems* ***sbyong ba gsum*** *pa* </> ***bdag dge ba sgrib pa med pa*** *zhes bya ba la sogs pa ste/ gang gi phyir bdag sa bcu thams cad du ye shes kyi tshogs legs par bsags pa lta zhes bya bar sbyar ro//* ***dge ba sgrib pa med pa*** *zhes bya ba ni 'dod chags dang bcas pa'i gnas ngan len bsrabs par byed cing dbral bar dka' ba'i sgrib pa 'byed pa rdo rje lta bu'i ting nge 'dzin te/ ting nge 'dzin gyi bar mtshams med pas sgrib pa thams cad dang bral zhing de'i rten gnas gyur pa des thob par 'gyur ro zhes bya'o//* ***shi*** *ba tsam nyid dang ni rnam par bral ba nyid chos mthun pa nyid du 'dod do//* ***phun sum tshogs pa*** *ni rnam pa thams cad mkhyen pa'o//*

MSU [D243b1–2, P296b5–6]: *bdag ni mi mthun pa'i phyogs spangs pa sgrib pa med pa'i dge bas dge ba can yin na/ sangs rgyas nyid du* ***phun sum tshogs par ci'i phyir mi 'gyur snyam pa ni*** *sems* ***sbyong ba rnam gsum*** *pa ste/ sems rab tu 'dzin cing rnon por byed ces bya ba'i tha tshig go//*

35 BŚ (104c6–8): 是中有偈　人類得菩提　於念念中間　衆生無量故　至時應捨行, Pa (122c21–24): 此中説偈　人道中衆生　念念證菩提　處所過數量　故無下劣心, DG (295b22–24): 此中有偈　在於人道中　無量諸衆生　念念得菩提　故除退屈心, H (142b29–c2): 此中有頌　人趣諸有情　處數皆無量　念念證等覺　故不應退屈.

MSBh [D160b2–3, P193a6–7]: ***de phyir zhum par mi bya'o*** *zhes bya ba ni sems zhum pa nyid du sems gnas par mi bya'o zhes bya ba'i tha tshig* bsam pa gang gis legs yid kyis//

C24a2

sbyin pa la sogs byed pa yi//

DT24a2

bsam pa de thob brtan rnams kyi[37]//

sbyin pa la sogs nyid du brjod//[38]<2//>

---

go// ji ltar bdag gis bla na med pa'i byang chub mngon par rdzogs par 'tshang rgya bar mi nus zhes don de lta bur byung ba'o//

MSU [D243b2–5, P296b6–297a2]: *don de nyid tshigs su bcad pa rnams kyis sdud de/* ***gang phyir sems can dpag med pa// mir gyur skad cig re re la// rdzogs pa'i byang chub thob gyur pa//*** *zhes bya ba la sogs pa'o//* ***zhum pa*** *zhes bya ba ni sems gang ba'o// de mi bya zhes bya ba'i tha tshig ste/ bdag gis bla na med pa yang dag par rdzogs pa'i byang chub mngon par rdzogs par 'tshang rgya bar mi nus so// snyam du bdag la nus pa med par bsam par mi bya ba ste/ ji skad du/*

gang dag kha cig bde bar gshegs pa'i go 'phang thob gyur pa//
de yang shin tu dman pa'i gnas skabs der ni lhung bar gyur//
khyod ni nyam ngar lhung yang bdag la smad par mdzad ma gyur//
bdag smod ro yin skyes bu skyid pa 'jig par byed//

ces bshad pa lta bu'o//

H-MSU (414b15–18): 如有頌言

無量十方諸有情　念念已證善逝果　彼既丈夫我亦爾　不應自輕而退屈.

This verse seems to be the mutilated version of the Tibetan translation of stanza 8 of Triratnadāsa's *Gunāparyantastotra*. The correct text (according to Prof. Hahn's critical edition) runs as follows:

gang su la la dag gis bde gshegs go 'phang brnyes pa de dag kyang//
'di bas shin tu smad pa'i gnas skabs dag tu lhung ba byung nyo zhes//
de slad khyod kyis nyam ngar lhung ba'i tshe yang bdag nyid smad ma mdzad//
bdag la smod pa mi rung skyes bu dar ba zhum (zhugs?) par bgyis pa lags//

36 Cf. MSA X. 11, p. 52, *ll.* 17–20:

manuṣabhūtāḥ saṁbodhiṁ prāpnuvanti pratikṣaṇam/
aprameyā yataḥ sattvā layaṁ nāto 'dhivāsayet//

tribhiḥ kāraṇair layo na yuktaḥ/ yato manuṣabhūto bodhiṁ prāpnuvanti/ nityaṁ prāpnuvanti/ aprameyāś ca prāpnuvanti/

37 D, C, T, Y, L, Na *kyi*; P, N *kyis*

38 BŚ (104c9–10): 隨心所行施　清淨無垢心　彼得心止(em. to 正)事　勇健布施成, Pa (122c25–26): 善心人信樂　能生施等度　勝人得此意　故能修施等, DG (295b25–26): 善心人專意　能行布施等　勝人得此意　亦能行施等, H (142c3–4): 諸淨心意樂　能修行施等　此勝者已得　故能修施等.

MSBh [D160b3–6, P193a7–b4]: ***legs yid kyis*** *zhes bya ba ni mi dge ba dang lung du ma bstan pa'i sems ma yin zhes bya ba'i tha tshig ste/ 'di ltar lung du ma bstan pa ni rnam par gyeng pa'i sems kha cig gis sbyin pa la*

P27b3

dge dang ldan pa[39] shi ma thag//

’dod bzhin phun sum tshogs lus ’thob//

spangs pa dge ldan N26a4 ’phral du yang//

phun sum tshogs de cis mi ’thob//[40]<3//>

---

sogs pa byed pa’o// de bzhin du mu stegs pa la sogs pa mi dge ba’i sems kyis sbyin pa la sogs pa byed pa <byang chub sems dpa’ ni de lta> ma yin te/ bla na med pa yang dag par rdzogs pa’i byang chub ’dod pas so// yang na de’i bsam pas dge ba’i rtsa ba mchog thob pa ni brtan pa rnams so// ***sbyin pa la sogs pa byed pa yi*** *zhes bya ba la/ de la de’i bsam pa ci ’dra ba cig thob nas* ***sbyin pa la sogs pa*** *pha rol tu phyin pa goms par byas pas de’i mi mthun pa’i phyogs ser sna la sogs pa spangs pa’i sems thob pa zhes bya ba’i tha tshig go//* ***bsam pa de thob brtan rnams kyi// sbyin pa la sogs nyid du brjod*** *// ces bya ba ni* ***sbyin pa la sogs*** *pa kho nar brjod pa’o//* ***sogs*** *pa smos pas ni tshul khrims la sogs pa nas/ shes rab kyi pha rol tu phyin pa rnams gzung ngo//*

MSU [D243b5–244a1, P297a2–6]: ***bsam pa gang gis*** *zhes bya ba’i* ***bsam pa*** *de ni sngar bshad zin to// chags pa med par sbyin pa la ’jug pa’i rgyu yin no//* ***legs yid kyis*** *zhes bya ba ni dge ba’i sems rnams kyis yin gyi/ mi dge ba dang lung du ma bstan pa’i sems rnams kyis ni ma yin te/ ji ltar ’jig rten pa dge ba dang mi dge ba dang lung du ma bstan pa rnam par gyengs pa’i sems dang ldan pa rnams kyang srid pa dang longs spyod ’dod pas sbyin pa la sogs pa la ’jug pa ltar/ byang chub sems dpa’ rnams ni de lta ma yin te/ bla na med pa yang dag par rdzogs pa’i byang chub don du gnyer ba’i phyir ro//* ***bsam pa de thob*** *ces bya ba ni rang gi ngang gis ’byung ba’i* ***bsam pa*** *ji skad smos pa gang gis pha rol tu phyin pa rnams sgom pa de* ***thob*** *pa’o//* ***brtan rnams kyi*** *zhes bya ba ni byang chub sems dpa’ rnams kyi ste/ gang gi phyir* ***sbyin pa la sogs*** *pa* ***nyid du brjod*** *pa yin gyi de ni mi mthun pa’i phyogs ni ma yin par nges par byas pas mi mthun pa’i phyogs spong bas bsgrim mi dgos par ’jug pa nyid bstan to//* ***sogs*** *pa smos pa ni tshul khrims la sogs pa’i pha rol tu phyin pa khong du chud par bya’o//*

39 D, C, T, L, Na *pa*; P, N, Y *par*

40 BŚ (104c11–12): 善者滅身已　自勢隨所心　善者滅身已　彼勢云何不, Pa (122c27–28): 若善人死時　即得勝富樂　滅位圓淨善　此義云何無, DG (295b27–28): 善人於死時　隨心得果報　既有滅位善　果報云何無, H (142c5–6): 善者於死時　得隨樂自滿　勝善由永斷　圓滿云何無.

MSBh [D160b6–7, P193b4–6]: ***’dod bzhin phun sum tshogs lus ’thob//*** *ces bya ba ni ’du shes med ’du shes med min skye mched kyi bar* ***’thob*** *pa ste/ ’gyur ro zhes bya ba’i tha tshig go//* ***spangs pa*** *zhes bya ba ni sgrib pa* ***spangs pa’o//*** ***phun sun tshogs de*** *zhes bya ba ni sangs rgyas nyid ces bya*

MS III. 6

yid la byed pa spangs pas nyan thos dang rang sangs [C24a3] [P27b4] rgyas kyi[41] yid la byed pa yongs su spong ba [DT24a3] dang/[42] yid gnyis dang som nyi spangs pas theg pa chen po la the tshom thams cad the tshom med pa dang/[43] chos [N26a5] la[44] mngon par zhen pa spangs pas thos pa dang bsam pa'i [P27b5] chos la ngar 'dzin pa dang nga'ir[45] 'dzin par mngon par zhen pa yongs su spong ba [C24a4] dang/[46] rnam par rtog pa spangs pas

---

ba'i tha tshig go//

MSU [D244a1–3, P297a6–8]: ***dge dang ldan pa shi ma thag*** *ces bya ba ni 'jig rten pa'i dge bas* ***dge*** *ba can shi ba'o//* ***'dod bzhin phun sum tshogs lus 'thob*** *ces bya ba ni 'jig rten pa rnams srid pa'i rtse mo'i bar du yang skye bar 'gyur zhes bya ba'i tha tshig go//* ***spangs pa dge ldan*** *zhes bya ba ni sgrib pa* ***spangs pa'****i dge bas* ***dge ba*** *dang ldan pa rnams zhes bya ba'i tha tshig go//* ***phun sum tshogs de*** *zhes bya ba ni ji ltar 'dod pa'i sangs rgyas nyid do//*

41 P, N, Y, L, Na *kyi*; D, C, T om.

42 BŚ (104c13): 捨聲聞緣覺心滅念故, Pa (122c29–123a1): 由滅除四處障故由捨離聲聞獨覺思惟故, DG (295c28): 遠離聲聞 辟支佛思惟故 思惟則滅, H (142c7): 由離聲聞獨覺作意斷作意故.

MSU [D244a3, P297b1]: ***yid la byed pa spangs pas*** *zhes bya ba ni nyan thos dang rang sangs rgyas kyi theg pa* ***yid la byed pa*** *'dor ba'i phyir ro//*

43 BŚ (104c13–14): 於大乘中一切有疑無疑故 滅疑或, Pa (123a1–2): 邪思惟滅於大乘中生信心及決了心故 滅一切邪意及疑, DG (295c28–29): 於大乘中一切疑無疑故 邪意及疑則滅, H (142c7–8): 由於大乘諸疑離疑 以能永斷異慧疑故.

MSBh [D161a1, P193b7]: ***yid gnyis dang som nyi spangs pas*** *zhes bya ba ni zab cing rgya che ba'i theg pa chen po la* ***yid gnyis dang som nyi spangs pa'****o//*

MSU [D244a3–4, P297b1–2]: ***yid gnyis dang som nyi spangs pas*** *zhes bya ba ni theg pa chen po'i zab pa nyid dang rgya che ba nyid la* ***yid gnyis*** *phyin ci log dang the tshom med par bya'o//*

44 Y om.

45 P, Y, L, Na *nga'ir*; D, C, T, N *nga yir*

46 BŚ (104c14–15): 聞思諸法除我相我我所相執故 滅法慢者, Pa (123a2–3): 是所聞思諸法中 捨離我及我所邪執故 是故滅除法執, DG (295c29–296a1): 於聞思法中離我我所執故 法執則滅, H (142c8–9): 由離所聞所思法中我我所

mdun na [DT24a4] gnas pa dang bzhag pa'i mtshan ma thams cad yid la mi byed [N26a6] cing rnam par mi [P27b6] rtog pa'i phyir ro//[47]

'dir tshigs su bcad pa/[48]

執斷法執故.

MSBh [D158b3–4, P190b5–6]: ***thos pa dang bsam pa'i chos la ngar 'dzin pa dang nga'ir 'dzin par mngon par zhen pa yongs su spong ba*** *zhes bya ba ni* ***chos la mngon par zhen pa*** *tsam spong bar bzhed pa'o//* [D161a2, P193b8–194a1] ***chos la mngon par zhen pa spangs pas*** *zhes bya ba ni ji snyed thos pa dang bsams pa'i chos rnams la bdag tu 'dzin pa dang bdag gir 'dzin pa yod kyi bar 'jug par mi 'gyur ro//*

MSU [D244a4–5, P297b2–3]: ***chos la mngon par zhen pa spangs pas*** *zhes bya ba ni* ***thos pa dang bsam pa'i chos la ngar 'dzin pa dang nga'ir 'dzin par mngon par zhen pa*** *spang bar bya ste/ mngon par rtogs pa'i bar du gcod pa'i phyir rang snyam to// ngas khong du chud do// nga'i thos pa'o// nga'i don to// zhes mngon par zhen par mi bya'o//*

47 BŚ (104c15–16): 前所住及安一切相 不念不分別故 及滅分別者, Pa (123a3–4): 安立現前住一切相思惟悉不分別是故能滅除分別, DG (296a1–2): 現前住安立一切相 思惟不分別故 則滅分別, H (142c9–10): 由於現前現住安立一切相中 無所作意無所分別斷分別故.

MSBh [D158b4–5, P190b6–8]: ***rnam par rtog pa spangs pas mdun na gnas pa dang bzhag pa'i mtshan ma thams cad yid la mi byed cing rnam par mi rtog pa*** *zhes bya ba ni sbyor ba las byung ba'i rnam par mi rtog pa'i ye shes la gnas pa'i tshul bzhin yid la byed pa'i gnas skabs la gnas pa thams cad du mnyam par bzhag pa'i sems so//* [D161a2–3, P194a1–3] ***rnam par rtog pa spangs pas*** *zhes bya ba ni gang gzugs la sogs pa mdun na gnas pa dang/ gang yang mnyam par bzhag pas rus pa'i phung po la sogs pa dmigs par 'gyur ba'i mtshan ma thams cad yid la mi byed pas rnam par brtag par bya ba la rnam par mi rtog pa'i thabs kyis 'jug par 'gyur gyi/ gzhan du rnam par rtog par 'gyur na 'jug par mi 'gyur ro//*

48 Cf. MSA XIX. 50, p. 169, *ll*. 9–17:

purataḥ sthāpitaṁ yac ca nimittaṁ yat sthitaṁ svayam/
sarvaṁ vibhāvayan dhīmān labhate bodhim uttamām//

tatra purataḥ sthāpitaṁ nimittaṁ yac chrutacintābhāvanāprayogenālambanīkṛtaṁ parikalpitam/ sthitaṁ svayam eva yat prakṛtyālambanībhūtam ayatnaparikalpitam/ tasya vibhāvanā vigamo 'nālambanībhāvaḥ/ akalpanā tadupāyo nimittapratipakṣaḥ/ tad cobhayaṁ kramād bhavati/ pūrvaṁ hi sthāpitasya paścāt svayaṁ sthitasya/ tatra caturviparyāsānugataṁ pudgalanimittaṁ vibhāyan yogī śrāvakabodhiṁ pratyekabodhiṁ vā labhate/ sarvadharmanimittaṁ vibhāvayan mahābodhim/ etena yathā tattvaṁ parijñāya mokṣāya saṁvartate yathābhūtaṁ parijñānam/ tat

mtshan ma gang zhig mdun bzhag dang//

gang yang bdag nyid gnas pa rnams//

kun la blo ldan mi rtog na//

byang chub [C24a5]dam pa 'thob par 'gyur//[49]

MS III. 7A

gang gis ji ltar[50] [DT24a5][P27b7]'jug ce na/[51]

thos pa'i bag chags [N26a7]kyi rgyu las byung ba/ tshul bzhin yid la byed pas bsdus pa/ chos dang don snang ba </> lta ba dang bcas pa'i yid kyi brjod pa dang/[52]

---

paridīpitam/

49 BŚ (104c16–18): 是中有偈 在前隨所除 相念自住處 智盡不分別 得上菩提爾, Pa (123a4–7): 此中說偈 現住及安立 一切相思惟 智人不分別 故得無上覺, DG (296a2–5): 此中有偈 安立及自住 所有現前相 一切不分別 智人得勝覺, H (142c11–13): 此中有頌 現前自然住 安立一切相 智者不分別 得最上菩提.

50 MSBh, MSU, L, Na *ji ltar*; D, C, T, P, N, Y *ji skad*

51 BŚ (104c19): 以何云何入, Pa (123a8): 緣法及義爲境 何因何方便得入, DG (296a25): 因何入云何入, H (142c14): 由何云何而得悟入.

MSU [D244a7–b1, P297b6–b7]: ***gang gis ji ltar 'jug ce na*** *zhes bya ba ni byed pa dang 'di ltar bya ba 'dri ba'o// 'di ltar 'jug par byed pa pos 'jug par byed pa na/ byed pa dang mngon par rtogs pa'i mtshan nyid kyi bya ba 'di lta bu dang 'di lta bu bya'o zhes bya ba 'di ltar bya ba gdon mi za bar dgos par 'gyur te/ des na gnyi ga ston to//*

H-MSU (414c23–26): 此中雙問 作具所作 由有作者入所作業 應知定有能入之具 自現觀相是所作事 決定應有如是如是所作方便 是故今當二俱解釋.

52 BŚ (104c19–20): 彼聞習業 寂靜思惟所攝 法義現見意言, Pa (123a8–10): 由聞熏習種類正思惟所攝 顯現似法及義 有見意言分別故, DG (296a25–26): 聞熏習所生 正思惟所攝故 似法及義顯現有見意言, H (142c15–16): 由聞熏習種類 如理作意所攝似法似義有見意言.

MSBh [D161a4–5, P194a3–5]: ***gang gis ji ltar 'jug*** *pa de bstan par bya ste/ de la* ***thos pa'i bag chags kyi rgyu las byung ba*** *zhes bya ba ni* ***thos pa'i bag chags kyi*** *rjes su mthun pa'o// gang du 'jug pa'i gnas ni sngar bstan pa ste/ de yang theg pa chen po'i* ***bag chags*** *las yang dag par* ***byung ba****'i phyir yongs su grub pa'i ngo bo nyid kyis bsdus pa nyid blta* yongs su tshol ba bzhi ste/ ming dang don dang [P27b8] ngo bo nyid dang bye brag tu btags [C24a6] pa'i[53] yongs su tshol ba rnams dang/[54] yang [DT24a6 N26b1] dag pa ji lta ba bzhin du yongs su shes pa bzhi ste/ ming dang dngos po dang ngo bo nyid dang khyad par du btags pa dang ngo bo nyid [P28a1] dang khyad par[55] yang dag pa ji lta ba bzhin du yongs su shes pa rnams kyis 'jug ste/ de dag mi dmigs pa'i phyir ro//[56]

---

bar bya'o//

MSU [D244b1, P297b7–8]: ***thos pa'i bag chags kyi rgyu las byung ba*** *zhes bya ba la sogs pas ni byed pa ston to//*

H-MSU (414c28–29): 此中先辨能入之具 種類之聲 即因言説是爲因義.

53 Y, Na *pa'i;* D, C, T, P, N, L *pa*

54 BŚ (104c20): 四種求 名義性勝安求等, Pa (123a10–11): 由四種尋思 謂名義自性差別假立尋思, DG (296b1): 有四種求 謂名義自性差別 假説相求, H (142c4): 由四尋思 謂由名義自性差別假立尋思.

55 The four Chinese translations of MS has no the phrase: *dang ngo bo nyid dang khyad par*. See n. 56 below.

56 BŚ (104c20–22): 四種如實知故 名事性勝安性勝 如實知彼不覺見故, Pa (123a12–13): 由四種如實智 謂名義自性差別如實智 四種不可得故, DG (296b4–5): 復有四種如實知 謂名事自性差別 假相説中如實知 彼自性差別不可得故, H (142c17–19): 及由四種如實遍智 謂由名事自性差別 假立如實遍智 如是皆同不可得故.

MSBh [D161a7–b1, P194b1]: *gang yang dag par dpyod pa ni* ***yongs su tshol ba'****o// gang mi dmigs pa ni* ***yang dag pa ji lta ba bzhin du yongs su shes pa'****o//*

MSU [D244b1–4, P297b8–298a4]: ***yongs su tshol ba bzhi*** *dang* ***yang dag pa ji lta ba bzhin du yongs su shes pa bzhi*** *zhes bya bas ni 'di ltar bya ba ston to// sbyor ba'i dus na ni yongs su tshol ba ste/ nges par rtog pa'i rnam pa'i lta ba* </> *dmigs pa med pa'i rnam par 'jug pa'i yongs su rtog pa'o// dmigs pa med par nges pa'i ye shes ni 'bras bu'i rang bzhin te/ yan dag pa* ***ji lta ba bzhin du yongs su shes pa'****o// de la* ***ming*** *ni gzugs zhes bya ba la sogs pa'i tha tshig go//* ***ming*** *de* ***yongs su tshol ba*** *ni yid kyi brjod pa tsam nyid du rtog pa ste/ yid kyi brjod pa las gud na med pas btags par yod pa'i phyir ro// dngos po yongs su tshol ba ni ji ltar ming gi tshogs la sogs pas phung po dang/ khams la sogs par brjod pa de bzhin du yongs su grub pa med par rtog pa ste/ rigs dang rigs can gyi 'brel ba tha dad na de dang ldan pa'i brjod pa mi rung ba'i phyir ro// ...* [D244b7–245a1, P298b1] ***de dag mi dmigs pa'i phyir ro*** *zhes bya ba ni ming la sogs par* ***mi dmigs par*** *nges pa'i* ***phyir ro*** *zhes bya ba'i tha tshig*

MS III. 7B

’di ltar byang [C24a7] chub sems dpa’ [N26b2] rnam [DT24a7] par rig pa tsam la ’jug [P28a2] par brtson pa de lta bu[57] de yi ge dang don snang ba’i yid kyi brjod[58] pa de la yi ge’i ming de yang yid kyi rtog[59] pa tsam du zad par yang dag par rtog go// yi ge la brten pa’i don de yang yid kyi[60] brjod[61] pa tsam du zad pa [P28a3] de nyid du yang dag par rtog go// [C24b1, N26b3] ming de yang [DT24b1] ngo bo nyid dang khyad par du btags par zad pa tsam du yang dag par rtog go//[62]

de’i phyir yid kyi brjod pa[63] tsam du zad pa nyid du dmigs shing </> ming dang bcas pa’i don ngo bo [P28a4] nyid dang khyad par du

---

go//

57 P, N, Y, L, Na *de lta bu*; D, C, T *de lta bu de ltar gyur pa*

58 P, N, Y, L, Na *brjod*; D, C, T *rjod*

59 D, C, T, P, N, Y, Na *rtog*; L *brjod*

60 D, C, T, Y, L, Na *kyi*; P, N *kyis*

61 P, N, Y, L, Na *brjod*; D, C, T *rjod*

62 BŚ (104c22–24): 如是彼菩薩唯入記故順修 彼名義現見(em. to 相?)意言 彼名意言唯正觀 彼名所依義唯意言正觀 然彼名性勝安唯觀, Pa (123a13–18): 若菩薩已入已解如此等義 則修加行爲入唯識觀 於此觀中意言分別似字言及義顯現 此中是字言相 但意言分別得如此通達 此義依名言唯意言分別 亦如此通達此名義自性差別 唯假説爲量 亦如此通達, DG (296b5–9): 菩薩如是如實爲入意言唯識故修行 於彼似字義意言中 知彼名字 唯是意言 知彼名所依義亦唯意言 卽知彼名自性及差別唯是假相說, H (142c19–23): 以諸菩薩如是如實爲入唯識勤修加行 卽於似文似義意言推求文名唯是意言 推求依此文名之義亦唯意言 推求名義自性差別唯是假立.

MSU [D244b4–6, P298a4–6]: *ming gi dngos po brjod par bya ba’i don gang yin pa ming la brten pa’i brjod par bya ba de la yang yid kyi brjod pa tsam du zad par rtog par byed de/ phyir rol gyi rnam par ’dzin pa las zlog cing/ nang gi yan lag tu nye bar rtog par byed do// gzugs la sogs pa zhes bya ba’i tshig de yang na ni ngo bo nyid du btags pa’i rang bzhin du ’gyur te/ lus dang tshor ba zhes bya ba la sogs pa ste/ gang zag btags pa ltar med bzhin du yang ngo bo nyid du ’dogs pa’i phyir ro// yang na ni khyad par du btags pa’i mtshan nyid de/ mi rtag pa dang sdug bsngal ba zhes bya ba la sogs pa ste/ med bzhin du khyad par ’dogs pa’i phyir ro//*

63 P, N, Y, L, Na *brjod*; D, C, T *rjod*

btags pa dang bcas shing/ ngo bo nyid dang khyad par du bcas pa [N26b4] don gyi mtshan nyid du mi dmigs [C24b2] pa na/ [DT24b2] yongs su tshol ba bzhi dang yang dag pa ji lta ba bzhin du yongs su [P28a5] shes pa bzhi po dag gis yi ge dang don snang ba'i yid kyi rnam par rtog[64] pa de dag la rnam par rig pa tsam ṅyid du 'jug go//[65]

MS III. 8A[66]

rnam par rig pa tsam nyid de la [N26b5] 'jug ces ni ji skad bya[67]/ ci 'dra bar ni 'jug [P28a6] ce na/[68]

---

64 D, C, T, Na *rtog*; P, N, Y *rtogs*, L *brjod*. BŚ: 意言, Pa: 意言分別, DG: 意言, H: 意言. See the following note.

65 BŚ (104c24–27): 於後唯意言不覺已有名彼義有性勝安有性勝義相不見已 此四種求及四種觀 見知已彼名義現相意言中唯記入, Pa (123a18–22): 次於此位中但證得唯意言分別 是觀行人不見名及義 不見自性差別假說 由實相不得有自性差別義 已由四種尋思及四種如實智 於意言分別顯現似名及義 得入唯識觀, DG (296b9–12): 是時證得唯有意言 則於名及義自性差別假相說中 不見有性差別義相 故由四種求及四種如實知 於彼似名及義意言中 得入唯識, H (142c23–26): 若時證得唯有意言 爾時證知若名若義自性差別皆是假立 自性差別義相無故 同不可得 由四尋思及由四種如實遍智 於此似文似義意言 便能悟入唯有識性.

66 Aramaki has reconstituted sections 8, 9, and 12 into Sanskrit based upon Tibetan and Chinese translations. Harada has also reconstituted the 8, 9, and some other sections into Sanskrit based upon Tibetan and Chinese translations and Aramaki's Skt. text. In the followiing, Aramaki's text is given. However, when Harada's text deffers from Aramaki's, Sanskrit reconstituted by Harada is shown in the parenthesis. 8A: *tasyāṁ vijñaptimātratāyāṁ* (*tāṁ vijñaptimātratāṁ*) *praviśatīti katamāyāṁ kīdṛśāyāṁ* (*katamāṁ kīdṁśāṁ*) *praviśati/ tanmātre nimittadṛṣṭidvayatve nānākāratve ca* (*tanmātratāṁ ca sanimittadṛṣṭidvayatāṁ ca nānākāratāṁ ca*) *praviśati/ nāmārthasvabhāvaviśeṣaprajñaptisvabhāvaviśeṣārthānāṁ ṣaḍvidhānām anarthatvāt* (*anarthatvāc ca*)*/ teṣāṁ grāhyagrāhaka-bhāvenopasthānāt/ sārdhaṁ* (*sāhityena ca*) *nānākārārthābhāsotpādāt/* See Aramaki 1963, p. 45., and Harada 1997, p. 132.

67 D, C, T, P, Y, L, Na *bya*; N *byed*

68 BŚ (104c27): 彼記事中入已 爲當唯入, Pa (123a22): 於唯識觀中入何法

de tsam [C24b3] nyid dang/ rgyu [DT24b3] mtshan dang lta ba dang bcas pa gnyis dang/ sna tshogs kyi rnam pa nyid[69] la ’jug ste/[70] (i) ming dang (ii) don dang (iii) ngo bo nyid dang (iv) khyad par du btags [P28a7, N26b6] pa dang (v) ngo bo nyid dang (vi) khyad par gyi don rnam pa drug don med pa nyid dang/[71] de dag gzung ba dang ’dzin pa’i dngos por nye bar gnas [C24b4] pa dang/[72] lhan [DT24b4] cig tu sna tshogs kyi[73] <rnam pa’i>[74] don snang ba ’byung ba’i phyir ro//[75]

如何法得入, DG (296b20): 此唯識觀入何法　似何法入, H (142c27): 於此悟入唯識性中　何所悟入　如何悟入.

MSU: [D245a2–3, P298b3–4] *gal te don med pa’i phyir rnams par rig pa tsam nyid la ’jug na/* ***rnam par rig pa tsam nyid de la ’jug ces <ni> ji skad bya*** *zhes bya bas spong bar byed de/ de nyid ’di’i don yin par bsams pa’o//*

69 P, N, Y, L, Na *nyid*; D, C, T *gnyis*

70 BŚ(104c27–28): 彼有相見二事及種種事入, Pa (123a23): 但入唯量相見二法種種相貌, DG (296b20–21): 謂入唯量故　相及見爲二故　種種相故, H (142c28): 入唯識性相見二性及種種性.

71 BŚ (104c28–29): 名義性勝義　六種相無義故, Pa (123a23–24): 名義自性差別假説自性差別義　六種相無義故, DG (296b21–22): 名義自性差別但假立自性差別六種事無事故, H (142c28–143a1): 若名若義自性差別假　自性差別義　如是六種義皆無故.

72 BŚ (104c29): 彼可取能取事現處故, P (123a24–25): 由此能取所取非有爲義故, DG (296b22–23): 爲能取及所取體而住故, H (143a1): 所取能取性現前故.

73 D, C, T, Y, L, Na *kyi*; P, N *kyis*

74 Y, L, Na add *rnam pa’i*, according to the Chinese translations. See n. 75 below.

75 BŚ (104c29–105a1): 不斷種種相義現　相所生故, Pa (123a25–26): 一時顯現似種種相貌及生故, DG (296b23): 一時似種種相事生故, H (143a1–2): 一時現似種種相義而生起故.

MSBh [D161b1–2, P194b2]: *de la* ***de tsam nyid*** *ces bya ba ni rnam par rig pa tsam nyid do//* ***rgyu mtsham dang lta ba dang bcas pa gnyis*** *zhes bya ba ni* ***rgyu mtsham dang lta ba dang bcas pa****’i rnam par shes pa bstan te/ ...* [D158b6, P190b8–191a2] ***lhan cig tu sna tshogs kyi rnam pa’i don snang ba ’byung ba’i phyir ro*** *zhes bya ba ni ming dang tshig dang yi ge’i* ***sna tshogs kyi rnam pa snang ba ’byung ba’i phyir*** *dang/ de la brten pa’i don* ***sna tshogs kyi rnam pa snang ba ’byung ba’i phyir ro//***

MS III. 8B[76]

mun khung na sbrul du snang ba'i thag pa bzhin du 'jug ste/[77] dper na med pa'i phyir thag pa la sbrul ni nor ba ste/[78] de'i don rtogs pa

P28a8 N26b7

MSU [D245a3–6, P298b4–299a1]: *de dgag pa'i phyir* ***de tsam nyid*** *ces bya ba smos so// rnam par rig pa'i don gyis kyang don med pa nyid yin gyi/ phyi rol 'ba' zhig gis ni ma yin no// gal te don med pa nyid yin na skye mched bcu gnyis la sogs pa bshad pa dang/ 'jig rten pa'i don gyi tha snyad kyi rjes su zhugs ba ji lta bu zhe na/ de'i phyir* ***rgyu mtshan dang lta ba dang bcas pa gnyis*** *zhes bya ba 'di smos te/ don med bzhin du yang phyi rol gyi don du snang ba'i rnam par rig pa ni don mngon par brjod pa'i bag chags kyi dbang gis 'grub la/ rnam par rig pa snang ba yang lta ba zhes bya bar btags pas 'gal ba med do// ci rgyu mtshan dang lta bar snang ba'i rnam par rig pa 'di dag rigs gzhan du gyur pa nyid ces 'jug par byed dam/ 'on te ma yin zhe na/ de'i phyir* ***sna tshogs kyi rnam pa nyid la 'jug*** *ces bya ba smos te/ rnam par shes pa gcig nyid gzung ba dang 'dzin pa'i dngos por rnam pa tha dad pas dus gcig tu rnam pa sna tshogs su snang ngo zhes 'jug go//* ***sna tshogs*** *zhes bya ba ni shes pa gcig nyid rnam pa mang por rang gis rig go// rtog pa rnam pa 'di gsum rnam par dgrol ba'i skabs kyis* ***ming*** *la sogs pa* ***don rnam pa drug don med pa nyid*** *ces bya ba la sogs pa gsum bstan to//*

76 Skt. reconstituted by Aramaki: *andhakāra iva rajjuḥ sarpena pratibhāsate* (*andhakāre sarpapratibhāsarajjuvat [praviśati]*)/ *tad yathā rajjau* (*rajjvāṁ*) *sarpo bhrāntir asattvāt/ tadarthāvabuddhā asati* (*asatyāṁ*) *sarpamatiṁ vyāvartya rajjumatau tiṣṭhanti/ sā ca sūkṣmākāreṇa vibhāvyamānā* (*sūkṣmaprakāraṁ kṛtvā*) *bhrāntir varṇagandharasa-spraṣṭavyalakṣaṇatvāt/ yathemāṁ matiṁ niśritya rajjumatir api nivāryā* (*tatra yathā varṇādi* (or *etad*) *matiniśrayā rajjumatir api nivāryā*)/ *tathaiteṣu ṣaḍvidheṣv akṣarārthapratibhāsamanojalpeṣu* (*vyañjanārtha-pratibhāsamanojalpeṣu*) *sarpamativat ṣaḍvidheṣu sadartheṣv apakṛṣṭeṣu* (*ṣaḍvidhe 'bhūtārthe 'pakṛṣṭe*) *vijñaptimātramatir api vibhāvyā pari-niṣpannasvabhāvamatyā* (*pariniṣpannasvabhāvamatiniśrayā*)/ See Aramaki 1963, p. 45., and Harada 1997, pp. 132–133.

77 MSBh [D161b2–3, P194b4]: *de la ngo bo nyid gsum la 'jug pa ni thag pa'i dpes bstan to//*

MSU [D245a6–7, P299a1–2]: ***ci 'dra bar ni 'jug*** *ces gang smos pa de'i dper/* ***mun khung na sbrul du snang ba'i thag pa bzhin du 'jug*** *ces bya ba la sogs pa smos te/ dpes ngo bo nyid gsum rtogs par ston to//*

78 MSU [D245a7–b1, P299a2–3]: ***dper na med pa' phyir thag pa la sbrul ni nor ba ste/*** *de bzhin du ming la sogs pa don rnam pa drug yin yi ge dang don du snang pa'i yid kyi brjod pa gzhan gyi dbang la ming la sogs pa*

rnams ni med pa la sbrul gyi blo ldog cing/ thag pa'i blor gnas so//[79] de yang rnam C24b5 pa phra mor bya na nor ba DT24b5 ste/ kha dog dang dri dang ro dang P28b1 reg bya'i[80] mtshan nyid yin pa'i phyir ro// de la ji ltar kha dog la sogs pa'i blo la brten te/ thag pa'i blo yang N27a1 bzlog par bya ba de bzhin du yong su grub pa'i ngo bo nyid kyi blo la brten te/ yi ge dang don rnam pa drug P28b2 snang ba'i yid kyi[81] brjod[82] C24b6 pa de dag la/ DT24b6 sbrul gyi blo bzhin du rnam pa drug la yang dag pa'i don bsal na/ rnam par rig pa tsam gyi blo yang rnam par N27a2 gzhig par bya ba yin no//[83]

---

yang nor ba yin no//

H-MSU (415c5–6): 如是似名似義意言　依他起上名等六種　遍計所執亦非眞實　以無有故.

79 BŚ (105a1–3): 闇中如見繩謂蛇現相故　所謂如繩蛇不實非衆生故　如是覺義者非有迴蛇意唯住繩意, Pa (123a26–28): 譬如闇中藤顯現似蛇　猶如於藤中蛇　即是虛實不有故　若人已了別此藤義　先時蛇亂智不緣境起　即便謝滅唯藤智在, DG (296b23–25): 如闇中繩似蛇　譬如繩中蛇　是妄以不有故　若見實義則無有妄　蛇智則滅唯繩智在, H (143a2–4): 如闇中繩顯現似蛇　譬如繩上蛇非眞實　以無有故　若已了知彼義無者　蛇覺雖滅繩覺猶在.

MSU [D245b1, P299a3]: *de la ji ltar thag pa'i blo la brten nas* ***med pa la*** *'khrul pa'i phyir* ***sbrul gyi blo ldog*** *pa de bzhin du gzhan gyi dbang la brten nas ming la sogs pa kun brtags pa'i don rnam pa drug gi blo rnam par ldog go//*

80 P, N, Y, L, Na *bya'i*; D, C, T *pa'i*

81 D, C, T, Y, L, Na *kyi*; P, N *mi*

82 Y, L *brjod*; D, C, T, P, N, Na *rtog*. BŚ: 意言, Pa: 意言分別, DG: 意言, H: 意言.　See n. 83 below.

83 BŚ (105a3–6): 彼亦微思量色香味觸相故　是中依慧繩慧亦迴成　如是此諸六種相名現相　意言中如繩慧　六種相實義實處唯記慧　亦思量成就性慧故, Pa (123a28–b5): 此藤智由微細分析虛空無實境　何以故　但是色香味觸相故　若心緣此境　藤智亦應可滅　若如此見已伏滅　六相顯現　似名及義　意言分別塵智不生　譬如蛇智　於伏滅六相義中　是唯識智亦應可伏滅　譬如藤智由依眞如智故, DG (296b25–29): 若細分析繩亦不實　以色香味觸相故　於中依止色等智故　繩智亦得除滅如是如是　彼似字及義六種相意言　如蛇智以知彼六種相無實義　此唯識智亦須除滅　由成就性智故, H (143a4–8): 若以微細品類分析此又虛妄　色香味觸爲其相故　此覺爲依繩覺當滅　如是於彼似文似

MS III. 9[84]

de ltar byang chub sems dpa' 'di yid kyi brjod[85] P28b3 pa snang ba'i don gyi mtshan nyid la 'jug pas kun brtags pa'i ngo bo nyid la 'jug pa yin no//[86] C24b7 DT24b7 rnam par rig pa tsam la 'jug pas gzhan gyi dbang gi ngo

---

義六相意言　伏除非實六相義時　唯識性覺　猶如蛇覺亦當除遣　由圓成實自性覺故.

MSU [D245b1–3, P299a3–6]: *ji ltar kha dog dang dri la sogs pa la brten nas cha shas su bshig na* ***thag pa'i blo yang*** *ldog ste/ de skad du/* (**Hastavāla-prakaraṇa* k. 1)

thag pa sbrul du shes pa las// thag par mthong nas don med do//
de yi cha mthong de la yang// shes pa sbrul ltar rnam par 'khrul//

ces bshad do// de ***bzhin du rnam pa drug la yang dag pa'i don bsal na*** *zhes bya ba la/* ***bsal ba*** *ni phral ba ste/ med ces bya ba'i tha tshig go// don yang dag pa ma yin pa rnam pa drug po med pa'i mtshan nyid yongs su grub pa la brten nas gzhan gyi dbang 'khrul pa yang bzlog par bya ba yin te/ bsal bar bya ba yin no//*

84 Skt. reconstituted by Aramaki: *evaṁ ayaṁ bodhisattvo manojalpābhāsārthalakṣaṇapraveśena parikalpitasvabhāve praviṣṭaḥ* (*parikalpitasvabhāvaṁ praviśati*)*/ vijñaptimātrapraveśena paratantrasvabhāve praviṣṭaḥ* (*paratantrasvabhāvaṁ praviśati*)*/ kathaṁ pariniṣpannasvabhāve* (*pariniṣpannasvabhāvaṁ*) *praviśati/ vijñaptimātrasaṁjñām api vyāvartya* [*praviśati*])*/ sā manojalpaḥ* (*teṣāṁ manojalpānāṁ*) *śrutadharmavāsanānvayaḥ* (*śrutadharmavāsanānvayānāṁ*)*/ tadā* (*tadā tatra*) *vibhūtārthasaṁjño bodhisattvaḥ* (*vibhūtārthasaṁjñe bodhisattve*)*/ na sarvārthābhāsotpādasyāvakāśo 'sti/ tena vijñaptimātrābhāso 'pi notpadyate/ tataḥ sarvārthanirvikalpakanāmni* (*sarvārthanirvikalpanāmni*) *tiṣṭhan dharmadhātau pratyakṣayogena tiṣṭhati/ tadāsya bodhisattvasya samasamālambyālambakanirvikalpajñānam* (*samasamālambyālambakajñānaṁ nirvikalpam*) *utpadyate/ evaṁ saty* (Harada om. *saty*) *ayaṁ bodhisattvaḥ pariniṣpannasvabhāve praviṣṭaḥ* (*pariniṣpannasvabhāvapraviṣṭaḥ*)*/* See Aramaki 1963, p. 45., and Harada 1997, p. 133.

85 P, N, Y, MSBh, MSU, L, Na *brjod*; D, C, T *rjod*

86 MSBh [D161b3–4, P194b5–6]: ***yid kyi brjod pa snang ba'i don gyi mtshan nyid la 'jug pas*** *zhes bya ba ni don gang yin pa de kun tu brtags pa tsam yin no zhes de ltar* ***kun*** *tu* ***brtags pa la 'jug par*** *'gyur ro//*

MSU [D245b3–4, P299a6–7]: ***yid kyi brjod pa snang ba'i don gyi mtshan nyid la 'jug pas*** *zhes bya ba ni* ***yid kyi brjod pa*** *'di don du snang gi/ kun brtags par bya ba'i don ni med do zhes* ***kun brtags pa la 'jug go//***

bo nyid la ’jug pa yin no//[87]

[N27a3] yongs su grub pa’i ngo bo nyid la [P28b4] ji ltar ’jug ce na/[88]

rnam par rig pa tsam gyi ’du shes kyang bzlog nas ’jug ste/ de’i tshe byang chub sems dpa’ don gyi[89] ’du shes rnam par bshig pa de la yid kyi [DCT25a1] brjod[90] pa thos[91] pa’i chos kyi bag chags kyi [P28b5] rgyu las byung ba de dag [N27a4] don du snang ba thams cad ’byung ba’i skabs med pa yin no//[92] des na rnam par rig pa tsam du snang ba yang

---

87 DG-MSBh (296c18–19): 入唯識故者　此之意言唯識所攝　得入依他性, H-MSBh (351c22–24): 悟入唯識故悟入依他起性者　舉其唯識即取意言　了知一切唯意言性　由此悟入依他起性.

MSU [D245b4–5, P299a7–8]: ***rnam par rig pa tsam la ’jug pas*** *zhes bya ba ni rnam par rig pa tsam ’di ma rig pa’i dbang gis ’khrul te don med bzhin du ’khrul pa don gyi rnam par snang ngo zhes* ***gzhan gyi dbang la ’jug*** *go//*

88 BŚ (105a6–8): 如是此菩薩意言現相義相事入　分別性入　成唯主記入故　他性　云何成就性入, Pa (123b5–7): 如此菩薩由入似義顯現意言分別相故　得入分別性　由入唯識義故　得入依他性　及云何得入眞實性, DG (296c10–11): 此菩薩如是入似義相意言故　得入分別性　入唯識故　得入依他性　云何入成就性, H (143a9–11): 如是菩薩悟入意言似義相故　悟入遍計所執性　悟入唯識故　悟入依他起性　云何悟入圓成實性.

89 D, C, T, Y, L, Na *gyi*; P, N *gyis*

90 P, N, Y, L, Na *brjod*; D, C, T *rjod*

91 Y, L, Na *thos*; D, C, T, P, N *thob*

92 BŚ (105a8–10): 迴唯記想　彼者是諸意言　聞法習者　彼爾時分別義相　菩薩一切義現相生無有餘成, Pa (123b7–10): 若捨唯識想已　是時意言分別　先所聞法熏習種類　菩薩已了別伏滅塵想　似一切義顯現　無復生緣故不得生, DG (296c12–13): 若滅離唯識想　彼聞法熏習所生意言　是時菩薩滅離義想　似一切義 無有生處故, H (143a11–13): 若已滅除意言聞法熏習種類唯識之想　爾時菩薩已遣義想　一切似義無容得生故.

MSBh [D161b4–6, P194b7–195a1]: ***don du snang ba thams cad ’byung ba’i skabs med pa yin no*** *zhes bya ba ni ji ltar rnam par rig pa tsam gyi rnam par yang mi ’byung na de don gyi rnam par snang ba ’byung ba lta ci smos te/ de’i phyir rnam par rig pa tsam nyid du brtags na yang don du ’gyur bas/ de’i phyir de las gzhan pa de bzhin nyid mngon sum nyid du ’gyur ba yin no// gnas skabs de ni brjod par nus pa ma yin te/ so so rang gis rig par bya ba yin pa’i phyir ro//*

MSU [D245b5–6, P299a8–b1]: *yongs su grub pa la ’jug pa’i skabs kyi*

mi 'byung ste/[93]

gang gi[94] tshe don thams cad la rnam par mi rtog[95] pa'i ming P28b6 la gnas shing/ chos C25a2 DT25a2 kyi[96] dbyings la mngon sum gyi tshul gyis gnas pa de'i tshe/ N27a5 byang chub sems dpa' de'i dmigs par bya ba dang dmigs par byed pa mnyam pas mnyam pa'i ye shes P28b7 rnam par mi rtog pa 'byung ste/[97] de ltar na byang chub sems dpa' 'di yongs su grub pa'i ngo bo nyid la zhugs pa yin C25a3 no//[98]

---

don gyi 'du shes rnam par bshig pa *zhes bya ba smos te/* ***don gyi 'du shes*** *bsal zhes bya ba'i tha tshig go//* ***don du snang ba thams cad 'byung ba'i skabs med pa yin no*** *zhes bya ba ni* ***don du snang ba*** *gang gis kyang skyed mi nus so zhes bya ba'i tha tshig go//*

93 BŚ (105a10–11): 是故唯記現相亦不生, Pa (123b10): 是故似唯識意言分別亦不得生, DG (296c13–14): 是故似唯識顯現亦不得生, H (143a13): 似唯識亦不得生.

MSU [D245b6, P299b1–2]: ***des na rnam par rig pa tsam du snang ba yang mi 'byung*** *zhes bya ba ni gzung ba med na 'dzin pa med pa'i phyir te/ rnam par rig pa tsam don du byas nas* ***mi 'byung*** *zhes bya ba'i tha tshig go//*

94 D, C, T, Y, L, Na *gi*; P, N *gis*

95 D, C, T, Y, L, Na *rtog*; P, N *rtogs*

96 D, C, T, N, Y, L, Na *kyi*; P *kyis*

97 MSU [D245b6–246a2, P299b2–6]: ***don thams cad la rnam par mi rtog pa'i ming la gnas shing*** *zhes bya ba la sogs pas ni* ***ming*** *gi spyod yul mdo la sogs pa'i chos gang yin pa de dag gis ma 'bags pa la 'di thams cad ni* ***ming*** *tsam mo zhes bya bar rnam par* ***gnas shing*** *ste/ ji skad du/*

> *thams cad ming tsam kho na ste// rtog pa thams cad 'jug pa med//* (Cf. MAV V. 18ab, p. 67, *l.* 1: *sarvasya nāmamātratvaṁ sarvakalpāpravṛttaye//*)
>
> *ming du snang ba'i rnam rig la// ming zhes nye bar 'dogs par byed//*

ces bshad pa lta bu'o// ***chos kyi dbyings la mngon sum gyi tshul gyis gnas*** *so zhes bya ba ni so so rang gis* ***mngon sum du*** *byed pas* ***gnas*** *kyi mos pas ni ma yin no//* ***dmigs par bya ba dang dmigs par byed pa mnyam pas mnyam pa'i ye shes*** *zhes bya ba ni ji ltar* ***dmigs par bya ba*** *med pa de bzhin du* ***dmigs par byed pa*** *yang med pas* ***dmigs par bya ba dang dmigs par byed pa*** *gnyis* ***mnyam pas mnyam pa*** *nyid do//*

98 BŚ (105a11–13): 是故一切義無分別事名住　已於法界如現見隨住　爾時彼菩薩同等念已　生無分別念智　是故此菩薩名爲入成就性, Pa (123b10–14): 由

MS III. 10

DT25a3
'dir tshigs su bcad pa/[99]

N27a6
chos dang gang zag chos dang don//

P28b8
bsdus pa dang ni rgyas dang rigs//

ma dag pa dang dag dang mtha'//

rab tu dbye bas ming gi yul//[100]

此義故　菩薩唯住無分別　一切義名中由無分別智　得證得住眞如法界　是時菩薩平等平等能緣所緣無分別智生　由此義故菩薩得入眞實性, DG (296c14–17): 即住不分別一切義名中　正證法界相應而住　是時菩薩於能緣所緣平等平等無分別智生　卽是菩薩入成就性, H (143a13–16): 由是因緣住一切義無分別名　於法界中便得現見相應而住　爾時菩薩平等平等所緣能緣　無分別智已得生起　由此菩薩名已悟入圓成實性.

MSU [D246a2–3, P299b6–8]: ***de ltar na <byang chub sems dpa'> 'di yongs su grub pa'i ngo bo nyid la zhugs pa yin no*** *zhes bya ba ni 'jug pa'i byed pa po'i spyod pa med par gyur pa'i mthar thugs ston to// <kun> brtags pa dang gzhan gyi dbang la 'jug pa ni lhag ma dang bcas pa'i phyir 'jug pa'i bya ba mthar thug pa ma yin pas byed pa po nyid du brjod par 'dod pas 'jug par bstan pa yin no//*

99 MSBh: [D162a1, P195a3–4] ***gang gi tshe don thams cad la rnam par mi rtog pa'i ming la gnas shing*** *zhes bya ba ni de'i ming ci rnam pa ji snyed ces bya ba'i tha tshig las de'i ming gi bye brag tshigs su bcad pas bstan to//*

MSU: [D246a3–4, P299b8] ***don thams cad la rnam par mi rotg pa'i ming la*** *zhes gang bshad pa yul dang bcas pa'i ming de rab tu dbye ba ni tshigs su bcad pas ston te/*

100 BŚ (105a13–16): 於中有偈　法衆生法義　同別有性義　不淨淨盡至　分別名境界, Pa (123b14–16): 此中說偈　法人及法義　性略及廣名　不淨淨究竟　十名差別境, DG (296c29–297a2): 此中有偈　法人及法義　若廣若略性　不淨淨究竟　是名境差別, H (143a17–19): 此中有頌　法補特伽羅　法義略廣性　不淨淨究竟　名所行差別.

MSBh: [D162a1–3, P195a4–8] ***chos*** *kyi ming ni gzugs dang tshor ba dang mig ces bya ba la sogs pa'o//* ***gang zag*** *gi ming ni sangs rgyas bshes gnyen dang dad pas rjes su 'brang ba zhes bya ba la sogs pa'o// yang* ***chos*** *kyi ming ni mdo sde la sogs pa'o//* ***don*** *gyi ming ni chos de dag la brten pa'i don to//* ***bsdus pa****'i ming ni sems can zhes bya ba lta bu'o//* ***rgyas*** *pa'i ming ni de dag nyid re re nas brjod pa lta bu'o//* ***rigs*** *kyi ming*

MS III. 11

de ltar na byang chub sems dpa' 'di shes bya'i mtshan nyid la rnam par rig pa tsam nyid du 'jug pas [P29a1] zhugs pa yin [C25a4] te/ der [DT25a4] zhugs pas sa [N27a7] rab tu dga' ba la zhugs pa yin te/ chos kyi dbyings legs par rtogs pa yin/ de bzhin gshegs pa'i rigs su skyes pa yin/ [P29a2] sems can thams cad

---

*ni yi ge'i phyi mo rnams so// **ma dag pa**'i ming ni so so'i skye bo rnams kyi'o// **dag** pa'i ming ni slob pa rnams kyi'o// **mtha**r thug pa rnams kyi ming ni gang 'dres pa'i chos la dmigs pa'o//*

[D158b7–162a4, P191a3–195b1]: *mdor bsdus na byang chub sems dpa'i ming la dmigs pa ni rnam pa bcu ste/ 'di lta ste **chos** kyi ming ni mig la sogs pa'o// **gang zag** gi ming ni bdag dang sems can la sogs pa'o// **chos** ni gsung rab yang lag bcu gnyis su gtogs pa'o// **don** ni gsung rab yang lag bcu gnyis po de'i don gang yin pa'o// ming **bsdus** pa ni chos thams cad ni 'dus byas dang 'dus ma byas zhes bya la sogs pa'o// ming **rgyas** pa ni gzugs dang tshor ba la sogs pa dang nam mkha' la sogs pa'o// **rigs** kyi ming ni dang po yi ge a nas yi ge ha'i mthar thug pa'i bar ro// **ma dag** pa'i ming ni don dang bcas pa'i so so'i skye bo'o// **dag pa**'i ming ni bden pa mthong ba rnams kyi'o// **mtha**r thug pa'i ming ni gang 'dres pa'i chos la dmigs pa'i 'jig rten las 'das pa dang/ de'i rjes las thob pa'i ye shes gnyis kyis dmigs ste/ rnam pa sna tshogs kyi chos thams cad la brten nas sa bcu pa lta bu'o// de la don thams cad ni 'dres pa'i chos la dmigs pa'i ye shes kyi dmigs pa'o// de lta bu'i rnam pa ni byang chub sems dpa'i ming gi yul yin no//*

MSU [D246a4–7, P299b8–300a5]: ***chos** zhes bya ba ni gzugs la sogs pa'o// **gang zag** ces bya ba ni lha sbyin dang dad pas rjes su 'brang zhes bya ba la sogs pa'o// **chos** zhes bya ba ni sangs rgyas kyi gsung rab mdo sde dang dbyangs kyis bsnyad pa'i sde la sogs pa'o// **don** zhes bya ba ni de'i brjod par bya ba ste/ pha dang ma ni gsad byas shing/ rgyal po gtsang spra can gnyis dang/ yul 'khor 'khor dang bcas bcom nas/ mi ni dag pa nyid du 'gyur/ zhes bya ba la sogs pa'o// **bsdus pa** zhes bya ba ni chos thams cad bdag med pa zhes bya ba la sogs pa'o// **rgyas** pa zhes bya ba ni gzugs bdag med pa zhes bya ba la sogs pa'o// **rigs** zhes bya ba ni yi ge'i 'bru a zhes bya ba la sogs pa ste/ tshig dang ngag gi rgyu yin pa'i phyir ro// **ma dag pa** zhes bya ba ni so so'i skye bo rnams te/ nyon mngons pas dri ma can du gyur pa'i phyir ro// **dag pa** zhes bya ba ni 'phags rnams te/ dri ma spangs pa'i phyir ro// **mtha'** zhes bya ba ni bsdus pa la dmigs pa ste/ shes rab kyi pha rol tu phyin pa dang/ sa bcu la sogs pa bsdus pa'i don la dmigs pa'i phyir ro//*

la sems mnyam pa dang byang chub sems dpa' thams cad la sems mnyam pa dang [C25a5] sangs rgyas thams cad la [DT25a5, N27b1] sems mnyam pa thob pa yin te/[101] de ni de'i mthong ba'i lam yin no//[102]

---

101 MSBh [D162a4–6, P195b1–4]: ***sems can thams cad la sems mnyam pa*** *yin zhes bya ba ni gang gi phyir bdag ji lta ba bzhin du sems can thams cad mya ngan las bzla'o zhes sems pa'o// ...* ***sangs rgyas thams cad la sems mnyam pa*** *zhes bya ba ni gang gi phyir sangs rgyas rnams kyi chos kyi sku'i gnas skabs des* ***thob par*** *gyur pa ste/ de thob pas* ***sangs rgyas thams cad la sems mnyam pa thob par*** *gyur pa'o//* [D159a3–5, P191a8–b2] ***sems can thams cad la sems mnyam pa*** *nyid ni bdag dang gzhan mnyam pa nyid du rtogs pas bdag la ji lta ba bzhin du de dag la yang sdug bsngal zad par 'dod pa'o//* ***byang chub sems dpa' thams cad la sems mnyam pa*** *nyid ni byang chub sems dpa' thams cad dang sbyor pa'i bsam pa mnyam pa'o//* ***sangs rgyas thams cad la sems mnyam pa thob pa*** *ni de dag dang chos kyi dbyings kyi bdag nyid tha mi dad par mthong ba'o//*

MSU [D246a7–b5, P300a5–b3]: ***chos kyi dbyings legs par rtogs pa yin*** *zhes bya ba ni de mngon sum du byed pa'i phyir ro//* ***de bzhin gshegs pa'i rigs su skyes pa yin*** *zhes bya ba la* ***de bzhin gshegs pa'i rigs*** *ni chos kyi dbyings yin te/ de rtogs pa dang de la dmigs pa'i ye shes khyad par can bskyed pa dang/ sngon gyi gnas gyur pa dang gnas gzhan bskyed pa'i phyir der* ***skyes pa yin*** *te/ ...* ***sems can thams cad la sems mnyam pa thob pa yin*** *zhes bya ba ni thams cad la bdag med par mnyam pa nyid du mthong ba'i phyir te/ ji skad du/ sems can thams cad ni de bzhin gshegs pa'i snying po'o zhes gsungs pa lta bu'o//* ***byang chub sems dpa' thams cad la sems mnyam pa*** *zhes bya ba ni de dag gi gnas gang yin pa de 'dag gi yang yin no snyam pa'i phyir ro//* ***sangs rgyas thams cad la sems mnyam pa thob pa yin te*** *zhes bya ba ni de dag chos kyi sku gang yin pa de bdag gis kyang thob po snyam pa'i phyir ro//*

102 BŚ (105a17–20): 如是此菩薩智及相唯記入故　名爲入成　彼入已名爲住歡喜地　善達法界及生如來家　得一切衆生平等心　得一切菩薩等心　是彼菩薩見道行, Pa (123b17–21): 如此菩薩由入唯識觀故　得入應知勝相　由入此相得入初歡喜地　善通達法界　得生十方諸佛如來家　得一切衆生心平等　得一切菩薩心平等　得一切諸佛如來心平等　此觀名菩薩見道, DG (297a18–22): 此菩薩如是入唯識故　得入應知相　由入應知相故　即得入歡喜地　善通達法界得生如來家　得一切衆生平等心　得一切菩薩平等心　得一切佛平等心　此卽是菩薩得見道, H (143a20–23): 如是菩薩悟入唯識性故　悟入所知相　悟入此故入極喜地　善達法界生如來家　得一切有情平等心性　得一切菩薩平等心性　得一切佛平等心性　此卽名爲菩薩見道.

MS III. 12[103]

P29a3
ci’i phyir yang rnam par rig pa tsam de la ’jug ce na/[104]

’dres pa’i chos la dmigs pa ’jig rten las ’das pa’i zhi gnas dang lhag mthong gi shes pa de dang de’i rjes la[105] thob pa sna tshogs C25a6 kyi[106] rnam par rig pa’i shes pas/ N27b2 DT25a6, P29a4 kun gzhi rnam par shes pa’i sa bon rgyu mtshan dang bcas pa[107] thams cad spang nas/ chos kyi sku la reg pa’i sa bon spel te/ gnas gyur nas </> sangs rgyas kyi[108] chos thams cad yang dag par ’grub P29a5 pa’i sgo nas/ thams cad mkhyen pa’i ye shes C25a7 thob par bya ba’i N27b3 phyir DT25a7 ’jug go//[109]

---

103 Skt. reconstituted by Aramaki: *punaḥ kimarthaṁ tasyāṁ vijñapti-mātratāyāṁ praviśati/ saṁbhinnadharmālambanena tena lokattareṇa śamathavipaśyanājñānena tatpṛṣṭhalabdhanānākāravijñaptijñānena ca sanimittaṁ sarvālayavijñānanimittabījaṁ vihāya dharmakāyasparśabījaṁ saṁvardhyāśrayaṁ parāvartya sarvabuddhadharmasamudāgamena sarva-jñajñānaprāptyarthaṁ praviśati/ tac ca pṛṣṭhalabdhajñānaṁ sarvālaya-vijñānaprabhūteṣu sarvavijñaptinimitteṣu māyādyupamatvasaṁdarśanena prakṛtyāviparītaṁ bhūtam/ tena sa bodhhisattvo māyākara iva māyākṛta-dharmeṣu nimitteṣu sahetuphaleṣu deśayann api sarvakālam aviparītaḥ/* See Aramaki 1963, p. 52.

104 BŚ (105a20): 佛以何義故入彼唯記處, Pa (123b22): 復次何故菩薩入唯識觀, DG (297b3): 復次何故入唯識觀, H (143a24): 復次爲何義故入唯識性.
MSU [D246b6, P300b4]: ***ci’i phyir yang rnam par rig pa tsam de la ’jug ce na*** *zhes bya ba ni dgos pa ’dri ba ste/*

105 Y, L, Na *la*; D, C, T, P, N *las*

106 Na adds *rnam pa’i* after *tshogs kyi*, according to the four Chinese translations. See n. 109 below.

107 Na adds *...’i rgyu mtshan* according to MSBh. See n. 109 below.

108 D, C, T, Y, L, Na *kyi*; P, N *kyis*

109 BŚ (105a20–23): 離法念彼出世間定慧智　藉得種種相記智同相一切阿梨耶識因種子滅故　法觸種子增長已轉身　一切佛法集故　入一切智智, Pa (123b22–27): 由縁極通法爲境出世奢摩他毘鉢舍那智故　由無分別智後所得種種相識爲相智故　爲滅除共本阿黎耶識中一切有因諸法種子　爲生長能觸法身諸法種子　爲轉依　爲得一切如來正法爲得一切智智故　入唯識觀, DG (297b3–7): 爲縁通相法故　出世奢摩他毘鉢舍那智故　彼後得種種相識智故　滅有因相阿梨耶識一切因相種子故　增長得觸法身種子故　轉依止故出生一切佛法故　爲得一切智智故　入唯識觀, H (143a24–28): 由縁總法出世止觀智故

rjes la thob pa'i ye shes[110] de ni kun gzhi rnam par shes pa <las>[111] thams cad rab tu skye ba dang rnam par rig pa'i mtshan ma thams cad la sgyu ma lta P29a6 bu nyid la sogs par kun tu lta bas rang bzhin gyis phyin ci log <pa med>[112] par 'byung ngo// des na byang chub sems dpa' de sgyu ma N27b4 byas pa'i C25b1 DT25b1 chos rnams la sgyu ma mkhan bzhin du rgyu dang 'bras bur bcas pa ston pa la yang dus P29a7 thams cad du phyin ci log med pa yin no//[113]

由此後得種種相識智故　爲斷及相阿賴耶識諸相種子　爲長能觸法身種子　爲轉所依　爲欲證得一切佛法　爲欲證得一切智智　入唯識性.

MSBh: [D162a7–b1, P195b6–7] *gang* ***kun gzhi rnam par shes pa*** *kun nas nyon mongs pa'i chos rnams kyi* ***sa bon*** *can no// yang* ***rgyu mtshan*** *smos pa ni de'i* ***sa bon*** *de dag gi dmigs pa'i rgyu mtshan bstan pa'i don to// de ltar byas nas* ***sa bon*** *de dag rgyu dang 'bras bu dang bcas par spangs pa bstan par 'gyur ro//*

MSU [D247a2–5, P300b8–301a4]: ***kun gzhi rnam par shes pa'i sa bon rgyu mtshan dang bcas pa thams cad*** *ces bya ba ni gzugs la sogs par snang ba'i bag chags sgo bar byed pa* ***dang bcas pa*** *rnams te/ rgyu dang 'bras bur bcas pa'i* ***sa bon*** *rnams spangs pa bstan to// ...* ***gnas gyur nas*** *zhes bya ba ni de bzhin nyid rtogs pas sems dang sems las byung ba rnams dri ma med par 'byung ba 'am/ de bzhin nyid rnam par dag pas te/ stobs dang mi 'jigs pa la sogs pa* ***sangs rgyas kyi chos thams cad <yang dag par> 'grub pa'i sgo nas*** *so//* ***thams cad mkhyen pa'i ye shes thob par bya ba'i phyir*** *zhes bya ba ni dri ma med cing thogs pa med pa'i* ***ye shes*** *brnyes par bya ba'i phyir ro//*

110 MSU, Y, L, Na *ye shes*; D, C, T, P, N *shes pa*. The four Chinese translations have 智 (wisdom, *ye shes*). See n. 113 below.

111 MSBh, L, Na *las*; D, C, T, P, N, Y om.

112 MSBh, Y, L, Na *pa med*; D, C, T, P, N om.

113 BŚ (105a23–26): 藉彼所得智一切阿梨耶識相處如幻等見故　性不顛倒行是故彼菩薩如幻師所作　義處相同因果唯有説　一切時不顛倒成, Pa (123b27–c2): 無分別智後所得智者　於本識及所生一切識識及相識相中由觀似幻化等譬自性無顛倒　由此義故　菩薩如幻師於一切幻事自了無倒　於一切相因縁及果中若正説時常無偏倒, DG (297b14–17): 復次彼後得智　於阿梨耶識所生一切識性相中　由見如幻等故　自然不復顛倒　是故猶如幻師於幻事中菩薩於諸相中設説因果　一切時亦得無倒, H (143a28–b2): 又後得智於一切阿賴耶識所生一切了別相中　見如幻等性無倒轉　是故菩薩譬如幻師　於所幻事於諸相中　及説因果常無顛倒.

MS III. 13

rnam par rig pa tsam nyid la ’jug pa de la ting nge ’dzin bzhi la gnas pa’i nges par ’byed[114] pa’i cha dang mthun pa bzhi ji ltar blta N27b5 zhe na/[115]

(1) yongs su tshol ba bzhi po C25b2 de dag gis don med DT25b2 P29a8 par bzod pa chung ngu’i tshe snang ba thob pa’i ting nge ’dzin te/ nges par ’byed pa’i cha dang mthun pa dro bar gyur pa’i gnas yin no//[116]

MSU [D247a5–6, P301a4–6]: ***rjes la thob pa’i ye shes de*** *zhes bya ba la sogs pa la/* ***kun gzhi rnam par shes pa <las> thams cad rab tu skye ba*** *zhes bya ba ni rgyur gyur pa rnams so//* ***rnam par rig pa’i mtshan ma thams cad la*** *zhes bya ba ni ’bras bur gyur ba rnams la ste/ gzhan gyi dbang gi ngo bo nyid ji lta ba bzhin du mthong ba’i phyir gzung ba dang ’dzin par snang ba rnams la phyin ci log dang nor ba med par rtog go//*

114 D, C, T, Y, L, Na *’byed*; P, N *byed*

115 BŚ (105a26–27): 彼以記入中　四種禪定所依四種攢相法云何知, Pa (123c3–4): 是時正入唯識觀位中　有四種三摩提　是四種通達分善根依止菩薩云何應見, DG (297b25–26): 於此入唯識觀中　有四種三摩提　爲四種通達分依止　云何可見, H (143b3–4): 於此悟入唯識性時　有四種三摩地　是四種順決擇分依止　云何應知.

116 BŚ (105a27–29): 四種求故　非不身無義無忍中得光明三昧　暖相依, Pa (123c4–6): 由四種尋思　於下品無塵觀忍光得三摩提　是暖行通達分善根依止, DG (297b26–28): 由四種求義故　下品無塵忍得明三摩提　爲暖行通達分所依止, H (143b4–6): 應知由四尋思於　下品無義忍中有明得三摩地　是暖順決擇分依止.

Harada’s Skt. reconstitution of this paragraph: *tābhiś catasṛbhiḥ paryeṣaṇābhir arthābhāvamṛdukṣāntivelāyām ālokalabdasamādhir āśrayo nirvedhabhāgīyasyoṣmagatasya/* (Harada 1997, p. 141, n. 26)

MSBh [D159a6, P191b3–4]: ***don med par*** *shes pa ni* ***snang ba thob pa*** *zhes bya ba’i sgras bstan to//* ***snang ba thob pa’i ting nge ’dzin*** *zhes bya ba ni don med pa la yang dag par brten pa’i* ***ting nge ’dzin*** *gyis mthong ba’o//*

MSU [D247b4–5, P301b4–5]: ***don med par bzod pa chung ngu’i tshe*** *zhes bya ba ni* ***don med par bzod pa chung ngu’****o//* ***snang ba*** *ni gsal ba ste/* ***don med par*** *shes par bya’o// de ’dod pa’i phyir* ***thob pa*** *ste/ des na* ***snang ba thob pa’i ting nge ’dzin*** *ni* ***snang ba thob*** *ces bya ba’i tha tshig go//*

(2) bzod pa[117] chen po'i tshe </> snang ba mched pa'i ting nge 'dzin te </> rtse mo'i gnas so//[118]

(3) [P29b1] yang dag pa ji lta ba [N27b6] bzhin du yong su shes pa bzhi po dag [C25b3] la rnam par rig pa [T25b3 D25b3] tsam nyid du zhugs pa dang/ don med pa la nges pa ni/ de kho na'i don gyi[119] phyogs gcig la zhugs pa'i rjes su song ba'i[120] ting nge 'dzin te/ bden pa'i [P29b2] rjes su mthun pa'i bzod pa'i gnas so//[121]

---

117 L adds *don med par* before *bzod pa*, according to H and MSBh. See n. 118 below.

118 BŚ (105a29): 增忍中光明增長三昧上依, Pa (123c6–7): 於最上品無塵觀忍光增三摩提　是頂行通達分善根依止, DG (297b28–29): 若增上忍增明三摩提　爲頂行通達分所依止, H (143b6–7): 於上品無義忍中有明增三摩地　是頂順決擇分依止.

Skt. reconstituted by Harada: *adhimātrakṣāntivelāyāṁ vṛddhāloka-samādhir āśrayo mūrdhanaḥ/* (Harada 1997, p. 141, n. 26)

MSBh [D159a6–7, P191b4]: *don med par* ***bzod pa chen po'i tshe*** *zhes bya ba la de la* ***bzod pa*** *ni 'dod pa ste/ mngon par 'dod pa'o//*

119 D, C, T, P, Y, L, Na *gyi*; N *gyis*

120 *rjes su song ba'i* should be omitted. See n. 121 below.

121 BŚ (105a29–b2): 四種中如實觀知　入唯記中　以無義決定心　眞實中入一切三昧　依順諦忍, Pa (123c7–9): 於四種如實智　菩薩已入唯識觀了別無塵故　正入眞義一分通行三摩提　是隨非安立諦忍依止, DG (297b29–c2): 由四種如實知故　得入唯識決定塵無所有　此入眞實義一分三摩提　是順諦忍所依止, H (143b7–9): 復由四種如實遍智已入唯識　於無義中已得決定　有入眞義一分三摩地　是諦順忍依止.

Skt. reconstituted by Harada: *caturṣu yathābhūtaparijñāneṣu vijñapti-mātratāpraviṣṭo 'rthābhāvaniścitas tattvārthaikadeśapraviṣṭ[ānu- gat]a-samādhiḥ satyānulomāyāḥ kṣānter āśrayaḥ/* (Harada, 1997, p. 143, n. 27)

MSBh [D159b1–2, P191b7–8]: ***bden pa'i rjes su mthun pa'i bzod pa'i gnas*** *zhes bya ba la/ chos bdag med pa ni* ***bden pa*** *zhes bya'o// de'i* ***rjes su mthun pa*** *gang yin pa'i* ***bzod pa*** *ni* ***bden pa'i rjes su mthun pa'i bzod pa'o//***

MSU [D247b7–248a2, P301b8–302a2]: *don ni gang yang med do zhes bya bar nges pa ni* ***de kho na'i don gyi phyogs gcig la zhugs pa'i ting nge 'dzin*** *to// gzung ba tsam gyi dngos po 'gog pa'i phyir* ***phyogs gcig*** *nyid de/ 'di ltar don med par khong du chud pa yin gyi/ rnam par rig pa tsam yang med par ni ma yin no// de nyid kyi phyir de ni* ***bden pa'i***

(4) gang gi ’og tu N27b7 rnam par rig pa tsam gyi[122] ’du shes rnam par ’jig pa de ni/ de ma thag pa’i C25b4 ting nge ’dzin te/ DT25b4 ’jig rten pa’i chos kyi mchog gi gnas su blta’o//[123]

ting nge ’dzin ’di P29b3 dag ni mngon par rtogs pa dang/ nye ba pa yin par blta bar bya’o//[124]

MS III. 14

de ltar sa la zhugs te mthong ba’i N28a1 lam thob pa’i byang chub sems dpa’ rnam par rig pa tsam nyid la zhugs pa bsgom pa’i lam la ji ltar C25b5 sbyor zhe na/[125]

***rjes su mthun pa’i bzod pa’i gnas** yin no// **rjes su mthun pa** ni nye ba’i phyir te/ des gzung ba med pa la brten nas ’dzin pa yang med par rtogs par ’gyur ba’i phyir ro//*

122 D, C, T, Y, L, Na *gyi*; P, N *gyis*

123 BŚ (105b2–3): 自此後唯記相思量彼是次第三昧　依世間上法見, Pa (123c10–11): 此三摩提最後刹那　了伏唯識想　轉名無間三摩提　應知是世第一法依止, DG (297c2–3): 此三摩提最後唯識想除　是無間三摩提　世第一法所依止, H (143b9–10): 從此無間伏唯識想　有無間三摩地　是世第一法依止.

Skt. reconstituted by Harada: *yasmād ūrdhvaṁ* (or *yasyānantaraṁ*) *vijñaptimātrasaṁjñā vibhāvyate sa ānantaryasamādhir laukikāgra-dharmasyāśrayo dṛśyate/* (Harada 1997, p. 149, n. 35)

124 BŚ (105b3–4): 故此諸三昧近入地應知, Pa (123c11–12): 四種三摩提 是菩薩入非安立諦觀前方便, DG (297c3–4): 應如是見此諸三摩提　是正位邊應知, H (143b10–11): 應知如是諸三摩地　是現觀邊.

Skt. reconstituted by Harada: *ete samādhayo ’bhisamayāntikā draṣṭavyāḥ/* (Harada 1997, p. 149, n. 35)

MSU [D248a2, P302a2–3]: ***ting nge ’dzin ’di dag ni mngon par rtogs pa dang nye ba <pa> yin par** zhes bya ba ni **mngon par rtogs pa**’i dus na ’byung ba yin par zhes bya ba’i tha tshig go//*

125 BŚ (105b4–5): 如是入地得見諦道　菩薩唯入記　云何行修道, Pa (123c12–14): 若菩薩如此入初地已得見道　得通達入唯識　云何菩薩修習觀行入於修道, DG (297c16–17): 如是入地菩薩　入唯識故得見道　云何發起修道, H (143b12–13): 如是菩薩已入於地　已得見道　已入唯識　於修道中云何修行.

DT25b5 ji ltar rnam P29b4 par gnas pa bstan pa byang chub sems dpa'i sa bcu[126] mdo sde thams cad bsdus pa nyid du nye bar gnas pa rnams la 'dres pa la N28a2 dmigs pa 'jig rten las 'das pa dang de'i rjes la thob pa'i zhi gnas dang lhag mthong gi shes P29b5 pas/ bskal pa bye ba khrag khrig brgya C25b6 stong DT25b6 phrag mang por goms par byas pa'i phyir de gnas gyur nas/ sangs rgyas kyi sku rnam pa gsum thob par bya ba'i phyir sbyor ro//[127]

MS III. 15

nyan N28a3 thos rnams kyi[128] mngon par rtogs[129] pa gang yin pa dang P29b6 byang chub sems dpa' rnams kyi mngon par rtogs pa gang yin

---

126 P, N, Y, L, Na om. *pa*; D, C, T *pa*

127 BŚ (105b5–8): 隨所分別說十地　攝一切修多羅現事住故　以雜念出世間　及藉彼得定慧智故　無量百千億習故　如是身轉已　爲得三種佛身　爲得故修行, Pa (123c14–20): 如佛廣說　所安立法相於菩薩十地　由攝一切如來所說大乘十二部經故得現前　由治所說通別二境　由生起緣極通境出世無分別智　及無分別智後所得奢摩他毘鉢舍那智　由無量無數百千俱胝大劫中依數數修習　由昔及今所得轉依　爲得三種佛身更修加行, DG (297c17–20): 隨所成立說十地一切修多羅攝取現住事　通相法爲緣　出世間及後得奢摩他毘鉢舍那智　無量百千俱胝那由他劫數習故　爲轉依止得三種佛身故修行, H (143b13–16): 於如所說安立十地攝一切經皆現前中　由緣總法出世後得止觀智故　經於無量百千俱胝那庾多劫　數修習故　而得轉依　爲欲證得三種佛身精勤修行.

MSBh [D162b5–163a1, P196a6–b1]: ***'dres pa la dmigs pa*** *zhes bya ba ni mkhas pas* ***dmigs pa'****i gnas la dmigs pa'o//* ***'jig rten las 'das pa*** *zhes bya ba ni rnam par mi rtog pa'o//* ***de'i rjes la thob pa*** *zhes bya ba ni rnam par bzhag pa ste/ de ni 'jig rten pa zhes brjod par bya ste/ 'di ltar 'jig rten pa dang rjes su mthun pa'i phyir ro// ...* ***de gnas gyur nas*** *zhes bya ba ni 'dres pa la dmigs pa'i ye shes kyi bye brag gnas gyur pa'o//* ***sangs rgyas kyi sku rnam pa gsum thob par*** *zhes bya ba ni* ***sangs rgyas kyi sku rnam pa gsum thob par*** *'gyur ba zhes sbyar bar bya'o//*

128 D, C, T, Y, L, Na *kyi*; P, N *kyis*

129 D, C, T, Y, L, Na *rtogs*; P, N *rtog*

pa 'di gnyis bye brag ci yod ce na/[130]

[DT25b7] nyan thos [C25b7] kyi mngon par rtogs pa las khyad par bcus byang chub sems dpa'i mngon par rtogs pa khyad par du [N28a4 P29b7] 'phags par blta bar bya ste/[131]

(1) dmigs pa'i khyad par ni </> theg pa chen po'i chos la dmigs pa'i phyir ro//[132]

(2) nye bar brten[133] pa'i khyad par ni/ bsod nams dang ye shes kyi [DT26a1] tshogs chen pos brten[134] pa'i phyir ro//[135]

(3) rtogs pa'i khyad par ni/ [P29b8] gang zag dang chos la bdag med par rtogs pa'i phyir ro//[136]

---

130 BŚ (105b8–9): 所有諸聲聞證道法　及此諸菩薩　此二有何差別勝, Pa (123c20–21): 是聲聞見道是菩薩見道　此二見道差別云何, DG (297c29–298a1): 聲聞入正位　菩薩入正位　此二有何差別, H (143b16–17): 聲聞現觀菩薩現觀有何差別.

131 BŚ (105b9–10): 聲聞證入中菩薩證入有十一種勝事應知, Pa (123c21–22): 聲聞菩薩見道應知有十一種差別　何者爲十一, DG (298a1–2): 聲聞正位有十種差別　與菩薩正位異應知, H (143b17–18): 謂菩薩現觀與聲聞異　由十一種差別應知.

132 BŚ (105b10–11): 一者念勝　念大乘法故, Pa (123c22–23): 一由境界差別　謂縁大乘法爲境, DG (298a2): 一所縁差別　大乘法爲縁故, H (143b18–19): 一由所縁差別　以大乘法爲所縁故.

MSU [D248a5–6, P302a7]: ***dmigs pa'i khyad par*** *ni theg pa chen po'i chos la byang chub sems dpa' thos pa las byung ba la sogs pa'i shes rab gsum gyis dmigs te/ nyan thos kyi theg pa'i chos la ni ma yin no//*

133 Y, L, Na *brten*; D, C, T *brtan*, P, N *brtas*

134 Y, L, Na *brten*; D, C, T, P, N *brtan*

135 BŚ (105b11): 二者淳至勝　大功德助集淳至故, Pa (123c23–24): 二由依止差別　謂依大福徳智慧資糧爲依止, DG (298a2–3): 二住持差別　大福智資糧住持故, H (143b19–20): 二由資持差別　以大福智二種資糧爲資持故.

MSU [D248a6, P302a8]: ***bsod nams kyi tshogs*** *ni sbyin pa dang tshul khrims dang bzod pa la sbyor ba rnams so//* ***ye shes kyi tshogs*** *ni thos pa la sogs pa ste/*

136 BŚ (105b12): 三者證勝　衆生法無我證故, Pa (123c24–25): 三由通達差別　謂通達人法二無我, DG (298a3–4): 三通達差別　通達人法無我故, H (143b20–21): 三由通達差別　以能通達補特伽羅法無我故.

(4) [N28a5] mya ngan las 'das pa'i khyad par ni/ mi gnas pa'i mya ngan las 'das pa yongs su 'dzin pa'i phyir ro//[137]

(5) sa'i khyad par ni/ sa bcus [DT26a2] nges par 'byung ba'i phyir ro//[138]

(6) [C26a2, P30a1] yongs su dag pa'i khyad par ni/ nyon mongs pa'i bag chags spong ba dang sangs rgyas kyi zhing yongs su sbyong [N28a6] ba'i phyir ro//[139]

(7) sems can thams cad dang bdag sems mnyam pa nyid [P30a2] thob pa'i khyad par ni </> sems can yongs su smin par byed par sbyor

---

MSU [D248a7, P302b1–2]: ***rtogs pa'i khyad par*** *ni nyan thos ni gang zag la bdag med pa tsam mngon par rtogs par byed do// byang chub sems dpa'i ni gang zag dang chos la bdag med pa mngon par rtogs par byed do//*

137 BŚ (105b12–13): 四者涅槃勝　攝取不住涅槃故, Pa (123c25–26): 四由涅槃差別　謂攝無住處涅槃以爲住處, DG (298a4): 四涅槃差別　攝取無住著涅槃故, H (143b21–22): 四由涅槃差別　攝受無住大涅槃故.

MSBh [D163a1, P196b1–2]: ***mya ngan las 'das pa'i khyad par*** *ni zhes bya ba ni 'di ltar byang chub sems dpa' rnams* ***mi gnas pa'i mya ngan las 'das pa*** *'dzin par byed kyi nyan thos ni ma yin no//*

MSU [D248a7–b2, P302b2–3]: ***mya ngan las 'das pa'i khyad par*** *ni byang chub sems dpa' rnams kyi ni* ***mi gnas pa'i mya ngan las 'das pa*** *ste/ shes rab dang snying rje'i thabs kyis yongs su zin pas 'khor pa dang mya ngan las 'das pa'i mtha' la mi gnas pa'i phyir ro// nyan thos ni 'dus ma byas kyi mya ngan las 'das pa la gnas so//*

138 BŚ (105b13): 五者地勝　十地盡至故, Pa (123c26–27): 五由地差別　謂依十地爲出離, DG (298a5): 五地差別　依十地出離故, H (143b22–23): 五由地差別　依於十地而出離故.

MSU [D248b2, P302b3–4]: ***sa'i khyad par*** *ni byang chub sems dpa' ni sa bcu po dag gis nges par 'byung ngo// nyan thos rnams la ni sa rnams par gzhag pa med do//*

139 BŚ (105b13–14): 六者淨勝　煩惱習滅佛世界令淸淨故, Pa (123c27–28): 六七由淸淨差別　謂滅煩惱習氣　及治淨土爲淸淨, DG (298a5–6): 六淸淨差別　煩惱斷及佛淨刹 (em. to 刹淨) 故, H (143b23–24): 六七由淸淨差別　斷煩惱習淨佛土故.

MSBh [D163a1–2, P196b2–3]: ***yongs su dag pa'i khyad par*** *ni zhes bya ba la/ 'di ltar byang chub sems dpa' rnams* ***bag chags*** *dang bcas pa'i* ***nyon mongs pa*** *rnams* ***spong ba dang sangs rgyas kyi zhing yongs su sbyong ba*** *yin gyi nyan thos rnams ni ma yin no//*

ba rgyun [DT26a3] mi gcod pa'i phyir ro//[140]

(8) skye ba'i khyad par ni </> de bzhin gshegs pa'i rigs su skye ba'i phyir ro//[141]

(9) skye 'byung [C26a3] gi khyad par ni/ [N28a7] sangs rgyas kyi [P30a3] 'khor gyi dkyil 'khor du dus thams cad du skye 'byung yongs su 'dzin pa'i phyir ro//[142]

(10) 'bras bu'i khyad par ni </> stobs bcu dang mi 'jigs pa dang sangs [DT26a4] rgyas kyi chos ma 'dres pa [C26a4] 'bras bu yon tan tshad med pa [P30a4] 'grub pa'i phyir ro//[143]

---

140 BŚ (105b14–15): 七者一切衆生同得記心勝　化衆生行不斷絶故, Pa (123c28–29): 八由於一切衆生得平等心差別　謂爲成熟衆生不捨加行功德善根, DG (298a6–7): 七得一切衆生與自身平等心差別　起成熟衆生行不休息故, H (143b23–24): 八由於自他得平等心差別　成熟有情加行無休息故.

MSU [D248b4–5, P302b6–7]: ***sems can thams cad dang bdag sems mnyam pa nyid thob pa'i khyad par*** *ni byang chub sems dpa' ni bdag dang gzhan mnyam pa nyid thob pas* ***sems can yongs su smin par bya ba'i sbyor ba rgyun mi gcod*** *do// nyan thos ni bdag dang gzhan tha dang du skye pas bdag gi don nyid la sbyong gyi/ gzhan gyi don la mi sbyong ngo//*

141 BŚ (105b15–16): 八者生勝生　如來家故, Pa (124a1): 九由受生差別　謂生如來家爲生故, DG (298a7–8): 八生差別　生如來家故, H (143b25): 九由生差別　生如來家故.

MSU [D248b5–6, P302b7–303a1]: ***skye ba'i khyad par*** *ni byang chub sems dpa' ni de bzhin gshegs pa'i rigs chos kyi dbyings su skyes nas sangs rgyas su 'gyur te/ 'khor los sgyur ba'i rigs su skyes pa'i gzhon nu mtshan dang ldan pa bzhin no// nyan thos ni de lta ma yin te/ ma rabs kyi rigs bran khor gyi bu bzhin no//*

142 BŚ (105b16–17): 九者取生勝　佛世界會中一切時取生故, Pa (124a1–3): 十由顯現差別　謂於佛子大集論(em. to 輪) 中常能顯現爲攝受正法, DG (298a8–9): 九化現差別　佛集輪中一切時化現所攝故, H (143b25–26): 十由受生差別　常於諸佛大集會中攝受生故.

143 BŚ (105b17–18): 十者果勝　十力四無畏十八不共佛法無量功德成就故, Pa (124a3–4): 十一由果差別　謂十力無畏不共如來法　及無量功德生爲果故, DG (298a9–10): 十果差別　十力無畏不共佛法等無量功德果成就故, H (143b26–28): 十一由果差別　十力無畏不共佛法無量功德果成滿故.

MS III. 16

N28b1
'dir tshigs su bcad pa/

ming dang dngos gnyis phan tshun du//
glo bur yin par yongs su btsal//
btags pa rnam pa gnyis po la//
de tsam nyid du btsal bar bya//[144]<1//>[145]

MSU [D248b7–249a1, P303a2–4]: ***'bras bu'i khyad par*** *ni byang chub sems dpa'i 'bras bu ni stobs la sogs pa yon tan gyi tshogs kyis brgyan pa lhun gyis grub par sems can gyi don byed nus pa chos kyi sku thob pa'o// cig shos kyi 'bras bu ni zag pa dang bcas pa'i skye ba med pa'o//*

144 Cf. MSA XIX. 47, p. 168, *ll.* 18–24:

āgantukatvaparyeṣā anyonyaṁ nāmavastunoḥ/
prajñapter dvividhasyātra tanmātratvasya caiṣaṇā//

caturvidhā paryeṣaṇā dharmāṇām/ nāmaparyeṣaṇā vastuparyeṣaṇā/ svabhāvaprajñaptiparyeṣaṇā/ viśeṣaprajñaptiparyeṣaṇā ca/ tatra nāmno vastuny āgantukatvaparyeṣaṇā nāmaparyeṣaṇā veditavyā/ vastuno nāmny āgantukatvaparyeṣaṇā vastuparyeṣaṇā veditavyā/ tadubhayābhisaṁbandhe svabhāvaviśeṣaprajñaptyoḥ prajñaptimātratvaparyeṣaṇā svabhāvaviśeṣaprajñaptiparyeṣaṇā veditavyā/

MSBh [D163a2–3, P196b4–5]: ***ming dang dngos gnyis phan tshun du// glo bur yin par yongs su btsal//*** *zhes bya ba la/* ***ming*** *ni don la glo bur ba yin la/* ***don*** *ni ming la glo bur ba ste/ ...* ***yongs su btsal*** *zhes bya ba ni mnyam par bzhag pas blta bar bya'o//*

MSU [D249a2–3, P303a5–7]: ***de tsam nyid du btsal bar bya//*** *yul gang du zhe na/* ***btags pa rnams pa gnyis po la//*** *zhes bya ba smos te/ ngo bo nyid du btags pa dang khyad par du btags pa'o// ji ltar zhe na/ 'di ni btags pa tsam ste tha snyad btags par zad kyi 'di la ngo bo nyid dang khyad par du btags pa ni med do zhes bya bar sbyar ro//*

145 BŚ (105b18–21): 是中有偈　迭互作客事　於事名所求　唯求彼諸事　分別二所安, Pa (124a4–6): 此中説兩偈　名義互爲客　菩薩應尋思　應觀二唯量及彼二假説, DG (298a14–16): 此中有偈　推尋名及義　各各互爲客　推尋二唯量　二施設亦然, H (143b29–c2): 此中有二頌　名事互爲客　其性應尋思　於二亦當推　唯量及唯假.

[P30a5]yang dag ji bzhin yongs shes pas//

[DCT26a5]don med par ni rtog gsum dang//

de med phyir yang de med par//

[N28b2]mthong ba gsum la ’jug pa yin//[146]<2//>[147]

MS III. 17

’di lta ste </> yang rnal ’byor gyi[148] rnam par dbye ba las gdams pa’i tshigs su bcad pa/[149]

---

146 MSBh [D163a7–b1, P197a2–4]: ***gsum la ’jug pa*** *zhes bya ba ni ngo bo nyid* ***gsum la ’jug pa****’o// de la ming dang don gnyis phan tshun glo bur ba nyid du mthong bar gyur na kun tu brtags pa’i ngo bo nyid la shugs pa yin no// ming gi ngo bo nyid brtags pa dang/ khyad par du brtags pa tsam du mthong ba na gzhan gyi dbang gi ngo bo nyid la shugs pa yin no// brtags pa de nyid <ma> mthong ba na yong su grub pa la zhugs pa yin te/ de lta bu ni gsum la ’jug pa yin no//*

MSU [D249a4–7, P303a7–b4]: ***don med par*** *zhes bya ba ni* ***don*** *dang bral ba’o//* ***rtog gsum*** *zhes bya ba ni ming du* ***rtog*** *pa dang/ ngo bo nyid du btags par* ***rtog*** *pa dang/ khyad par du btags par* ***rtog*** *pa’o//* ***de med phyir*** *zhes bya ba ni* ***don med*** *pa’i* ***phyir*** *ro//* ***don med par*** *zhes bya ba ni rtog pa rnam pa gsum* ***med par*** *mthong ba’o//* ***gsum la ’jug pa yin*** *zhes bya ba ni ngo bo nyid* ***gsum la ’jug pa****’o// tshigs su bcad pa dang po’i phyed kyis ni ming dang dngos po gnyis gcig la gcig glo bur yin par mthong nas kun brtags pa’i ngo bo nyid la zhugs pa yin no// tshigs su bcad pa dang po’i phyed ’og mas ni ngo bo nyid dang/ khyad par du brtags pa rtogs pa tsam nyid du mthong nas gzhan gyi dbang gi ngo bo nyid mngon par rtogs pa yin no// tshigs su bcad pa gnyis pa rangs pas ni rtog par zad kyi/ dngos por ni ma yin no zhes rtog pa rnams kyang med par mthong bas yongs su grub pa la ’jug go// gzhan du na ni dag pa dang ma dag pa med pas bcings pa dang thar ba mi ’grub bo//*

147 BŚ (105b22–23): 如實知見故　離義分別三　見彼是非事　彼無二所執, Pa (124a7–8): 從此生實智　離塵分別三　若見其非有　得入三無性, DG (298a17–18): 從此生實知　三分別無義　若見彼非有　即入三無性, H (143c3–4): 實智觀無義　唯有分別三　彼無故此無　是即入三性.

148 D, C, T, Na *gyi*; P, N, Y, L om. *gyi*

149 BŚ (105b24): 喻若順分別　復有教授偈, Pa (124a9): 又正教兩偈　如分別觀論說, DG (298b6): 復有教授偈　如觀行差別論說, H (143c5): 復有教授二頌

byang [P30a6] chub sems dpa' mnyam gzhag pas//

gzugs brnyan yid du mthong ba ni//

don [DT26a6] gyi[150] 'du shes bzlog nas su//

rang gi[151] 'du shes [C26a6] nges par gzung//[152]<1//>[153]

如分別瑜伽論說.

150 D, C, T, Y, L, Na *gyi*; P, N *gyis*

151 D, C, T, Y, L, Na *gi*; P, N *gis*

152 MSBh [D163b1–3, P197a5–7]: ***gzugs brnyan yid du mthong ba ni**// zhes bya ba la/ chos dang don du snang ba gang yin pa'i **gzugs brnyan** de **yid** yin no zhes **mthong ba**'o// … **don gyi 'du shes bzlog nas su**// **rang gi 'du shes nges par gzung**// zhes bya ba ni de'i dus na **don gyi 'du shes** bor nas rang gyi sems nyid chos dang don gyi rnam pa de yin par gzung zhes bya ba'i tha tshig go//*

MSU [D249a7–3, P303b4–8]: *su zhig de ltar yongs su tshol nas 'bras bu thob pa dang su la de skad bstan pa de'i dbang du byas nas tshigs su bcad pa/ **byang chub sems dpa' mnyam gzhag pas**// **gzugs brnyan yid du mthong ba ni**// zhes bya ba la sogs pa'o// chos dang don du snang ba ting nge 'dzin gyi **gzugs brnyan** gang yin pa de **yid** yin par **mthong ba** ste/ ji skad du*

rnam par shes pa ni dmigs pa rnam par rig pas rab tu phye ba can no//

zhes ngas bshad do zhes der gsungs pa lta bu'o//

*sus mthong zhe na/ **byan chub sems dpa' mnyam gzhag pas**// zhes bya ba ste/ sems rtse gcig pas so// **don gyi 'du shes bzlog nas su**// zhes bya ba ni gzugs brnyan de las **don gyi 'du shes** bsal nas so// **rang gi 'du shes nges par gzung**// zhes bya ba ni bdag gi **mnyam** par **gzhag pa**'i sems 'di nyid chos dang don lta bur so sor snang ngo snyam du'o//*

153 BŚ (105b25–26): 鏡像意於後　菩薩在諸定　迴彼義想已　憶持自想事, Pa (124a10–11): 菩薩在靜位　觀心唯是影　捨離外塵相　唯定觀自想, DG (298b7–8): 菩薩靜心中　得見其心影　滅除於義想　但觀於自想, H (143c6–7): 菩薩於定位　觀影唯是心　義相既滅除　審觀唯自想.

Cf. AS, p. 82, *ll*. 20–21:

pratibimbaṁ manaḥ paśyan bodhisattvaḥ samāhitaḥ/
vyāvarttya viṣaye saṁjñāṁ svasaṁjñām upadhārayan//

de ltar nang du sems [N28b3] gnas so//

gzung ba med pa [P30a7] rab rtogs byos//

de phyir 'dzin pa med rtogs byos[154]//

des na dmigs pa med la[155] reg//[156]<2//>[157]

MS III. 18

'di lta ste/ theg pa chen po'i mdo sde'i rgyan las/ gzhan yang mngon par [DT26a7] rtogs pa'i tshig su bcad pa dag [P30a8] 'byung ba/[158]

---

154 P, N, Y, L, Na *byos*; D, C, T *kyis*

155 D, C, T, L, Na *la*; P, N, Y *par*

156 MSBh [D163b4–5, P197a8–b2]: ***gzung ba med pa rab rtogs byos***// *zhes bya ba ni* ***gzung ba med par*** *shes par gyis shig ces bya ba'i tha tshig go*// ***de phyir 'dzin pa med rtogs byos***// *zhes bya ba ni gang gi phyir gzung bar bya ba'i don yod pa ma yin pas 'dzin par byed pa'i sems nyid kyang rigs pa ma yin pa nyid du 'gyur ro*//

MSU [D249b3–4, P303b8–304a2]: ***de ltar nang du sems gnas so***// *zhes bya ba ni de'i tshe de'i sems nyid la* ***sems gnas*** *pa yin no zhes bya ba'i tha tshig go*// ***gzung ba med pa rab rtogs byos***// *zhes bya ba ni* ***gzung ba med par*** *shes par bya ba'o*// ***de phyir 'dzin pa med rtogs byos***// *zhes bya ba ni gzung ba med na* ***'dzin pa*** *mi 'thad pa'i phyir ro*// ***des na dmigs pa med la reg***// *ces bya ba ni de gnyi ga'i ngo bo nyid dmigs pa dang bral ba'i de bzhin nyid khong du chud de rab tu rtogs pa'o*//

157 BŚ (105b27–28): 住心如是内　知無所可取　於後無能取　無分別知爾, Pa (124a12–13): 菩薩住於内　入所取非有　次觀能取空　後觸二無得, DG (298b9–10): 如是心住内　知所取非有　即無能取者　故證無所有, H (143c8–9): 如是住内心　知所取非有　次能取亦無　後觸無所得.
Cf. AS, p. 82, *ll*. 22–23:

evam ātmasthacitto 'sau grāhyābhāvaṁ vibodhayet/
tataś ca grāhakābhāvaṁ nopalambhaṁ spṛśettataḥ//

158 BŚ (105b29): 更復有證道偈　所謂大乘莊嚴論中説, Pa (124a14): 復有大乘莊嚴經論所説五偈　爲顯此道, DG (298b21–22): 復有入正位別偈　如大乘經莊嚴論中所説, H (143c10): 復有別五現觀伽他　如大乘經莊嚴論説.

byang chub [C26a7] sems dpa'[159] [N28b4] bsod nams ye shes kyi//

tshogs rnams mtha' yas pha rol med bsags te//

chos la sems pa[160] legs par rnam[161] nges phyir//

don gyi rnam pa brjod pa'i rgyus byung [P30b1] rtogs//[162]<1//>[163]

brjod pa tsam du don ni nges [DT26b1] shes nas//

de 'dra ba yi[164] sems tsam nyid la gnas//

[C26b1] [N28b5] de bas gnyis kyi mtshan nyid bral ba yi[165]//

chos kyi dbyings ni mngon sum nyid du 'gyur//[166]<2//>[167]

---

159 P, N, Y, L, Na *dpa'*; D, C, T *dpas*
160 D, C, T, Y, L, Na *pa*; P, N *dpa'*
161 D, C, T, Y, L, Na *rnam*; P, N *snang*
162 Cf. MSA, VI. 6, p. 23, *ll.* 26–27 and p. 24, *ll.* 7–9:

> *saṁbhṛtya saṁbhāram anantapāraṁ jñānasya puṇyasya ca bodhisattvaḥ/ dharmeṣu cintāsuviniścitatvāj* (Lévi: *-suviniśritatvāj*) *jalpānvayām arthagatiṁ paraiti//*

ekena saṁbhṛtasaṁbhāratvaṁ dharmacintāsuviniścitatvaṁ samādhiniścitya bhāvanāt manojalpāc ca teṣāṁ dharmāṇām arthaprakhyānāvagamāt tatpraveśaṁ darśayati/ asaṁkhyeyaprabhedakālaṁ pāram asya paripūraṇam ity anantapāraṁ/

MSU [D249b4–250a1, P304a2–8]: ***bsod nams kyi tshogs*** *ni sbyin pa la sogs pa pha rol tu phyin pa gsum mo//* ***ye shes kyi tshogs*** *ni shes rab kyi pha rol tu phyin pa'o// brtson 'grus ni gnyi gar gtogs so// bsam gtan ni tshad med pa la dmigs pa ni* ***bsod nams kyi tshogs*** *so// gzhan ni* ***ye shes kyi*** *yan lag go// ...* ***chos la sems pa legs par rnam nges phyir*** *// zhes bya ba ni ting nge 'dzin gyi rjes la mdo'i sde la sogs pa la shin tu nges pa'i phyir te/ the tshom med pa'i phyir ro//* ***don gyi rnam pa brjod pa'i rgyus byung rtogs*** *// zhes bya ba ni don rnams kyi rgyu ni yid kyi brjod pa yin par shes pa ste/ ji skad du chos rnams brjod pa'i bag chags las byung ste zhes bya ba la sogs pa gsungs pa lta bu'o// ... tshigs su bcad pa 'dis ni tshogs kyi lam bstan to//*

163 BŚ (105c1–2): 助集無邊行　功徳智菩薩　法思善決定　語言達義盡, Pa (124a15–16): 菩薩生長福及慧　二種資糧無量際　於法思惟心決故(em. to 定)　能了義類分別因, DG (298b23–24): 菩薩具滿無邊際　福徳智惠之資糧　法中思量善決已　則了義類意言生, H (143c11–12): 福徳智慧二資糧　菩薩善備無邊際　於法思量善決已　故了義趣唯言類.
164 D, C, T, L, Na *yi*; P, N, Y *yis*
165 D, C, T, Na *yi*; P, N, Y, L *yis*

[P30b2] sems las gzhan med par ni blos rtogs nas//

de phyir sems kyang med pa nyid du rtogs//

blo dang ldan pas gnyis po med rtogs nas//[DT26b2]

de dang mi ldan chos kyi dbyings la [N28b6]gnas//[168]<3//>[169]

---

166 Cf. MSA VI. 7, p. 24, *ll*. 1–2 and 9–12:

arthān sa vijñāya ca jalpamātrān saṁtiṣṭhate tannibhacittamātre/
pratyakṣatām eti ca dharmadhātus tasmād viyukto dvayalakṣaṇena//

dvitīyena manojalpamātrān arthān viditvā, tadābhāse citta-mātre 'vasthānam iyaṁ bodhisat<t>vasya nirvedhabhāgīyāvasthā/ tataḥ pareṇa dharmadhātoḥ prayakṣato gamane dvayalakṣaṇena viyukto grāhyagrāhakalakṣaṇena iyaṁ darśanamārgāvasthā/

MSBh [D164a3, P198a2–3]: ***de 'dra ba yi sems tsam nyid la gnas***// *zhes bya ba ni gang gi phyir de ni 'di ltar don du snang ba 'di dag ni* ***sems tsam nyid*** *do zhes bya bar shes pa'o//*

MSU: [D250a1–3, P304b1–4] ***de bas gnyis kyi mtshan nyid bral ba yi// chos kyi dbyings ni mngon sum nyid du 'gyur***// *zhes bya ba ni don med par rtogs pa sngon du 'gro ba'i sems tsam la gnas nas bzung ba dang 'dzin pa'i* ***mtshan nyid*** *gnyis dang* ***bral ba*** *gnyis su med pa'i* ***chos kyi dbyings ni mngon sum <nyid> du 'gyur*** *te/ nges par skyes pa'i phyir ro// tshigs su bcad pa 'dis ni sbyor pa'i lam bstan to//*

167 BŚ (105c3–4): 彼知正義已　說住彼定心　法界現意故　是以離二相, Pa (124a17–18): 已知義類但分別　得住似義唯識中　故觀行人證法界　能離二相及無二, DG (298b25–26): 彼知諸義唯意言　即住似義唯心中　如是正證法界已　是故遠離二種相, H (143c13–14): 若知諸義唯是言　即住似彼唯心理　便能現證眞法界　是故二相悉蠲除.

168 Cf. MSA VI. 8, p. 24, *ll*. 3–4 and 12–16:

nāstīti cittāt param etya buddhyā cittasya nāstitvam upaiti tasmāt/
dvayasya nāstitvam upetya dhīmān saṁtiṣṭhate 'tadgatidharmadhātau//

tṛtīyena yathāsau dharmadhātuḥ pratyakṣatām eti tad darśayati/ kathaṁ cāsau dharmadhātuḥ pratyakṣatām eti/ cittād anyad ālaṁbanaṁ grāhyaṁ nāstīty avagamya buddhyā tasyāpi cittamātrasya nāstitvāva-gamanaṁ grāhyābhāve grāhakābhāvāt/ dvaye cāsya nāstitvaṁ viditvā dharmadhātau avasthānam 'tadgatir grāhyagrāhakalakṣaṇābhyām rahita evaṁ dharmadhātuḥ pratyakṣatām iti/

MSBh [D164a4–6, P198a4–6]: ***sems las gzhan med par ni blos rtogs nas// de phyir sems kyang med pa nyid du rtogs***// *zhes bya ba la/* ***sems las gzhan*** *pa'i dmigs par bya ba'i don* ***med*** *la de med pas dmigs par byed pa'i sems kyang med pa nyid 'thob ste/ de gnyis kyi med pa nyid byang chub sems dpas rtogs nas/* ***de dang mi ldan chos kyi dbyings la gnas***// *zhes bya ba ste/ don de dag dang sems bral bar gyur ces bya ba'i tha*

C26b2 P30b3

rtog[170] med[171] shes stobs mnyam pa'i rjes song bas//

blo dang ldan pas kun nas rtag par yang//

de'i gnas thibs po nyes pa[172] bsags pa sel//

rtsi sman chen pos dug ni sel ba bzhin//[173]<4//>[174]

---

tshig go//

MSU [D250a3–5, P304b3–6]: ***sems las gshan med par ni blos rtogs nas// de phyir sems kyang med pa nyid du rtogs//*** *zhes bya ba ni* ***sems las gzhan*** *pa dmigs par bya ba'i don med de/ de med pas dmigs par byed pa yang mi 'thad de zhes bya bar sbyar ro// ...* ***de dang mi ldan chos kyi dbyings la gnas//*** *zhes bya ba ni gzung ba dang 'dzin pa dang bral ba la zhes bya ba'i tha tshig go// ... tshigs su bcad pa 'dis ni mthong ba'i lam bstan to//*

169 BŚ (105b5–6): 離心無有餘　善知心亦無　知二既是無　正住於法界, Pa (124a19–20): 若離於心知無餘　由此卽見心非有　智人見此二不有　得住無二眞法界, DG (298b27–28): 以知心外無有他　故得知心亦非有　智者了知二俱無　卽住無二法界中, H (143c15–16): 體知離心無別物　由此即會心非有　智者了達二皆無　等住二無眞法界.

170 P, N, Y, L, Na *rtog*; D, C, T *rtogs*

171 Na om.

172 MSBh, MSU, Y, L, Na *pa*; D, C, T, P, N *par*

173 Cf. MSA VI. 9, p. 24, *ll.* 5–6 and 16–20:

akalpanājñānabalena dhīmataḥ samānuyātena samantataḥ sadā/
tadāśrayo gahvaradoṣasaṁcayo mahāgadeneva viṣaṁ nirasyate//

caturthena bhāvanāmārgāvasthāyām āśrayaparivartanāt pāramārthika-jñānapraveśaṁ darśayati/ sadā sarvatra samatānugatenāvikalpa-jñānabalena yatra tatsamatānugataṁ paratantre svabhāve tadāśrayasya dūrānupraviṣṭasya doṣasaṁcayasya dauṣṭhulyalakṣaṇasya mahā-gadeneva viṣasya nirasanāt/

MSBh [D164a7–b1, P198a8–b2]: ***de'i gnas thibs po nyes pa bsags pa <sel>//*** *zhes bya ba ni kun nas nyon mongs pa'i chos de'i* ***gnas*** *te rgyu'o//* ***thibs po*** *zhes bya ba ni rjes su rtogs par dka' ba nyid do//* ***nyes pa bsags pa*** *zhes bya ba ni kun nas nyon mongs pa'i chos rnams kyi bag chags kyi ngo bo zhes bya ba'i don to//*

MSU [D250a5–7, P304b6–305a2]: ***rtogs med shes stobs*** *zhes bya ba ni rnam par mi rtog pa'i ye* ***shes*** *kyi mthus so// ...* ***thibs po*** *ni shes par dka' shing rtogs par dka' pa ste/* ***<nyes pa bsags pa ni>*** *kun nas nyon mongs pa'i chos kyi bag chags kyi mdzod kun gzhi'o// ... tshigs su bcad pa 'dis ni bsgom pa'i lam bstan to//*

174 BŚ (105c7–8): 不分知力故　同時常同行　彼身窟聚患　如象滅諸毒, Pa (124a21–22): 由無分別智慧人　恒平等行遍一切　染衣(em. to 依)稠密過聚

DT26b3
thub pas gsungs pa'i legs chos legs bzhag pa//
P30b4 N28b7
rtsa ba chos dbyings bcas la des blo bzhag//
C26b3
dran pa'i rgyud ni rtog pa tsam shes nas//

yon tan rgya mtsho'i pha rol brtan[175] myur 'gro//[176]<5//>[177]

性　遣滅如藥能除毒, DG (298b29–c1): 智者無分別智力　平等順行常普遍所依稠密罪惡聚　如大伽陀拔衆毒, H (143c17–18): 慧者無分別智力　周遍平等常順行　滅依榛梗過失聚　如大良藥銷衆毒.

175 D, C, T, Y, L, Na *brtan*; P, N *bstan*

176 Cf. MSA VI. 10, p. 24, *ll*. 21–26:
paramārthajñānamahātmye ślokaḥ/

> *munivihitasudharmasuvyavastho matim upadhāya sa mūladharmadhātau/*
> *smṛtigatim* (Lévi: *-matim*) *avagamya kalpamātrāṁ vrajati guṇārṇavapāram āśu dhīraḥ//*

buddhavihite sudharme suvyavasthāpite sa paramārthajñānapraviṣṭo bodhisat<t>vaḥ saṁpiṇḍitadharmālambanasya mūlacittasya dharmadhātau matim upanividhāya yā smṛtir upalabhyate tām sarvāṁ smṛtipravṛttiṁ kalpanāmātrām avagacchaty evaṁ guṇārṇavasya pāraṁ Buddhatvam āśu vrajatīty etat paramārthajñānasya mahātmyam/

MSBh [D164b1–4, P198b2–8]: ***thub pas gsungs pa'i legs chos legs bzhag pa// rtsa ba chos dbyings <bcas> la des blo bzhag//*** *ces bya ba la* ***rtsa ba*** *dang bcas pa'i sems kyis dmigs pa gang la* ***blo*** *nges par bzhag ste/ de bzhin nyid de la'o// ... tshigs su bcad pa de rnams kyi bsdus pa'i don ni dang pos ni tshogs kyi lam mo// gnyis pa'i phyed kyis ni sbyor ba'i lam mo// phyed phyi ma dang gsum pas ni mthong ba'i lam mo// bzhi pas ni bsgom pa'i lam mo// lnga pas ni mthar phyin pa'i lam mo//*

MSU [D250b1–2, P305a2–4] ***rtsa ba*** *zhes bya ba ni sa bcu pa ste/ mdo sde thams cad kyi ma mo yin pa'i phyir ro// de'i chos rnams ni chos gang dag la de 'jug pa'o//* ***chos*** *de dag gi* ***dbyings*** *ni stong pa nyid de/ de la rjes la thob pa'i ye shes kyis dran pa bzhag ste'o//* ***dran pa'i rgyud ni rtog pa tsam shes nas//*** *zhes bya ba ni* ***dran pa'i rgyud rtsa ba'i chos kyi dbyings*** *la 'jug pa'o//*

177 BŚ (105c9–11): 牟尼説善法　善住意思量　根本法界處　念至知意故　唯分別正取　速得功德處, Pa (124a23–24): 佛説正法善成立　安心有根於法界已知憶念唯分別　功德海岸智人至, DG (298c2–3): 牟尼善説諸正法　安心有根法界中　已知念行唯分別　智者疾至德海岸, H (143c19–20): 佛説妙法善成立　安慧并根法界中　了知念趣唯分別　勇猛疾歸德海岸.

Bibliography

In the Tibetan Texts and Chinese Texts sections below, in order to avoid making this Bibliography section too long, I have not included the Tibetan and Chinese texts mentioned in Chapter One of this book, and I have only included the Tibetan and Chinese texts which were used for my own edition of the Tibetan Text in Chapter three in this book.

Pali Text

Aṅguttara-Nikāya, The Pali Text Society, London, 1958.

Tibetan Texts

Co ne, Microfiche edition, The Institute for Advanced Studies of World Religions, New York.

sDe dge, *sDe dge* edition of the Tibetan Tripiṭaka, Hayashima, K., Takasaki, J., Yamaguchi, Z., and Ejima, Y. eds., Sekai Seiten Kankokai, Tokyo, 1977.

sNar thang, *sNar thang* edition of the Tibetan Tripiṭaka, kept in Ryukoku University Library, Kyoto.

Peking, Peking edition of the Tibetan Tripiṭaka, Suzuki, D. ed., Tibetan Tripiṭaka Research Institute, Tokyo-Kyoto, 1957–1961.

Taipei, Taipei edition of the Tibetan Tripiṭaka, Barber, A. W. ed., Taipei, 1991.

Chinese Texts

Shê ta ch'êng lun (攝大乘論), Buddhaśānta (佛陀扇多), tr., Taisho vol. 31, no. 1592, pp. 97a1–112b8.

Shê ta ch'êng lun (攝大乘論), Paramārtha (眞諦), tr., Taisho vol. 31, no. 1593, pp. 112b9–132c14.

Shê ta ch'êng lun pên (攝大乘論本), Hsüan-tsang (玄奘), tr., Taisho vol. 31, no. 1594, pp. 132c 15–152a18.

Shê ta ch'êng lun shih (攝大乘論釋), Paramārtha, tr., Taisho vol. 31, no. 1595, pp. 152a19–270b14.

Shê ta ch'êng lun shih lun (攝大乘論釋論), Dharmagupta and others (笈多共行矩等), tr., Taisho vol. 31, no. 1596, pp. 271a1–321a8.

Shê ta ch'êng lun shih (攝大乘論釋), Hsüan-tsang, tr., Taisho vol. 31, no. 1597, pp. 321a9–380a17.

Shê ta ch'êng lun shih (攝大乘論釋), Hsüan-tsang, tr., Taisho vol. 31, no. 1598, pp. 380a18–449b26.

Modern Works

Akashi, Etatsu

1932 "西藏訳掌中論和訳" (Japanese Translation of the Tibetan Translation of the *Hastavālaprakaraṇa*), RDR vol. 304, pp. 1–30.

Aramaki, Noritoshi

1963 "摂大乗論の依他起性" (Relative Reality as Expounded in the *Mahāyānasaṁgraha*), IG vol. 4-5, pp. 26–67.

1964 "摂大乗論第二章第三十二節" (*Mahāyānasaṁgraha* 2.32), IBK vol. 12-2, pp. 788–791.

Bagchi, S.

1970 *Mahāyānasūtrālaṁkārabhāṣya*, Buddhist Sanskrit Texts vol. 13, Mithila Insti- tute, Darbhanga.

Beal, Samuel

1906 Record of the Western Kingdoms, Trubner & Co., London.

Bendall. C. and Possin, de La Valée

1905 "A Text-book of the Yogācāra School, An English Summary with Notes and Illustrative Extracts from Other Buddhistic Works," Le Muséon vol. 24, pp. 38–52.

1906 "A Text-book of the Yogācāra School, An English Summary with Notes and Illustrative Extracts from Other Buddhistic Works," Le Muséon vol. 25, pp. 213–230.

1911 "*Bodhisattvabhūmi*; Sommaire et notes," Le Muséon vol. 30, pp. 155–191.

Candra, Lokesh

1959 *Tibetan-Sanskrit Dictionaly*, International Academy of Indian Culture, Delhi.

Chiba, Koji

2001 "『秘儀分別摂疏』覚え書 (1)" (A Memo about *Vivṛtaguhyārthapiṇḍavyākhyā* (1)), KJDKK vol. 8, pp. 209–216.

2002a "『秘儀分別摂疏』覚え書 (2)" (A Memo about *Vivṛtaguhyārthapiṇḍavyākhyā* (2)), NBK vol. 4, pp. 117–131.

2002b "如来の所分別についての一考察—『秘儀分別摂疏』覚え書 (3)" (A Study of *Kalpitatva* for *Tathāgata*: A Memo about *Vivṛtaguhyārthapiṇḍavyākhyā* (3)), KJDKK vol. 9, pp. 199–210.

2003 "『秘儀分別摂疏』における真如観について," IBK vol. 52-1, pp. 376–373 (119–122).

2004a "所分別と三昧についての一考察—『秘儀分別摂疏』覚え書 (4)"

(A Study of *Vikapla* and *Samādhi*: A Memo about *Vivṛtaguhyārthapiṇḍavyākhyā* (4)), KK vol. 37, pp. 79–85.

2004b "唯識説における Buddha-vacanatva について—『秘儀分別摂疏』覚え書 (5)" (On the *Buddha-vacanatva* in Vijñapti-matratā-vādin: A Study of *Vivṛtaguhyārthapiṇḍavyākhyā* (5)), KJDKK vol. 11, pp. 131–140.

2005 "『秘儀分別摂疏』の考察 (6)" (A Study of *Vivṛtaguhyārthapiṇḍavyākhyā* (6)), KJDKK vol. 12, pp. 107–117.

2006 "アーラヤ識縁起説における増益と損減—『秘儀分別摂疏』の考察 (7)—" (*Samaropa* and *Apavāda*, in Thought of *Pratītyasamutpada* based on *Ālayavijñāna*: A study of *Vivṛtaguhyārthapiṇḍavyākhyā* (7)), KJDKK vol. 13, pp. 167–175.

2007 "アーラヤ識の存在証明—『秘儀分別摂疏』の考察 (8)—" (Existence Proof of *Ālayavijñāna*: A Study of *Vivṛtaguhyārthapiṇḍavyākhyā* (8)), KJDKK vol. 14, pp. 131–140.

2008 "アーラヤ識の存在証明—『秘儀分別摂疏』の考察 (9)—" (Existence Proof of *Ālayavijñāna*: A Study of *Vivṛtaguhyārthapiṇḍavyākhyā* (9)), KJDKK vol. 15, pp. 103–114.

2009 "『秘儀分別摂疏』の考察 (10)" (A Study of *Vivṛtaguhyārthapiṇḍavyākhyā* (10)), KJDKK vol. 16, pp. 117–127.

2010 "『秘儀分別摂疏』の考察 (11)" (A Study about *Vivṛtaguhyārthapiṇḍavyākhyā* (11)), KJDKK vol. 17, pp. 149–184

Chimpa, L. and Chattopadhyaya, A.

1970 *Tāranātha's History of Buddhism*, Indian Institute of Advanced Studies, Simla.

Cordier, P.

1908 *Catalogue du fonds tibétain de la Bibliothéque nationale*, pts., Paris.

Das, Sarat Chandra

1985 A Tibetan-English Dictionary, Rinsen Book Co., Kyoto (First ed. Calcutta, 1902).

Demiéville, P.

1957 "Le Chapitre de la *Bodhisattvabhūmi* sur la Perfection du *Dhyāna*," Rocznik Orientalistyczny XXI, pp. 109–128 (rpt. in *Choix d'etudes bouddhiques*, Leiden Brill, 1973, pp. 300–319).

Dutt, Nalinaksha

1966 *Bodhisattvabhūmi*, Tibetan Sanskrit Works Series vol. VII, Patna.

Edgerton, Franklin

1985 Buddhist Hybrid Sanskrit Grammar and Dictionary, Rinsen Book Co., Kyoto (First ed. Yale University Press, 1953).

Frauwallner, Erich

1951 *On the Date of the Buddhist Master of the Law Vasubandhu*, Serie Orientale Roma.

1956 *Die Philosophie des Buddhismus*, Berlin.

1959 "Dignāga, Sein Werk und seine Entwicklung," WZKSO, vol. 3, pp. 129–130 and pp. 152–156.

Funahashi, Naoya

1978 "大乗荘厳経論（求法品）の原典の考察" (Notes on the Text of

the *Dharmaparyeṣṭyadhikāra* in the *Mahāyānasūtrālaṁkāra*), IBK vol. 27-1, pp. 51–57.

1982 "大乗阿毘達磨集論 (*Abhidharmasamuccaya*) 並びに *Abhidharmasamuccyabhāṣya* の和訳" (*A Japanese Translation of the Abhidharmasamuccaya and Abhidharmasamuccayabhāṣya*), OG vol. 62-3, pp. 29–41.

1985 "*Mahāyānasūtrālaṁkāra* Chapters I, II, III, IX and X, Revised on the basis of Nepalese Manuscript," in ネパール写本対照による大乗荘厳経論の研究 (*Studies in the *Mahāyānasūtrālaṁkāra*), Kokushokankokai, Tokyo.

1986 "大乗阿毘達磨集論 (*Abhidharmasamuccaya*) 並びに *Abhidharmasamuccyabhāṣya* の和訳 (2)" (*A Japanese Translation of the Abhidharmasamuccaya and Abhidharmasamuccayabhāṣya* (2)), OG vol. 66-1, pp. 17–31.

1990 "阿毘達磨集論 (*Abhidharmasamuccaya*) の諸問題—和訳と研究—" (Some Problems of the *Abhidharmasamuccaya*: A Japanese Translation and Study), OG vol. 70-1, pp. 1–16.

1991a "『大乗阿毘達磨集論』と初期唯識論書との前後について—十二有支と三雑染との関係を中心として—" (The *Mahāyāna Abhidharmasamuccaya* and Early Yogācāra Treatises: The Relationship between *Pratītyasamutpāda* and *Saṁkleśa*), BS vol. 54, pp. 15–37.

1991b "『大乗阿毘達磨集論』の一考察" (A Study of the *Abhidharmasamuccaya*), IBK vol. 40-1, pp. 28–34.

1995 "大乗阿毘達磨集論 (*Abhidharmasamuccaya*) と *Abhidharmasamuccyabhāṣya* の和訳並びに研究" (*A Japanese Translation and Study of the Abhidharmasamuccaya and Abhidharmasamuccayabhāṣya*), OG vol. 74-

4, pp. 37–46.

2000 “『大乗荘厳経論』の諸問題並びに第十一章求法品のテキスト校訂” (Some Problems in the *Mahāyānasūtrālaṁkāra* and Corrigenda of the *Mahāyānasūtrālaṁkāra* (Chapter XI)), ODKN vol. 52, pp. 1–69.

Goda, Hideyuki

1994 “無著造『禅定灯論』” (On *ālambana* in Asaṅga’s *Dhyānadīpanāmopadeśa*), IBK vol. 43-1, pp. 378–375 (147–150).

1995 “無着における *Buddhānusmṛti* について” (On *Buddhānusmṛti* in Asaṅga’s Commentaries), IBK vol. 44-1, pp. 387–384 (108–111).

1998 “無着における *Dharmānusmṛti* について” (On *Dharmānusmṛti* in Asaṅga’s Commentaries), IBK vol. 46-2, pp. 966–962 (95–99).

Griffiths, Paul

1986 *On Being Mindless*, Open Court, La Salle, Illinois.

Hakamaya, Noriaki

1969 “玄奘訳『摂大乗論釈』について—チベット訳との比較による一考察—” (Hsüan-tsang’s Translation of the *Mahāyānasaṁgrahopanibandhana*—Compared With its Tibetan Translation—), IBK vol. 18-1, pp. 140–141.

1970 “MS. に対する Asvabhāva 注釈の特徴—チベット訳を資料として—” (Some Features of Asaṅga’s *Mahāyānasaṁgrahopanibandhana* according to Its Tibetan Translation), IBK vol. 19-1, pp. 444–439 (46–51).

1973 “*Mahāyānasaṁgrahopanibandhana*, Its Tibetan and Chinese Text (1),” KDBK vol. 31, pp. 8–14.

1974a “*Mahāyānasaṁgrahopanibandhana*, Its Tibetan and

Chinese Text (2)," KDBK vol. 32, pp. 1–14.

1974b "On a Verse Quoted in the Tibetan Translation of the *Mahāyānasaṁgrahopanibandhana*," IBK vol. 32-2, pp. 1111–1107 (17–21).

1975 "*Mahāyānasaṁgrahopanibandhana*, Its Tibetan and Chinese Text (3)," KDBK vol. 33, pp. 15–33.

1976 "三種転依考" (On the *Triple āśraya-parivṛtti/-parāvṛtti*), BG vol. 2, pp. 46–76.

1978 "アーラヤ識存在の八論証に関する諸文献" (Materials for the Eight Proofs of the Existence of *Ālayavijñāna*), KDBKK vol. 36, pp. 1–26.

1979a "*Mahāyānasaṁgraha* における心意識説" (The Theory of *citta, manas* and *vijñāna* in the *Mahāyānasaṁgraha*), TBKK vol. 76, pp. 197–309.

1979b "*Viniścayasaṁgrahaṇī* におけるアーラヤ識の規定" (On the Stipulation of the *Ālayavijñāna* in the *Viniścayasaṁgrahaṇī*), TBKK vol. 79, pp. 1–79.

1983 "*Chos kyi sku la gnas pa'i yon tan la bstod pa* とその関連文献" (*Chos kyi sku la gnas pa'i yon tan la bstod pa* and Its related Materials), KDBR vol. 14, pp. 342–324 (9–27).

1986 "*Pūrvācārya* " (On the *Pūrvācārya*), IBK vol. 34-2, pp. 859–866

1993 新国訳大蔵経　大乗荘厳経論 (*New Japanese translation of the Chinese Tripiṭaka, *Mahāyānasūtrālaṁkāra*), Daizoshuppan, Tokyo.

2008 唯識文献研究 (*A Study of Texts on *Vijñaptimātra* Thought), Daizoshuppan.

Hakamaya, Noriaki, Keenan, J. P., Griffiths, P., and Swanson, P.

1989 *The Realm of Awakening: Chapter Ten of Asaṅga's Mahāyānasaṁgraha*, Oxford University Press, New York Oxford.

Harada, Waso

1993 "Dignāga の *Hastavāla-prakaraṇa* & *Vṛtti*—和訳とSkt. 還元訳の試み—" (Dignāga's *Hastavāla-prakaraṇa* and *Vṛtti*: Japanese Translation and Sanskrit Retranslation), RDBKN vol. 6.

1997a "「蛇・縄・色等」の比喩と入唯識性 (I)—MS III §§ 8–9 の和訳と訳註—" (*Analogy of "Snake, Rope, Colour, etc.," and Entrance into *Vijñaptimātratā* (1): Japanese Translation and Annotation of MS III. 8–9) in 渡邊隆生教授還暦記念 佛教思想文化史論叢 (*Buddhist Thought and History of Buddhist Culture, A Collection of Papers in Honour of Professor Watanabe Takao on the Occasion of his Sixtieth Birthday*, The Committee for the Commemoration of Professor Watanabe Takao's Sixtieth Birthday), Nagata Bunshodo, Kyoto, pp. 125–152.

1997b "「蛇・縄・色等」の比喩と入唯識性 (II)—MSU III §§ 8–9 の和訳と評註—" (*An Analogy of 'Snake, Rope, Colour, etc.' and Entrance into *Vijñaptimātratā* (2)), KRTDK vol. 43, pp. 135–175.

Hatano, Hakuyu

1975 瑜伽論菩薩地 (*The *Bodhisattvabhūmi* in the *Yogācārabhūmi*), Study Group of Tibetan Buddhist Text, Sendai.

Hayashima, Osamu

1973 "*Mahāyānasūtrālaṁkāra* における菩薩行の構造—第VI章 tattva を中心にして—" (The Structure of *Bodhisattva-*

pratipatti in the *Mahāyānasūtrālaṁkāra*), IBK vol. 21-2, pp. 983–980.

1977 "(*Chos yoṅs su thol baḥi skabs* or) *Dharmaparyeṣṭy* (*Adhikāra*), The XIth Chapter of the *Sūtrālaṁkāravṛtti-bhāṣya*, Subcommentary of the *Mahāyānasūtrālaṁkāra*," Part I, NDKR vol 26, pp. 19–61.

1978 "(*Chos yoṅs su thol baḥi skabs* or) *Dharmaparyeṣṭy* (*Adhikāra*), The XIth Chapter of the *Sūtrālaṁkāravṛtti-bhāṣya*, Subcommentary of the *Mahāyānasūtrālaṁkāra*," Part II, NDKR vol 27, pp. 73–119.

1979 "(*Chos yoṅs su thol baḥi skabs* or) *Dharmaparyeṣṭy* (*Adhikāra*), The XIth Chapter of the *Sūtrālaṁkāravṛtti-bhāṣya*, Subcommentary of the *Mahāyānasūtrālaṁkāra*," Part III, NDKR vol 28, pp. 37–70.

1982 "(*Chos yoṅs su thol baḥi skabs* or) *Dharmaparyeṣṭy* (*Adhikāra*), The XIth Chapter of the *Sūtrālaṁkāravṛtti-bhāṣya*, Subcommentary of the *Mahāyānasūtrālaṁkāra*," Part IV, NDKR vol 31, pp. 55–98.

1983a "(*Chos yoṅs su thol baḥi skabs* or) *Dharmaparyeṣṭy* (*Adhikāra*), The XIth Chapter of the *Sūtrālaṁkāravṛtti-bhāṣya*, Subcommentary of the *Mahāyānasūtrālaṁkāra*," Part V, NDKR vol 32, pp. 11–23.

1983b "*Tattva*, The VIth Chapter of the *Mahāyānasūtrālaṁkāra*," NDKR vol. 32, pp. 39–78.

1983c "「六波羅密」考—MSA XVI章を中心に—" (On the *ṣaṭ-pāramitā*, with Special Reference to Chap. XVI of the *Mahāyānasūtrlaṁkāra*), IBK vol. 32-1, pp. 456–453 (103–106).

1988 "『顕揚聖教論』に見られる極微説" (The Atomic Theory in

the *Hsien-yang sheng-chiao lun*), IBK vol. 37-1, pp. 426–421 (87–92).

1997a "『顕揚聖教論』「成不思議品　第十」について" (On the Tenth Chapter (*Acinta*) of the *Xianyang shengjiao-lun*), IBK vol. 46-1, pp. 349–345 (172–176).

1997b "『顕揚聖教論』研究序" (An Introductory Study of the Xianyang shengjiao-lun), NDKR vol. 54, pp. 23–52.

1997c 余、変異無常、転異無常 (On *anityatā* and *Trisvabhāva*), NDKR vol. 54, pp. 53–69.

2004 "菩薩と聖弟子声聞" (Bodhisattva and Ārya-Śrāvaka), IBK vol. 53-1, pp. 118–124.

Hikata, Ryusho

1954 "世親年代再考" (A Study of the Date of Vasubandhu), in 宮本正尊教授還暦記念論集 印度学仏教学論集 (Prof. Shoson Miyamoto's 60th Anniversary Commemorative Volume), Sanshodo, Tokyo, pp. 305–324.

Hirakawa, Akira

1973 *Index to the Abhidharmakośabhāṣya*, Part I, Sanskrit-Tibetan-Chinese, Daizoshuppan, Tokyo.

1977 *Index to the Abhidharmakośabhāṣya*, Part II, Chinese-Sanskrit, Daizoshuppan, Tokyo.

1978 *Index to the Abhidharmakośabhāṣya*, Part III, Tibetan-Sanskrit, Daizoshuppan, Tokyo.

1979 インド仏教史 下 (*History of Indian Buddhism*, vol. 2), Shunjusha, Tokyo.

Iwata, Taijyo

1981 初期唯識思想研究—世親造『摂大乗論釈』所知相章の漢蔵対照— (A Study of the Early Yogācāra Philosophy: Vasubandhu's *Mahāyānasaṁgrahabhāṣya*: A Comparison of the Chinese and Tibetan Translations: The *Jñeyalakṣaṇa* Chapter), Daizoshuppan, Tokyo.

1983 "笈多訳の『摂大乗論』について" (On Dharmagupta's Chinese Translation of Asaṅga's *Mahāyānasaṁgraha*), IBK vol. 31-2, pp. 801–805.

1992 "世親造『摂大乗論釈』所知依章の漢蔵対照（一）" (A Comparison of the Chinese and Tibetan Translations of the *Jñeyāśraya* Chapter of Vasubandhu's *Mahāyānasaṁgrahabhāṣya*), HBK vol. 18, pp. 1–54.

2000 "世親造『摂大乗論釈』所知依章の漢蔵対照（二）" (A Comparison of the Chinese and Tibetan Translations of the *Jñeyāśraya* Chapter of Vasubandhu's *Mahāyānasaṁgrahabhāṣya*), MDBK vol. 1, pp. 1–34.

2001 "世親造『摂大乗論釈』所知依章の漢蔵対照（三）" (A Comparison of the Chinese and Tibetan Translations of the *Jñeyāśraya* Chapter of Vasubandhu's *Mahāyānasaṁgrahabhāṣya*), MDBK vol. 2, pp. 17–37.

2003 "世親造『摂大乗論釈』所知依章の漢蔵対照（四）" (A Comparison of the Chinese and Tibetan Translations of the *Jñeyāśraya* Chapter of Vasubandhu's *Mahāyānasaṁgrahabhāṣya*), MDBK vol. 4, 2003, pp. 1–19.

Jaini, P. S.

1958 "On the Theory of Two Vasubandhus," BSOAS vol. 21-1, pp. 48–53.

Jäschke, H. A.

1965 *A Tibetan-English Dictionary*, Routledge & Kegan Paul Ltd., London (first ed. 1881).

Johnston, E. H. and Chowdhury, T.

1950 *The Ratnagotravibhāga Mahāyānottaratantraśāstra*,

JBORS vol. 36, Patna (rpt. Bihar Research Society, Patna, 1950, 1960).

Joshi, Lal. Mani

1978 "*Vajracchedikā prajñāpāramitāsūtra tathā ācārya asaṅgakṛtatriśatikākārikāsaptati*," *Bibliotheca Indo-Tibetica* 3, Sarnath, pp. 79–92.

Kajiyama, Yuichi

1969 仏教の思想 3 (Thought of Buddhism 3), Kadokawa-shoten, Tokyo.

Katano, Michio

1967 "摂大乗論に於けるアーラヤ識の相（lakṣaṇa）について" (Three Characteristics of *Ālayavijñāna* in the *Mahāyānasaṁgraha*), IBK vol. 16-1, pp. 175–178.

1968 "摂大乗論における声聞乗のアーラヤの異門" (The *Śrāvakayāna's* Synonyms of *ālaya* in the *Mahāyānasaṁgraha*), BGS vol. 8, pp. 46–61.

1975 インド仏教における唯識思想の研究—無性造『摂大乗論註』所知相章の解読— (*A Study of *Vijñaptimātra* Thought: An Annotated Translation of the *Jñeyalakṣaṇa* Chapter of Asvabhāva's Commentary on the *Mahāyānasaṁgraha*), Buneido, Kyoto.

1976 "無住涅槃としての転依" (Buddhist Thought of *Apratiṣṭhita-nirvāṅa* in India—An Annotated Translation of Asvabhāva's Commentary on the *Mahāyānasaṁgraha*, the Chap. IX—), OG vol. 56-2, pp. 37–49.

1977 "無性造「摂大乗論註」序章の解読" (The Annotated Translation of Asvabhāva's Commentary on the Intro ductory Chapter of the *Mahāyānasaṁgraha*), BGS vol. 27, pp. 37–54.

Katsube, T., Takahashi, H., and Matsunami, Y.

1981 "梵文声聞地" (The *Śrāvakabhūmi*: Sanskrit Text, Analysis and Japanese Translation), TDSBK vol. 3, pp. 1–44.

1982 "梵文声聞地" (The *Śrāvakabhūmi*: Sanskrit Text, Analysis and Japanese Translation), TDSBK vol. 4, pp. 1–27.

1984 "梵文声聞地" (The *Śrāvakabhūmi*: Sanskrit Text, Analysis and Japanese Translation), TDSBK vol. 6, pp. 1–30.

1985 "梵文声聞地" (The *Śrāvakabhūmi*: Sanskrit Text, Analysis and Japanese Translation), TDSBK vol. 7, pp. 37–68.

1986 "梵文声聞地" (The *Śrāvakabhūmi*: Sanskrit Text, Analysis and Japanese Trans- lation), TDSBK vol. 8, pp. 59–101.

1987 "梵文声聞地" (The *Śrāvakabhūmi*: Sanskrit Text, Analysis and Japanese Translation), TDSBK vol. 9, pp. 86–139.

1988 "梵文声聞地" (The *Śrāvakabhūmi*: Sanskrit Text, Analysis and Japanese Translation), TDSBK vol. 10, pp. 58–87.

1998 瑜伽論声聞地第一瑜伽処—サンスクリット語テキストと和訳— (*Śrāvakabhūmi*, Revised Sanskrit Text and Japanese Translation, The First Chapter), Sankibobusshorin, Tokyo.

Kritzer, Robert B.

1995 *Pratītyasamutpāda* in the *Abhidharmasamuccaya*: Conditioned Origination in the Yogācāra *Abhidharma*, Unpublished Ph.D. Dissertation, University of California, Berkeley.

1999 *Rebirth and Causation in the Yogācāra Abhidharma*, WSTB vol. 44, Wien.

Kataoka, Yugo

1959 "無著の順中論について" (On Asaṅga's *Shun chung lun*), SK vol. 4, pp. 151–161.

Keenan, John P.

1989 "Asaṅga's Understanding of *Mādhyamika*: Notes on the *Shung-chung-lun*," JIABS vol. 12-1, pp. 93–107.

1992 The Summary of the Great Vehicle, Numata Center for Buddhist Translation and Research, Berkeley.

Kawamura, Leslie S.

1991 "*Nirvikalpa-jñāna*: Awareness Freed From Discrimination," in *From Benares To Beijing: Essays on Buddhism and Chinese Religion in Honour of Prof. Jan Yün-Hua*, Shinohara, K. and Schopen, G., eds. Mosaic Press.

Lamotte, Étienne

1935 "L'*ālayavijñāna* (La Réceptacle) dans la *Mahāyāna-saṁgraha* (Chaptire II), Asaṅga et ses commentateurs," MCB vol. 3, pp. 169–255.

1973 *La Somme du Grand Véhicule D'Asaṅga* (*Mahāyāna-saṁgraha*) Tome I and II. Université du Louvain, Publications de l'Institut Orientaliste du Louvain 8, (first ed. 1938).

Lévi, Sylvain

1911 *Mahāyānasūtrāṁkāla*, Bibliothèque de l'École des Hautes Études, Paris.

Matsuda, Kazunobu

1984a "Vasubandhu 研究ノート (1)" (Notes on Vasubandhu (1)), IBK vol. 32-2, pp. 82–85.

1984b "Vasubandhu における三帰依の規定とその応用" (*Pre-*

scription for Taking refuge in the triratna and its Application in Vasubandhu), BGS vol. 39, pp. 1–16.

1985 "*Vyākhyāyukti* の二諦説—Vasubandhu 研究ノート (2)" (The Theory of Two Truths in *Vyākhyāyukti*: Notes on Vasubandhu (2)) IBK vol. 33-2, pp. 756–750 (114–120).

1988 "ダライラマ13世寄贈の一連のネパール系写本について—『瑜伽論』「摂決択分」梵文断簡発見記—" (*On the Series of Nepalese Manuscripts Presented by the 13th Dalai Lama: A Report of the Discovery of Sanskrit Fragments of the *Viniścayasaṁgrahaṇī* in the *Yogācārabhūmi*), NTGK vol. 34, p. 16–20.

Monier-Williams, Monier

1982 Sanskrit-English Dictionary, Oxford University Press (First ed. 1899)

Mukai, Akira

1976 "アサンガにおける大乗思想の形成と空観" (The Formation of the Mahāyāna Thought in Asaṅga), SK vol. 227, p. 128.

1979 "『顕揚聖教論』と『瑜伽師地論』" (On the *Śāsanodbhāvana* and the *Yogācārabhūmi*), BG vol. 8, pp. 39–68.

1981 "『瑜伽論』の成立とアサンガの年代" (On the Completion of the *Yogācārabhūmi* and the Date of Asaṅga), IBK vol. 29-2, pp. 680–686.

Muroji, Yoshihito

1986 "倶舎論 成業論 縁起経釈" (*Abhidharmakośa*, *Karmasiddhiprakaraṇa*, *Pratītyasamutpādavyākhyā*), MB vol. 156, pp. 53–82

Nagao, Gadjin M.

1943 "摂大乗論世親釈の漢蔵本対照" (*A Comparison of the Chinese and Tibetan Translations of Vasubandhu's Commentary on the *Mahāyānasaṁgraha*), TG vol. 13-2, pp. 119–175.

1958 *Index to the Mahāyāna-sūtrāṁkāra*, Part I, Nippon Gakujutsu Shinko-kai (Japan Society for the Promotion of Science), Kyoto.

1961 *Index to the Mahāyāna-sūtrāṁkāra*, Part II, Nippon Gakujutsu Shinko-kai (Japan Society for the Promotion of Science), Kyoto.

1964 *Madhyāntavibhāga-bhāṣya*, Suzuki Research Foundation, Tokyo, pp. 79–231.

1973 "金剛般若経" (*Vajracchedikāprajñāpāramitā-sūtra*) in 大乗仏典 (Mahāyāna Buddhist Texts), vol. 1, Chuokoronsha, Tokyo, pp. 5–71.

1978 "金剛般若経に対する無着の釈偈" (*Asaṅga's Commentary on the *Vajracchedikāprajñāpāramitā-sūtra*) in 中観と唯識 (*Mādhyamika and Yogācāra), Iwanamishoten, Tokyo, pp. 561–583.

1982 摂大乗論 和訳と注解 上 (*Mahāyānasaṁgraha*: A Japanese Translation and Annotation), Kodansha, Tokyo, vol. 1.

1987 摂大乗論 和訳と注解 下 (*Mahāyānasaṁgraha*: A Japanese Translation and Annotation), Kodansha, Tokyo, vol. 2.

1994 *An Index to Asaṅga's Mahāyānasaṁgraha, Part One*, Studia Philologica Buddhica, Monograph Series IX, The International Institute for Buddhist Studies, Tokyo.

Nagasawa Jitsudo

1955 漢訳二本対照チベット訳手量註和訳 (Japanese Translation of the Tibetan Translation of the *Hastavālaprakaraṇa*: Comparison with Two Chinese Translation), CG vol. 4, pp. 46–55 (reprint in 瑜伽行思想と密教の研究, Daito-shuppan, 1978, pp. 291–301).

Nakamura, Hajime

1980 *Indian Buddhism: A Survey with Bibliographical Notes*, SUFS Publication, Hirakata.

Nakamura, Zuiryu

1961 梵漢対照・究竟一乗宝性論研究 (A Study of the *Uttara-tantraratnagotravibhāga*), Sankibobusshorin, Tokyo.

Nishio, Kyoyu

1982 "無着造　解深密経疏に就いて" (*On Asaṅga's *Saṁdhinirmocanabhāṣya*), in 仏地経論之研究 (*Studies in the *Buddhabhūmyupadeśa*), vol. 2, Kokushokankokai, Tokyo, pp. 33–82.

Nishioka, Soshu

1981 "『プトゥン仏教史』目録部索引 II" (Index to the Catalogue Section of Bu-ston's "History of Buddhis" II), *Annual Report of the Institute for the Study of Cultural Exchange* vol. 5, The Institute for the Study of Cultural Exchange, Faculty of Letters, The University of Tokyo, Tokyo.

Obermiller, Eugéne

1931a *History of Buddhism by Bu-ston*, Heidelberg (rpt. Suzuki Research Foundation, Tokyo, 1961, 1986)

1931b "The Sublime Science of the Great Vehicle to Salvation," AO vol. 9, London, pp. 81–306.

Odani, Nobuchiyo

1983 "Sanskrit Text of the *Mahāyānasūtrālaṁkārabhāṣya* Chapter XIV" in 大乗荘厳経論の研究 (*Studies in the *Mahāyānasūtrālaṁkāra*), Buneido, Kyoto.

Ozawa, Kenju

1968 "順中論について" (On the *Shun-chung-lun*), IBK vol. 16-2, pp. 841–843.

1970 "順中論における我の解釈" (*Ātman* in the *Shun-chung-lun*), IBK vol. 18-2, pp. 907–909.

Powers, John

1992 *Two Commentaries on the Saṁdhinirmocana-sūtra by Asaṅga and Jñānagarbha*, Studies in Asian Thought and Religion vol. 13, The Edwin Mellen Press, Lewiston/Queenston/Lampeter.

Pradhan, Prahlad

1950 *Abhidharmasamuccaya of Asaṅga*, Visva-Bharati, Santiniketan.

1967 *Abhidharmakośabhāṣya of Vasubandhu*, K. P. Jayashwal Research Institute, Patna.

Rahder, J.

1926 *Daśabhūmikasūtra and Bodhisattvabhūmi*, Paris-Louvain, Appendice, pp. 1–28.

Rahula Wolpola

1966 "Asaṅga" in Encyclopedia of Buddhism, Colombo, pp. 133–136.

1971 *Le Compendium de la Super-doctrine (Abhidharma-samuccaya) d'Asaṅga*, Publications de l'École Française d'Extrême-Orient, LXX VIII, Paris (rpt. 1980).

Roth, G.

1975 "Observation on the First Chapter of Asaṅga's *Bodhisattvabhūmi*," *Indologica Taurinensia* 3–4, pp. 403–412 (rpt. in *Indian Studies*, 1987, pp. 165–174).

Ruegg, D. S.

1969 *La Théorie du Tathāgatagarbha et du Gotra*, Publication de l'École Française d'Extréme-Orient vol. LXX, Paris.

Saeki, Jyoin.

1940 新導：成唯識論, Horyuji, Nara.

Sakaki, Ryozaburo

1962 *Mahāyutpatti*: 梵蔵漢和四訳対校 翻訳名義大集, Kokusho-kankokai, Tokyo (rpt. 1981)

Sasaki, Gessho

1931 漢訳四本対照・攝大乗論 (*Comparison of the Four Chinese Translations of the *Mahāyānasaṁgraha*), Hobun- sha, Tokyo, (rpt. Rinsenshoten, Kyoto, 1977).

Schmithausen, Lambert

1967 "Sautrāntika-Voraussetzungen im *Viṁśatikā* und *Triṁśikā*," WZKSO vol. 11.

1969a "*Zur Literaturgeschichte der ältern Yogācāra-Schule*," ZDMG-supplementum I vol. 2, pp. 811–823.

1969b "*Der Nirvāṇa-Abschnitt in der Viniścayasaṁgrahaṇī der Yogācārabhūmiḥ*," Österreichische Akademie der Wissenschaften, Wien.

1971 "Philologische Bemerkungen zum *Ratnagotravibhāga*," WZKSO vol. 15, pp. 123–177.

1982 "Die Letzen Seiten der *Śrāvakabhūmi*," *Indological and Buddhist Studies— Volume in honour of Professor J. W.*

De Jong on his sixtieth Birthday—, Faculty of Asian Studies, Canberra, pp. 457–489.

1983 "The *Darśanamārga* Section of the *Abhidharmasamuccaya* and Its Interpretation by Tibetan Commentators (with special reference to *Bu ston rin chen grub*)," *Contributions on Tibetan and Buddhist Religion and Philosophy*, Steinkellner, E. and Tauscher, H., eds., Vienna, vol. 1, pp. 259–274.

1985 "Once Again *Mahāyānasaṁgraha* I. 8" in 雲井昭善博士古希記念 仏教と異宗教 (Buddhism and Its Relation to Other Religions, Essays in Honour of Dr. Shozen Kumoi on His Seventieth Birthday), Heirakujiśhoten, Tokyo, pp. 139–160.

1987 *Ālayavijñāna, On the Origin and the Early Development of a Central Concept of Yogācāra Philosophy*, Studia Philologica Buddhica, Monograph Series IV, The International Institute for Buddhist Studies, Tokyo.

Shimokawabe, Kiyoshi

1992 "An Emendation of the Tibetan Translation of Vasubandhu's Commentary on *Jñeyalakṣaṇapraveśa* of the *Mahāyānasaṁgraha*," HBK vol. 18, pp. 55–76.

1994 "チベット語訳世親釈『摂大乗論・入所知相分』和訳" (A Japanese Translation of the Tibetan Version of Vasubandhu's Commentary on *Jñeyalakṣaṇapraveśa* of the *Mahāyānasaṁgraha*), HBK vol. 20, pp. 107–122.

Suguro, Shinjyo

1976 "瑜伽論の成立に関する私見" (On the Establishment of the *Yogācārabhūmi*), OsG vol. 129, pp. 1–50.

1982 "唯識説の体系の成立" (*The Formation of the *Vijñapti-*

mātravāda System: With Special Reference to the *Mahāyānasaṁgraha*), KD vol. 8, pp. 77–112.

Shukla, Karunesha

1973 *Śrāvakabhūmi of Ācārya Asaṅga*, Tibetan Sanskrit Works Series vol. XIV, Patna.

Soma, Kazui

1986a "「菩薩地」真実義章試訳" (A Japanese Translation of the *Tattvārthapaṭala*, the Fourth Chapter of the *Bodhisattvabhūmi*), NB vol. 55, pp. 105–126.

1986b "梵文和訳「菩薩地」—種姓の章・発心の章—" (A Japanese Translation of the *Bodhisattvabhūmi* (1)), BK vol. 42, pp. 1–26.

1987 "梵文和訳「菩薩地」(２)—自利・利他の章—" (A Japanese Translation of the *Bodhisattvabhūmi* (2)), BK vol. 43, pp. 20–43.

Takakusu, Junjiro

1904 "Life of Vasubandhu," *T'oung Pao* II-5, pp. 269–296 (rpt. E. J. Brill, Leyden, 1904).

Takasaki, Jikido

1966 *A Study on the Ratnagotravibhāga (Uttaratantra), Being a Treatise on the Tathāgatagarbha Theory of Mahāyāna Buddhism*, IsMEO vol. 33, Roma.

1974 如来蔵思想の形成 (*The Formation of the *Tathāgatagarbha* Thought), Shunjusha, Tokyo.

1982 "瑜伽行派の形成" (*The Formation of Yogācāra school), KDB vol. 8, pp. 1–42.

1988 宝性論 (*The *Ratnagotravibhāva*), Kodansha, Tokyo.

Takemura, Makio

1975 "『摂大乗論』の三性説—世親釈の名の理解を手がかりに—"

(On *Svabhāvatraya* in the *Mahāyānasaṁgraha*), IBK vol. 23-2, pp. 752–755.

1976 "*Vijñapti* について—チベット訳『摂大乗論』の用例を中心に—" (On the Term *Vijñapti*, Based on Examples from the Tibetan Translation of the *Mahāyānasaṁgraha*), SK vol. 227, pp. 73–94.

Tatia, N.

1976 *Abhidharmasamuccayabhāṣya*, K. P. Jayashwal Research Institute, Patna.

Thomas, F. W. and Ui, H.

1918 "The Hand Treatise, A Work of Ārvadeva," JRAS, pp. 267–311.

Tora, F. and Dragonetti, C.

1980 "The *Hastavāla-nāmaprakaraṇavṛtti*," JRS vol. 8-1, 1980, pp. 18–31.

Tucci, G.

1956 *Minor Buddhist Text* I, IsMEO 9, Roma.

Ueda, Yoshifumi

1981 摂大乗論講読 (*Lectures on the *Mahāyānasaṁgraha*), Kodansha, Tokyo.

Ui, Hakuju

1932 印度哲学史 (*History of Indian Philosophy), Iwanamishoten, Tokyo.

1935 摂大乗論研究 (*A Study of the *Mahāyānasaṁgraha*), Iwanamishoten, Tokyo.

1958 陳那著作の研究 (*A Study of DignAga's Works), Iwanamishoten, Tokyo.

1959 宝性論研究 (*A Study of the *Ratnagotravibhāga*), Iwanamishoten, Tokyo (rpt. 1979).

1961a 梵漢対照 菩薩地索引 (*Index to the *Bodhisattvabhūmi*, Sanskrit-Chinese), Suzuki Research Foundation, Tokyo.

1961b 大乗荘嚴經論の研究 (*A Study of the *Mahāyāna-sūtrālaṁkāra*), Iwanamishoten, Tokyo, (reprint 1979).

1963 大乗仏典の研究 (*Studies in the Mahāyāna Buddhist Texts), Iwanamishoten, Tokyo.

1965a "決定藏論の研究" (*A Study of *Chyüeh Ting Tsang Lun*) in 印度哲学研究 (*Studies in Indian Philosophy), vol. 6, Iwanamishoten, Tokyo, pp. 541–789.

1965b "三無性論の研究" (*Study of the *San wu hsing lun*) in 印度哲学研究 (*Studies in Indian Philosophy), vol. 6, Iwanamishoten, Tokyo, pp. 205–358.

Warder, A. K.

1970 *Indian Buddhism*, Motilal Banarsidass, Delhi.

Watanabe, Chikafumi

2001 "*Mahāyānasaṁgraha* における菩薩道" (Bodhisattva's Path in the *Mahāyānasaṁgraha*), KDBgR vol. 13-1, pp. 39–54.

2002 "An Examination of Mind-talk (manojalpa) in *Mahāyānasaṁgraha* III," IBK vol. 50-1, pp. 31–35.

2003 "A Translation of *Mahāyānasaṁgraha* III. 1–4" in 瓜生津隆真博士退職記念論集 仏教から真宗へ (Essays in Honour of Prof. Dr. Ryushin Uryuzu's Retirement from Kyoto Women's University, "From Buddhism to [Pure Land] Shin Buddhism"), Nagata Bunshodo, Kyoto, pp. 157–176.

2004 "A Translation of *Mahāyānasaṁgraha* III. 5–7," *Nagoya Studies in Indian Culture and Buddhism, SAṀ-*

BHĀṢĀ, vol. 24, Nagoya University, Nogoya, pp. 99–114.

2005 "A Translation of *Mahāyānasaṁgraha* III. 8–11" in 小林圓照博士古希記念論集 禅学研究 (Studies in Zen Buddhism, Aspects of Buddhist Thought and Culture: Essays in Honour of Professor Ensho Kobayashi's 70th Year), Hanazono University, Kyoto, pp. 73–98.

2013 "Bodhisattva's Praxis and Philosophical Theories in *Mahāyānasaṁgraha* III," Journal of Asiatic Society of Mumbai vol. 85 in press.

Wayman, Alex

1961 *Analysis of the Śrāvakabhūmi Manuscript*, University of California Publications in Classical Philology vol. XVII, Berkeley.

Willis, Janice D.

1976 *A Study of the Chapter on Reality, based upon the Tattvārtha-Paṭalam of Asaṅga's Bodhisattvabhūmi*, Unpublished Ph.D. Dissertation, Columbia University.

1982 *On Knowing Reality*, Columbia University Press, New York.

Wogihara, Unrai

1930 *Bodhisattvabhūmi, A Statement of Whole Course of the Bodhisattva*, Sankibobusshorin, Tokyo, Completed in 1936, (rpt. 1971).

Yamaguchi, Susumu

1931 西藏譯「攝大乘論」(*Tibetan Translation of the *Mahāyānasaṁgraha*) in Sasaki's 漢訳四本対照・攝大乘論 (*Comparison of the Four Chinese Translations of the *Mahāyānasaṁgraha*), Hobunsha, Tokyo, (rpt. Rinsenshoten, Kyoto,

1977).

Yamamoto, Shohaku

1961 "無著の金剛經の釋論偈における三身思想" (The Theory of the Threefold Body in Asaṅga's *Vajracchedikākārikā*), IBK vol. 9-1, pp. 128–129.

Yeh, Ah-yueh

1975 唯識思想の研究—根本眞實としての三性説を中心にして— (A Study of the *Vijñānamātra* theory: from the Standpoint of the Three Natures as the *mūlatattva*), Toho Kenkyukai, Tokyo.

Yokoyama, Koichi

1971 "五思想より見たる弥勒の著作" (Maitreya's Writings as Seen from the Five Thoughts), SK vol. 208, pp. 27–52.

Yokoyama, Koichi and Hirasawa, T.

1997 *Dictionary of Buddhist Terminology (based upon Yogācārabhūmi)*, Sankibobusshorin, Tokyo.

Yoshimura, Hiromi

1998 "『摂大乗論』における入無相方便相" (*Asallakṣaṇānupraveśopāyalakṣaṇa* in the *Mahāyānasaṁgraha*), IBK vol. 36-2, pp. 336–343.

2002 "『摂大乗論』に引用される『大乗荘厳経論』XI, 24" (*Mahāyānasūtrālaṁkara* XI, 24 quoted in the *Mahāyānasaṁgraha*), IBK vol. 50-2, pp. 173–180.

Yuki, Reimon

1956 世親唯識の研究 (The *Vijñaptimātratā* Thought of Vasubandhu), Aoyamashoin, Tokyo, 1956, (rpt. Daizoshuppan, 1986).

Index

R